Chris Tarrant was born in Reading, educated at King's School in Worcester and obtained a BA Hons in English Literature at Birmingham University. He started his television career as a newsreader for ATV in the early 1970s and soon became a household name as producer and presenter of the hugely popular children's Saturday morning TV show *TISWAS*. Chris has presented *Tarrant on TV* since 1988 and *Who Wants To Be A Millionaire?* since September 1998. He has also hosted the Capital FM Breakfast Show in London since April 1987.

CHRIS TARRANT

Millionaire
Moments

timewarner
books

A *Time Warner* Book

First published in Great Britain in 2002
as a Time Warner Original by Time Warner Books

A CIP catalogue record for this book
is available from the British Library.

ISBN 0 316 72456 4

Typeset in Fournier by M Rules
Printed and bound in Great Britain by
Clays Ltd, St Ives plc

Time Warner Books UK
Brettenham House
Lancaster Place
London WC2E 7EN

www.TimeWarnerBooks.co.uk

Contents

Who Wants To Be A Millionaire?® The US experience

Showtime

For Briggsy

Introduction

WHO WANTS TO BE A MILLIONAIRE?®

The phenomenon

It's almost exactly four years to the day since I was last able to walk down a street anywhere in the British Isles without somebody somewhere winding down a car window and shouting, ''allo, Chrissy – wanna Phone-A-Friend?' It's no problem but, of course, each time I have to pretend that I've never, ever heard this before in my life! In my *TISWAS* days in the seventies, people used to shout, 'Gotta custard pie, Chris?' as if I somehow carried them, hidden away beneath my clothes, at all times. It comes with the territory. It's been happening to people like Brucie for years – I see it as the public's way of saying, we really like that show you're doing.

The *Who Wants To Be A Millionaire?* catchphrases seem to have seeped into the public consciousness not just of this country, but of the whole world. 'Phone-A-Friend' has been referred to in the House of Commons; 'Ask the Audience' and 'I'll go 50:50' have been used in the American Senate; in Japan, you hear the phrases, 'Is that your final answer?' and 'Do you want to Phone-A-Friend?' spoken around the country in high-speed staccato English.

When we filmed our first shaky pilot on 12 August 1998, with just over three weeks to go before transmission, not one of us had any idea that we were going to spawn an unprecedented international game-show phenomenon. Since the first-ever show was transmitted here in the UK by ITV on 4 September 1998, we have aired 276 programmes in the UK; 687 people have sat in the legendary hot seat; and in total £30,931,000 has been won. Since the programme was launched 37,973,366 calls have been made to the contestant recruitment line! After a long wait for the first £1,000,000 winner – Judith Keppel, a garden designer from Fulham, who won a million on 20 November 2000 – two subsequent contestants have been made millionaires as a result of the show: David Edwards, a teacher from Staffordshire, who won a million on 21 April 2001, and Robert Brydges, an ex-banker and writer of children's books, who got his million on 29 September 2001. In October 2000 Duncan Bickley lost the highest-ever sum on the show in the UK, when he got the £500,000 question wrong and dropped a vast £218,000, going back down to £32,000.

Six people have had the opportunity to see the £1,000,000 question, at which point they have quit and left with £500,000. Five people have left with no money at all. We have also run special celebrity editions of the show for charity during the past three years, in which just under £1,000,000 has been won by stars such as Carol Vorderman; Sky Sports presenters Andy Gray and Richard Keys; David Baddiel and Frank Skinner; Jonathan Ross and his wife Jane Goldman; and Christine and Neil Hamilton.

Who Wants To Be A Millionaire? has won a hat-trick of national TV awards; a comedy award from BAFTA –

puzzling because it's the straightest show I've ever done! – and many other international prizes.

In only its second week of release the *Who Wants To Be A Millionaire?* computer game created UK chart history by becoming the first-ever title to top the 'all-formats chart' – Playstation, PC and Dreamcast – in the same week. It proceeded to have a record eighteen weeks at the number-one spot on the chart. The game also became the fastest to sell one million copies in UK chart history, ahead of *Tomb Raider* and *Tomb Raider II*.

The superlatives go on and on. The *Who Wants To Be A Millionaire?* quiz books from publishers Boxtree have sold over a million copies, the *Who Wants To Be A Millionaire?* board game was the best-selling game for the third year running in 2001 and the on-line game has already proved a massive hit for ITC On-line, registering 1.1 million users since its launch last April – that's an average of four thousand new registrations every day, who between them have played the game over twenty-two million times! Other *Millionaire* games on the internet are played in excess of three quarters of a million times a month in nine different countries.

Mobile Millionaire is now the world's most popular mobile game and is available to over 300 million subscribers. It also won the Best Consumer Wireless Application or Service Award at the GSM World Congress – the Oscars of the wireless world!

We may not have known that the show would take the world by storm, but we certainly realised that *Who Wants To Be A Millionaire?* was a good game – even a great game. Like all great ideas, its success lies in its simplicity. Billy Cotton Jnr – for years Head of Light Entertainment at the BBC – said to me a couple of years ago, 'There have only been two perfect shows in my lifetime in television: *This Is Your Life* and *Who Wants To Be A Millionaire?*' He is right: *Millionaire* has the perfect format for a really exciting quiz; fifteen questions worth escalating amounts of money; four possible answers to each; three Lifelines to call on at any time; the choice to quit and take the money if you get stuck; the chance to win £1,000,000 if you never get stuck. That's it. In a couple of lines I've just told you everything you need to know about the game! The masterstroke is previewing each question and its four possible answers to allow contestants to decide whether or not to gamble the money they have already won. After all, who in their right mind would risk losing £500,000 before knowing what they'll be asked to win a million? This way, too, great suspense is created for the audience – they can empathise with the contestant's dilemma, and have a stab at answering the questions themselves.

David Briggs, for many years my producer at Capital Radio, is co-deviser of *Who Wants To Be A Millionaire?* One crucial element to its success is what David terms 'shoutability'. When we worked together on radio David dreamed up most of the competitions that I ran, and they all had people screaming abuse at the radio. They couldn't believe that so-and-so contestant could be so dumb as to not know such-and-such an answer. David's genius was to adapt this concept to TV – *Millionaire* possesses the ultimate 'shoutability' factor and in so many ways this is the key to its success. 'Shoutability' means the show is great family entertainment – it's a chance for Dad to show off, Mum to scream her disagreement and the kids to be amazed at how intelligent their parents actually are or, just as often, how much brighter they are than their parents! 'Shoutability' also means that the game feels wonderfully inclusive. A fishing mate of mine, who left school very early and has a fairly menial job, says he loves *Who Wants To Be A Millionaire?* because it gives him a great sense of superiority. He says, 'I may not be that bright, but I can't believe how stupid some of those people in that chair are!' Equally, of course, some of them are super-intelligent. But, whether bright or not so clever, every contestant knows that all around the country millions of people watching from the comfort of their living rooms are screaming at them, and they usually openly admit that they've done the same. They regularly tell me, 'My family sent me here to put my money where my mouth is.'

We gave away hundreds of thousands of pounds on Capital Radio during the Tarrant-Briggs years. We also learnt many lessons – some of them the hard way! We learnt about 'shoutability' and we learnt how to stretch a contestant almost to the point of snapping. We quickly realised that women are much better contestants than men: they are more open and honest with their emotions. If they are thrilled they don't care who knows it, whereas men are generally far more concerned about their image and sometimes don't like to show even gratitude: often during our competitions women would scream and sob with delight when they'd won a huge sum of money or an exotic holiday; men would simply grunt!

In 1996 David made the transition to TV, going to work on GMTV. Just before he left that we ran a competition that we both absolutely loved. It was called *Double or Quits*. Contestants were asked a question, starting at £1, and could double up their money each time they came up with a right answer. At any point, they could take the money and run or risk the lot and go on to the next question. Sounds familiar? Of course it does! Capital Radio got into a terrible panic – they were convinced that we were going to bankrupt the station. The reality was, of course, that sooner or later most people got a question wrong and lost the lot. And, of course, starting at £1, the stakes were pretty low (although it was amazing how quickly the doubling-up effect did build to serious money. I remember one guy got up to £12,000 before he went one question too far and blew it all).

After he left Capital, David would refer back to *Double or Quits*. 'I want to try and turn it into a TV format,' he always said, 'it's such a great idea.' He would ask me if I was interested in coming in on a TV version with him, and I always said that if he got the backing, I would make him a pilot show at the very least.

Then suddenly, early in the spring of 1998, Briggsy rang me out of the blue and told me that ITV had got very keen. They wanted to make a pilot with a company called Celador, which they were planning to call *Cash Mountain*. I knew Celador well – I'd worked with them before on several shows – and I knew that if Briggsy's idea was in their hands, it would be very professionally and painstakingly made: they've always insisted on the highest production levels, which proved vital in the months ahead. The months ahead, of course, were to change all our lives, no one's more than David Briggs's.

Just before the pilot Celador decided to change the show's title from *Cash Mountain* to *Who Wants To Be A Millionaire?* To my embarrassment, I remember saying to David, 'Oh God, that'll never catch on!' Looking back now, this is probably on a par for sheer stupidity with the guy from Decca Records who turned down the Beatles! Fortunately, I was overruled.

Paul Smith, the Managing Director of Celador, the company that produces the show, has said of that first pilot, 'It looked a bit like *Seaside Special* circa 1976.' But in most ways the basic game has barely changed, although back then question number one was worth £1. Initially we thought there was a nice symmetry about going from £1 to £1,000,000, but we soon realised that not many viewers were going to sit on the edge of their seat to see whether or not someone was going to win a quid. They were going to go out and make a cup of tea, or – worse – switch over to another channel. That idea was quickly dropped.

The most fundamental changes in those next three frantic weeks were the look and the sound of the show: the lighting and the music. The original music lacked any drama, and we knew that needed to change. To help us, we brought in composer Keith Strachan and his son Matthew, who came up with what turned out to be a revolution in the audio presentation of the genre. 'If you want drama,' said Keith, 'you need music throughout the show. A big, bold tune, almost orchestral in style. Something like a John Williams score for a Spielberg movie – something like *ET* or *Jaws*. I want to concentrate on brass and strings, rather than drums. I don't want anything plinky-plonky.' (This comes from the man who wrote Cliff Richard's 'Mistletoe and Wine'!)

There was certainly nothing plinky-plonky about the music that Keith went on to create for the show. It played for virtually the entire length of the programme and was incredibly effective in heightening the sense of drama in the studio. So this, and a whole new lighting design, were key elements in generating an on-set atmosphere of electric tension in time for show number one.

Brian Pearce, one of the most respected and experienced lighting directors in British television, was responsible for introduced 'varilites' to *Who Wants To Be A Millionaire?* Varilites have been used a lot in pop concerts (they were originally developed for Genesis's world tours) but rarely on television, and never before on quiz shows. They became crucial to the look and feel of the show – like the music, they helped generate and increase tension. Varilites are spotlights that remain light blue until the £1000 question, at which point they become progressively darker. When a contestant gets to question ten for £32,000, they black out, so that from there on in all eyes are entirely focused on the person in the hot seat and myself.

These changes between the pilot and the first transmitted show gave *Who Wants To Be A Millionaire?* a fantastically exciting edge; and Keith and Brian managed this massive revamp in less than twenty-one sleepless nights. Their results changed television game shows for ever.

Even though at the time of writing this book I've hosted nearly three hundred *Who Wants To Be A Millionaire?* shows, evening after evening I still find it as absorbing as it was on night one. If that wasn't the case, I'd have probably hung up my suit and tie a couple of years ago, but when a contestant wins any money, especially when it's an unexpectedly large amount, it's the nicest feeling in the world. Of course, the times when someone leaves with really big money are tremendous and certainly the three occasions when a contestant has left with £1,000,000 have been especially fantastic: they were nights none of us will ever forget. Each one of the £1,000,000 winners has been courageous, extraordinarily intelligent and very skilful. On these shows the atmosphere in the studio has been like the World Cup Final, with the whole audience standing on their seats applauding and cheering long after the game was over.

But there is a danger with these huge sums of money that people lose their sense of perspective. One or two contestants have left the show saying, 'Well, it was great but I *only* won £16,000!' C'mon, get real! Sixteen thousand pounds, tax free, is a huge amount of money – far more than you are likely to win on virtually any other game show in the world, and more than a lot of people in the UK take home in a year.

Many contestants have talked to me about the nagging worry of debt in their lives. We're not talking about the huge amounts of money that international businessmen borrow, make and lose on the stock market every day, but the sort of niggling debt that means that credit cards are a constant worry; cheques are always in danger of bouncing; the kids can't have things that their mates at school have; the car is falling apart but is too expensive to replace; holidays are a forbidden luxury. One woman told me that for as long as she could remember she had lain awake for part of the night worrying about money she owed and didn't have. So it's contestants in these kinds of straits more than any that I've really enjoyed having on the show. For many of them, even a comparatively low amount of money has been life-changing.

Of course, I tease our players. I push them; I make them sweat. Sometimes I make them doubt their own mind. It is fascinating trying to gauge how well each one will do. Perversely, the really bright contestants tend to find the questions easier as the money goes up. They're probably more likely to get stuck on an early question about a boy band, *Coronation Street* or Aston Villa than when asked later about the paintings of Michelangelo, the poetry of Alexander Pope or the geography of Outer Mongolia!

In the years before *Who Wants To Be A Millionaire?*, I had given away all kinds of prizes and what must add up to well over £1,000,000 to all sorts of people, from all sorts of places, on all sorts of shows, both on radio and television. The lucky ones yell with excitement as they are awarded big cheques or brand-new cars; the unlucky ones slope off with virtually nothing or something as forgettable as a pen! But – and I'm sure most game-show hosts would agree with this – I find it really hard to picture many of them in any detail. If we're honest, the majority of quiz contestants tend to fade from our memories pretty quickly.

I don't think it is any different for the viewer at home: if you think of all the game shows you've watched in your life, truthfully, how many of the contestants, even the big winners, do you actually remember? Probably very few. Very few, that is, until the arrival of *Millionaire*. As I've said many times before, the show is much more than a quiz – it's a drama! It's a soap opera. The people that make it into that hot seat are beamed into your living room, and their lives are laid bare in a matter of minutes. Normally quiz-show contestants are pre-selected in a series of auditions, but legally the very fact that people are paying for a phone call to get on the show means that *Millionaire* is open to literally anyone who will pay to make that call. In turn this means that the most unlikely people get on TV, in front of a huge audience, under the spotlight in unrelenting close-up. The show is all about their raw emotions, as they play for life-changing amounts of cash before our very eyes. 'It's the greatest ingredient on the show,' says

David Briggs. 'These are really ordinary people playing for extraordinary sums of money; and they continue to surprise and delight us, night after night.'

I meet the contestants during afternoon rehearsals, no more than a couple of hours before the show, then, at 7.30pm, the two of us together embark on a strangely intimate and yet completely public adventure. Whoever is in the hot seat knows, I hope, that I want them to win; that I genuinely feel for them – they are under tremendous pressure. For many of them, it's the best night of their life, the most memorable experience they will ever have gone through.

So this book is all about these amazing people: the big-money winners, the small-money winners; the big-money losers; but above all the truly unforgettable characters, no matter how much money they won or lost. From the youngest to the oldest; the brightest to the dumbest; the nicest to the nastiest, they are included simply because they stand out most clearly from my memories of the show. You will find that you will remember many of them yourself: you will have shared some of their triumphs or their tragedies from the comparative safe zone of your own living room.

To all the other hundreds who have gone through that extraordinary eyeball-to-eyeball experience with me, I'm sorry there wasn't enough space to include your big night in this book. We are delighted to have met you, and I hope that you have fond memories of your day with us!

WHO WANTS TO BE A MILLIONAIRE?®

Worldwide

The intrinsic simplicity and sheer human drama of the show has ensured that it is a success not only in Britain but all around the world. Elements of *Who Wants To Be A Millionaire?* have caught on, on an unprecedented scale.

The show's format has now been licensed or optioned in well over a hundred countries, as far apart culturally and geographically as Japan (*Who Wants To Be A Millionaire?* was the first Western game show ever bought by a Japanese television channel – Fuji in this case), Kazakhstan, Russia, India, Colombia, the Philippines, Germany, South Africa, Venezuela, Israel, China, Kenya and Australia. It has gone to number one in the ratings for at least a short, but often an extremely long period, in almost every country where it's been transmitted.

Of course, we are very proud that *Who Wants To Be A Millionaire?* is British. It has won the Queen's Award for Export Services to British Industry, and has spawned all sorts of other shows, like *The Weakest Link*, that, in style and look if nothing else, are very similar and would never have got on air in the countries they now go to, if *Millionaire* had not paved the way first.

It's by far the most successful game show that the Americans have ever bought from overseas, although it almost physically hurts them to admit it. The United States is, of course, the great creator of virtually all modern TV game shows. So when they buy a programme that goes straight to number one in the ratings right across the USA, they don't actually deny that it's British, but they are certainly not too keen to acknowledge it. I guested on a TV chat show in America a couple of years ago and most of the audience was genuinely amazed to be told that *Who Wants To Be A Millionaire?* had been invented by the Limeys.

Ratings in the USA have reached over thirty-two million viewers; the first celebrity show they ever did in the States gained the biggest audience for the ABC network since 1983.

One of my favourite stories of contestants from around the world is that of a struggling American musician who was down to his last $15 in the world when he learnt he'd made it on to the show. He hadn't even got a decent pair of trousers, so he told his local Gap that he was going to be on *Who Wants To Be A Millionaire?* and they lent him a nice new pair! He left the show $250,000 better off, and faithfully returned them on his journey home. Later in the book, too, there are a couple of other gems of stories which happened on the US show.

The overseas versions of *Millionaire* are virtually identical to the UK show. Celador's international team goes over to each country to which they have sold the programme in order to advise them how best to produce it successfully, but after that they are on their own. They cannot diverge from the basic format and rules of the game, but the joy of syndicating it internationally is that each foreign show takes on unique national characteristics.

Having said that, dozens of the foreign hosts mimic exactly what I do over here. They point their fingers in the same way; they have the same poker face; they have the same intonation, no matter what the language. I remember crawling back to civilisation after a week's fishing in the wilderness of Kazakhstan, finding what they called a five-star hotel – I think over here it might have got just about one AA spanner! – taking my first bath for a week (badly needed!) and turning on the TV only to hear some rather familiar theme music and to see a man, looking spookily similar to me, obviously telling a contestant in Kazakhstan that he could use a Lifeline – perhaps he should Phone-A-Friend. It was a very strange experience.

The overseas shows have spawned some stories that you really couldn't make up. On the eve of the presidential elections in Russia in 2000, the six candidates were invited to take part in a one-off charity edition of the show. Four candidates actually took up the offer, although president Putin was not among them! Russia was an interesting place to broadcast *Who Wants To Be A Millionaire?* The country has no real history of TV game shows and there were big problems with the Russian studio audience. After the first few nights on air, it became clear that the Ask the Audience Lifeline was proving disastrous because the majority vote was invariably wrong. It emerged that the audience didn't see why they should help the contestant in the chair and were deliberately giving the wrong answer, jealous that they hadn't made it into the hotseat! The production company and the host had their work cut out for them re-educating their audiences.

The Indian show is made in Bollywood, which is, of course, the Indian equivalent of Hollywood. The host is Amitabh Bacchan, a great Bollywood film legend. Many of the contestants are more interested in getting a chance to meet him than in winning the prize money! Before the first show Hindu priests were brought into the studio, ringing little bells and sprinkling holy water to bless the set. Everybody, including some of the lads from Celador out there to help the first show on its way, was anointed with a little red dot on their forehead.

The gap between rich and poor in India is enormous. They play there for a million rupees, which is about £100,000 sterling. It may not sound a huge amount but you could probably buy half of Calcutta with a hundred grand. A lot of people living in slum districts have no electricity, let alone a television, so a great tradition has arisen whereby hundreds, sometimes thousands of people, watch such programmes on a single television on the beach! *Who Wants To Be A Millionaire?* is the most popular show in the history of Indian television. There are no taxis to be had anywhere when it is on air – literally everybody stops and dives into the nearest house (or on to the nearest beach!) with a TV. Television's big rivals there are the cinema and cricket – audiences for both were badly hit when *Millionaire* first came on air.

The Hong Kong television company that bought the show wanted two hosts: one to ask the questions under the spotlight, and one to participate with the audience. We had to point out to them that this would be very confusing and disruptive and they finally begrudgingly agreed to use just the one. Each Chinese programme recording, filmed in Hong Kong but, of course, broadcast from Beijing, must be sent for government censorship before it can be screened and, three days before the first show was due to be transmitted, the Chinese government decided to slash the top prize money by half.

In Malaysia, the host is an actor famous for playing the roles of millionaires in TV dramas. For this and no other reason, he was chosen to play my role on *Millionaire*!

The Venezuelan host is also the president of the TV station and in Chile the programme is presented by a man called Don Francisco – a famous South American TV star who lives in Miami and flies in to Santiago by private jet for each programme. He wanted to turn *Millionaire* into a chat show because, in his words, 'That's what my audience want from me.' It was firmly pointed out to him by the makers of the programme that, no matter who he was, if he wanted to present *Millionaire*, he was obliged to host the game, and the game alone!

In Colombia, many contestants are very wary of appearing in the *Millionaire* hotseat. Understandably in this very volatile, dangerous country, they are terrified that, having won a huge amount of money in public, their chances of getting out of the studio alive will be much reduced. Those who are brave, or foolhardy enough, to come on to the show have been known to change their name after their appearance to offset the very real danger that they could be murdered, or kidnapped due to their win.

The first series in the Middle East was bought by Egypt. Initially it was filmed at Elstree Studios, in between our own recordings, using our set, our camera crews, even our warm-up man, Ray Turner, whose knowledge of Arabic is . . . non-existent. Contestants were flown into

Borehamwood from Cairo and a local Arab audience was recruited for each programme!

Saudi Arabian participants often quit with one, two or even three Lifelines left. To show ignorance is a mark of shame among Arabs and in such a culture it is almost a taboo to be seen to ask for help. So Saudi contestants would often rather leave with no money than suffer the public humiliation of being seen to Ask the Audience or Phone-A-Friend! Perhaps surprisingly, there are no rules forbidding women to appear on the show there.

In Turkey a million Turkish lira is worth less than a quid, so the show has been renamed *Who Wants To Be A Billionaire?* Apparently those who have been invited on often visit their local priest beforehand to ask him how much money they will win. However, human nature being what it is, even if the priest tells them they won't win much, they tend to ignore him and have a go anyway, on the off-chance.

When the Israeli show had its first £1,000,000 winner, the host danced around in the middle of the studio stripping, as a mark of respect!

In Iceland, because the population is only 250,000, the producers have had to reduce the number competing for the hot seat from ten to six: there is a real fear that in a few years they will literally run out of people to compete on the show. One of the country's favourite contestants was a priest from a tiny village. He promised his congregation that if he won a million kronur, he would build the village a new church. He won the million, and, as you would expect, was true to his word.

A German contestant recently declared on the show, 'If I get all fifteen questions right, all I want to do with the money is divorce my husband.' She was forced to quit before question fifteen, but she went ahead and divorced him anyway!

In the first year of *Who Wants To Be A Millionaire?* in Bulgaria the nearest television studio was over the border in Romania. Every week a convoy of buses would leave Sofia and head for Bucharest to record a run of shows. Inside were eight programmes' worth of contestants, plus friends and family. Each bus was emblazoned with the show's logo and branding – they were named the '*Millionaire* Caravans'.

The story of the show in Georgia has to be one of my favourites – for their sheer resilience and persistence in making a success of it despite a series of setbacks. The country suffers constant power cuts, sometimes as frequently as every five minutes, so it can take a whole day to record one episode. The facilities in their studio are basic: the lift carries only five people at a time, so getting the contestants, host and audience on to the set is a laborious process, to say the least. It's worth the effort, though: it's probably the most successful show ever transmitted on Georgian television.

One of the most deserving winners of all the tens of thousands from around the world comes from Georgia. A paraplegic with a life-threatening lung condition, he has to have his temperature regulated twenty-four hours a day and so for six years he had not left the safety of his own home. Having been selected to appear on the show, he had to be brought to the studio in an ambulance, and once he was there the temperature on set had to be monitored very carefully by his doctors. A specially developed machine was set up to enable him to complete Fastest Finger First, which this remarkable man proceeded to win. In the hot-seat, he succeeded in winning the equivalent of £125,000.

Such money has transformed his entire life: he was able to buy his first-ever computer and, having been unable to leave his house for years, let alone make new friends, he is now in contact with people all over the world via email and the internet. He has become a celebrity in Georgia – he was even asked to open an art exhibition and, when doctors advised him that it was too dangerous for him to leave his temperature-controlled flat again, a crew was allowed to film him in his home making the official opening speech there!

These are just some of the stories from around the world on *Who Wants To Be A Millionaire?*, and just some of hundreds of extraordinary ways in which the game has enriched the lives of all sorts of people in all sorts of countries.

Millionaire
Moments

Graham Elwell

On the night of 4 September 1998 the atmosphere on set was electric and everybody was showing distinct signs of nerves. Certainly myself, Paul Smith, David Briggs and ITV's new programming boss, David Liddiment, who had a brand-new ITV network schedule resting on the shoulders of this show – it had been his brave, slightly mad decision to launch the show by stripping it across prime time every night for ten days. Having done rather a lot of telly since ATV days in the early 1970s, I don't often get nervous any more but, I must say, that night I was really feeling it. There had been so much pre-hype about the show in the media; so many people seemed to want us to fail, or genuinely believed we *would* fail, that the pressure was tremendous.

At about a quarter past seven I did something very uncharacteristic. I quietly asked Ingrid, my wife, and Paul Vaughan, my manager, to leave my dressing room and give me ten minutes or so to get my head together before I went on the set.

Then suddenly it was 7.30pm – time to go. The floor manager came to collect me. The new theme music sounded for the first time anywhere in the world, the two hundred-strong studio audience cheered in anticipation – although none of them quite knew what to expect – and we were on air, to over ten million viewers. One of the many great things about *Millionaire* is that whether you are nervous or tired, the show has an energy of its own. Once it starts it's carried along by its own momentum, and some nights so am I!

I took the seat that was to become my second home for the next few years and introduced the show, aware that there was no going back now. In a flash we were into Fastest Finger First:

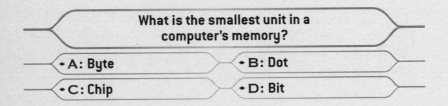

What is the smallest unit in a computer's memory?

• A: Byte   • B: Dot

• C: Chip   • D: Bit

Graham Elwell, our number-one contestant on the show, got the correct answer – Bit – in 0.69 seconds, and jumped up out of his seat like a jack-in-the-box. Graham was a twenty-seven-year-old student with manic, curly hair, and when I asked him what he'd do if he won a million quid, there was none of that nonsense about saving it for a rainy day or to get married, investing it sensibly or giving some of it to charity. He said quite openly and honestly, 'I'd blow the lot!' The audience gave him a huge cheer.

26

The first question was brought up on the screen:

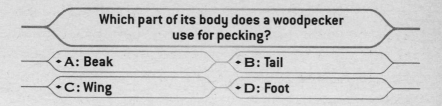

Which part of its body does a woodpecker use for pecking?

- ◆ A: Beak
- ◆ B: Tail
- ◆ C: Wing
- ◆ D: Foot

Not too demanding, I'm sure you'll agree. Graham went for 'beak'. It was the right answer. He'd won £100.

Looking back now on these early shows, it's interesting to observe how laboured we were over the first five questions. Even if they seem blatantly obvious to you, there remains the possibility that somebody out there simply does not know the answer. The phrase we coined: 'They're only easy if you know the answer' is very apt for *Who Wants To Be A Millionaire?* It doesn't matter if half the country is screaming the right answer at their TV screen, the bottom line is that you're in the chair and they're not and if you don't know it, you're up a creek without a paddle.

So I always am aware when asking these first five questions that, even if they seem incredibly easy, the person opposite me might struggle, for whatever reason. Not necessarily through lack of intelligence, sometimes it's just amazing what people don't know; how they can have lived for a long time and not come across a certain phrase or silly fact. But it does happen, and that is one of the many fascinations of the game.

So, on this first show, I was much slower through the early questions, giving each one far more weight and significance than we do now. I certainly didn't want our first contestant to go home with nothing. Not that Graham

Elwell was likely to. He turned out to be an extraordinarily bright, positive guy. He raced up to £16,000 without turning a hair and when he had given his answer to the £32,000 question I announced infuriatingly, in what has become very much a Tarrant trademark: 'We'll take a break now.' In those early days it seemed a pretty harsh thing to do to people, but then these were great sums of money, the like of which no one had ever been seen to win on television before. Paul Smith always reckoned that there should be pleasure on *Millionaire*, but there should be pain as well. Agonising pauses, dramatic music and making people wait across a three-minute break to see if they are right or wrong are all part of the pain. The pleasure is the enormous sense of relief when you are told that you are right and you go home with a huge cheque in your hand and a soppy grin on your face.

After the break I was delighted to tell Graham that he'd won £32,000 and still hadn't used a single Lifeline. He was ecstatic. I showed him the cheque, complete with the day's date on it. Writing a cheque out on air and showing it to the camera and the contestant was quite a first. Like a lot of things on *Millionaire*, it seems an obvious ploy now, but at the time it simply had never been done before. It was an inspired idea, there was something wonderfully immediate about the way the contestant could take it away that night, ready to pay it into the bank first thing the next morning. People all over the country were quickly sussing that this was a show that really could transform their lives.

At this point Graham, a struggling student, could definitely see that his life was about to change for the better. He was a guaranteed £32,000 better off; he hadn't had to think twice on any of the first ten questions; he still had three unused Lifelines; and he was only five questions away from winning £1,000,000. The audience in the studio and right across the country must have sensed that a £1,000,000 winner was suddenly a real possibility. But nobody watching the first few shows had any real idea how hard the questions would get from here on in.

The world now knows how long we waited for Judith Keppel and that is another story, but at this point, as it did so many times over the next couple of years, it looked like we might be about to give away the largest sum of money ever handed over on TV, to the first contestant on the first show.

In those days we had a glass case right at the front of the set, containing £1,000,000, to remind everybody, by its sheer bulk, of just how large an amount of money this was. I was always worried about the moment of opening the case to hand over the money because, although we'd practised it numerous times in rehearsals, it always seemed to me that there was every chance the money would go flying all over the place. Imagine the shambles – there could even have been a stampede among the audience, stuffing tenners down the front of their trousers and doing a runner. If I was in the audience I'm sure that's what I'd have done. In fact after the second series we dropped this idea altogether and settled for just writing out a cheque for £1,000,000 to anyone clever enough to give me fifteen correct answers.

Graham was finally forced to use a Lifeline on his eleventh question, for £64,000:

What was the first stately home in Britain to open its doors to the public?

- A: Longleat
- B: Beaulieu
- C: Wilton
- D: Blenheim

Graham went 50:50 and was left with 'Blenheim' and 'Wilton'. I wasn't certain but I thought it was most likely to be 'Blenheim'. Of course, I said nothing – for the first time in hundreds of nights I sat there with that idiotic, inscrutable mask across my face. Graham decided it was 'Wilton' and went for it. I was wrong, he was right. He won £64,000. The audience went wild. He was now only four questions away from winning £1,000,000.

The next question was a stinker:

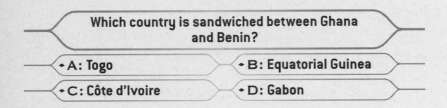

Like many contestants since, Graham reckoned there probably wasn't much point trusting the audience at this level. Instead he chose to phone his grandad, John, as his Phone-A-Friend. For those of you who don't really understand the mysteries of Phone-A-Friend, each contestant is allowed to choose a maximum of five friends. Obviously the best tactic is to select ones to represent different areas of general knowledge: one might be a sportsman; one might know all about pop music; another might teach English Literature, and so on. You'd have thought, strategically, the more people you have on call the better, but some players trust only two or three friends. One girl famously trusted only her dad; and one contestant, who I won't name, actually had no friends at all! Each one is told to stay by the phone as soon as the recording starts and if their contestant wins First Finger First our researchers ring them again to make sure they are still on red alert. In spite of this, over the years we have called several people whose phones were engaged; one or two who'd actually gone out; and at least one who'd left his phone on voicemail – what sort of friends are these? In such instances we eventually had to call a second choice. (In the main we have edited these moments out on the grounds of sheer dullness.)

On that first show we used an actual telephone to make the call to Grandad, our first-ever Phone-A-Friend. He answered immediately, I talked to him briefly and then had to physically hand the phone across to Graham, at which point the thirty-second clock started. This was another clumsy idea that we got rid of after just the one show.

Grandad John sadly didn't know the right answer. Graham still didn't want to risk asking the audience – he'd obviously seen them with the lights up and decided they were a waste of space. So, off he went home, with a huge cheque for £64,000.

It was an enormous sum of money – nothing like it had ever been given away on television before in the UK or probably anywhere in the world. We couldn't have had a better start to this brand-new series.

Oh, incidentally, the country squeezed between Ghana and Benin is Togo.

Rachel Mendez de Costa

The second *Who Wants To Be A Millionaire?* contestant could not have been more different from cool, calm Graham Elwell. Rachel Mendez de Costa, from Edgware in Middlesex, was just twenty years old. She was a bag of nerves whose eyes and trembling lips betrayed her every emotion. She was in the most dreadful lather, but absolutely adorable. Even though she got the Fastest Finger First correct in the mind-bogglingly quick time of 0.69 seconds, she seemed to doubt each of her answers and was almost afraid to speak out in case she was wrong!

She wanted the money to pay off her boyfriend's debts and to get a few quid together for their planned wedding, already booked two years ahead for May 2000. Clearly the money was crucial – every pound mattered to Rachel and her grinning fiancé in the audience. She got up to £500 without any real problem, despite her self-doubt. Then the klaxon sounded and Rachel became the first person to have to wait overnight to come back on the show.

These are sometimes long, excruciating waits for both the contestant and the audience at home. In these early days viewers right across the country couldn't wait to get home the next night to see how much further such-and-such a contestant would go. The talk on the buses, in the pubs and at work was, 'Did you see that bloke last night – he's on £16,000. I think he's gonna make the million!' This sort of discussion still continues four years later, but in those early, heady days the electrifying buzz surrounding the show made the start of each *Millionaire* unmissable. The audiences were huge and the anticipation was fantastic.

Rachel told me the following night that she had been through the most agonising twenty-four hours of her life. She was clearly in a far worse state of nerves than she had been the night before. She'd hardly slept a wink; had been constantly on the phone to her dad for reassurance; and was terrified that she was going to get the next question wrong and go home with nothing at all. She needn't have worried – she got question five correct straight away and, with a huge sigh of relief, knew that she was going to be at least £1000 better off when she got home.

But then things started to go wrong. Paul Smith said to me afterwards that it was the first time he realised how nerve-racking and tense this show could be. I certainly felt it too – it was then we realised what an incredible extra edge *Millionaire* has over almost all other game shows in the world. I have said, time and again, it's not really a game show, it's not really even a big-money show. Of course, the money is relevant but, above all, it's a drama, it's a soap, it's about perfectly ordinary people playing out their own personal dreams in close-up before our very eyes. Rachel went through the gamut of emotions that night on national television. The £2000 question, question number six, was:

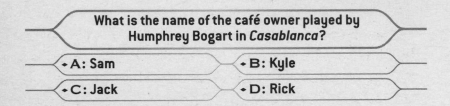

What is the name of the café owner played by Humphrey Bogart in *Casablanca*?

- ◆ A: Sam
- ◆ B: Kyle
- ◆ C: Jack
- ◆ D: Rick

At this point two thirds of the population of Britain must have been screaming 'Rick' at their television screens. A mate of mine told me later that he was in a pub that evening and the whole place was hollering the answer at the top of their voices. Sadly, Rachel couldn't hear any of them. There were big tears of sheer frustration in her eyes – she wasn't at all sure of the right answer. She went 50:50. 'Sam' and 'Rick' remained. Still she wasn't convinced and she asked the audience. Sixty-nine per cent of them went for 'Rick', 31 per cent went for 'Sam'. With absolutely no conviction at all, purely on the majority of the audience's say-so, she decided to play and went for 'Rick'. I told her it was the right answer and the audience went through the roof. She was pouring tears. She tried to drink a glass of water but she was visibly shaking and spilling her drink. She had £4000 but only one Lifeline left.

It was the essence of *Who Wants To Be A Millionaire?*, exactly why it's been such an international success.

She played the next question without a problem and got to £8000. On £8000 she said to me out loud, 'I feel sick' and used her final Lifeline on this question:

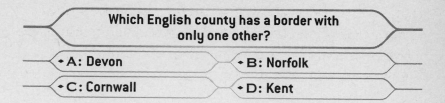

Which English county has a border with only one other?

- A: Devon
- B: Norfolk
- C: Cornwall
- D: Kent

She phoned her best friend, her dad Jack, who was in a hotel room. She had said to me earlier that her father was the one person she trusted completely. He had been hugely supportive of her coming on the show in the first place, and she would depend on him and him alone if she was in trouble. Rachel Mendez de Costa was in deep trouble, and Dad was her last Lifeline!

With a plaintive cry of 'Dad, please help me!', Rachel – along with the audience and, inwardly, myself – was horrified when Dad said, 'I'm sorry, love, I really don't know. I'm just no good at geography.' It was a distressing moment. Rachel had got to £8000, a lot of money, but clearly with her debts and dreams of her wedding, she had hoped for a lot more. With just a little bit of luck, or Dad being keener on geography when he was at school, she might have got further. But agonisingly, she was now forced to stop.

In what has become another Tarrant tradition on the show, I asked Rachel 'purely hypothetically' which one she would have gone for if so much had not been at stake. 'Cornwall,' she said to me. When I told her that it was the right answer, she looked aghast. She went away £8000 better off but visibly shattered. For Rachel and the audience it had been two days of raw emotion. But, over the years, these moments have been more deeply etched into the memories of the audience than many of the really big winners.

Life After *Who Wants To Be A Millionaire?*

Rachel says she remembers a feeling of nausea when she came off the set, having taken the money. Her legs gave way and she realised for the first time why we always have a nurse on standby at the studio. She got recognised a lot and says the money came at the perfect time. It went towards a new flat for her and her husband and they spent a weekend in Amsterdam. She says she can't watch the show any more and she feels sick whenever she hears of, thinks about or, especially, sees Cornwall!

John McKeown

Probably the character that most people remember from that thrilling first series was John McKeown. He was the forty-three-year-old sewage delivery driver from Glasgow, who arrived with his young son John Paul, since his wife was far too nervous to come down to London and sit in the audience. In fact, until she saw her husband on television with her own eyes, she said she didn't believe that he was really going to be on the show at all.

For a lot of people, John was an object lesson in how you don't need a university degree to have a tremendous breadth of general knowledge. At first John, with his very thick, gruff Glaswegian accent and general hard-man appearance, didn't seem likely to go far at all. I'm sure most of the audience thought that if he got to £1000 it would be a good result and he'd go away more than happy. It was fairly obvious that a Glaswegian sewage delivery worker – what a job that sounds! – wouldn't earn a lot of money and clearly he didn't need much of an intellect to do his job. However, as has happened since dozens of times, the audience and I slowly became aware that here was a guy with a tremendous wealth of knowledge, someone who would not want to waste a lot of the otherwise dull, futile time he would have on his hands between sewage deliveries.

John McKeown is an amazing man. His completely shaved head shone brightly under the studio lights and there was a real twinkle in his blue eyes as he steamed effortlessly through the early questions. During our chat at the top of the show, he had said jokingly that if he won some money all he really wanted in life was a hair transplant. He had also said, much more seriously, that his lifelong dream was to go to Lisbon and walk on the pitch where Celtic had won the European Cup in 1967. He said this with a burning fire in his eyes – he'd always wanted to go, but never thought he'd have the money to afford the trip.

John got to £1000 no problem. Then £2000. The £4000 question was this:

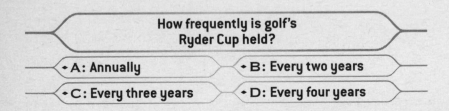

How frequently is golf's
Ryder Cup held?

A: Annually

B: Every two years

C: Every three years

D: Every four years

John used his 50:50 and he was left with 'every two years' or 'every three years'. He went for 'B'. It was the right answer and he raced to £4000.

For £8000 he was asked this question:

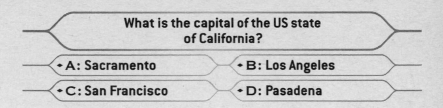

What is the capital of the US state of California?

◆ A: Sacramento   ◆ B: Los Angeles

◆ C: San Francisco   ◆ D: Pasadena

He decided to Ask the Audience, and they were very split on this. Thirty-eight per cent thought it was 'Sacramento', 36 per cent went for 'Los Angeles', 7 per cent even thought it was 'Pasadena', for God's sake! John went for 'Sacramento'. Spot on! He was £8000 better off.

With still one Lifeline in hand, he raced to £32,000. The audience were ecstatic. They absolutely loved him. So did I. This kind of money would change his whole life. It would certainly guarantee the trip to see the hallowed turf where Celtic had lifted the European Cup. But John wasn't finished yet.

The £64,000 question was a stinker:

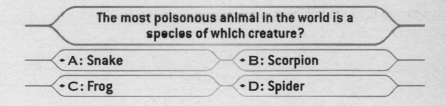

The most poisonous animal in the world is a species of which creature?

◆ A: Snake   ◆ B: Scorpion

◆ C: Frog   ◆ D: Spider

John didn't blink. He didn't waste his final Lifeline and said straight away 'It's "frog".' It was the right answer – the roof lifted off the studio. I pumped John's massive fist in delight, I was so thrilled for him. I seem to remember, to my horror, that I even slapped him playfully on his head. I'm sure if any man was ever foolish enough to try that in the pubs of his native Glasgow, they would be dead, and deservedly so. I still cringe at the memory, but it was a terrific moment. I was hugely proud of him and he was clearly delighted at his own triumph.

However, at that moment, of all moments, the klaxon went for the end of the show and we had to endure the suspense of a twenty-four-hour wait for our suddenly vulnerable-looking hard man to come back to play for £125,000. For John, indeed for all of us, it was an agonising twenty-four hours. The next night, predictably, the show got a huge audience.

I genuinely believe that if we hadn't run out of time on that first night, John might well have been our first £1,000,000 winner. He was flying; totally without nerve. But, as we've seen so often on the show since, people come back having had a night to think about the huge sums of money with which they are gambling, to worry about what they might win or might lose, and the next evening they almost invariably take the money and run. The sheer enormity of the amount they've already got sinks home, whereas at the time they're on a roll, they're intensely focused and really going for it. On the second night, time and again, they've lost that edge.

John came back to wild applause. For £125,000 I asked him:

> **Which of these artists has never had a UK number-one hit single?**
>
> ◆ A: Genesis ◆ B: Fleetwood Mac
> ◆ C: UB40 ◆ D: Marvin Gaye

John looked puzzled and used his last Lifeline to Phone-A-Friend. A very chirpy-sounding Scotsman called John

Dempster came on the line, but once John had read him the question he said, 'I'm really sorry, mate, I really don't know.'

McKeown looked at me sadly and said, 'I just can't risk this. I'm taking the money.' It was still a terrific moment – he went away with £64,000. His son John Paul came down from the audience to stand proudly beside his dad, who was clutching his enormous cheque – in his own words, 'several years' money'. A good few years of delivering sewage, I suspect!

Just as he was leaving, I spieled out my teaser routine: 'By the way, John, if you'd gone for any of these possibilities which one would you have chosen?' 'Genesis,' he said. It was the right answer. But John and his son were still utterly thrilled. They made for the nearest bar £64,000 better off . . . and I went with them!

Life After *Who Wants To Be A Millionaire?*

John says he still gets recognised nearly four years later. He can now do things that he could never have done before. He bought new furniture, a brand-new car and has been on a few holidays, including Gran Canaria and Tenerife. But, best of all, his local paper paid for him to go to Portugal and stand on that legendary Lisbon pitch where Celtic won the European Cup.

Matthew Asbury

One of the many emotionally draining nights – or two nights, to be precise – on *Who Wants To Be A Millionaire?* was spent in the company of a great young guy called Matthew Asbury. He was only twenty-six and worked in a factory, where he could hardly have been earning a fortune. He was clearly very brave, quite emotional and ever so slightly mad.

He told me that if he won 'the million' he had only one real ambition in life: to buy Geri Halliwell's Union Jack dress, an extremely skimpy little miniskirt and top, which, big, burly Matthew said, in all seriousness, he'd love to wear into the factory. He said he could just imagine the greeting he'd get from the rest of the lads. I think we all can.

But there was nothing remotely feminine about Matthew. He was a chunky lad and his dad was sitting up in the audience, not his wife Catherine, because she was expecting their first baby, which was a week overdue.

So, imagine the scenario: Catherine was in a maternity ward being comforted by Matthew's mother-in-law, while he and his dad were down in London on a TV game show. The pressure on Matthew to do well for his family must have been enormous. Catherine was, according to Matthew, very understanding about his absence, and was constantly fighting strange cravings for fish and chips, curry and dandelion and burdock. They sounded a great young family and everybody wanted Matthew to do his best and take some money away with him, but to do so as quickly as he could. Throughout the show we had a car sitting outside the studio ready to race him back up the motorway to his wife and soon-to-be new baby.

I've never got through the questions so fast in all my life. Matthew raced through the first five. He struggled a bit at the £300 mark, to remember who spoke the Cantonese language, settled correctly for the Chinese and finally reached £1000. Then he got a really hard question for £2000 and had to use up his first Lifeline – his 50:50:

> **What name is given to the lower part of an interior wall?**
>
> ◆ A: Stucco ◆ B: Quoin
> ◆ C: Dado ◆ D: Transom

Suddenly it looked as if Matthew might be going off to the hospital quite soon. His 50:50 left 'dado' and 'transom', which he said didn't help him much. Looking extremely nervy, Matthew phoned a friend, his mate Paul Montgomery. Paul was equally uncertain, although he did inform Matt, 'If I had a guess, I'd probably go for "dado"' – not really the sort of reassurance that Matthew was hoping for. But he went with Paul and, miraculously, it was the right answer.

With the audience on the edge of their seats, suddenly the klaxon sounded, leaving Matthew an agonising twenty-four-hour wait for his £8000 question. It was probably just as well that Catherine couldn't see the show from her maternity ward in Burnley.

Matthew dutifully raced back up the motorway with his dad, touched base with his wife and mother-in-law, to be reassured that the baby hadn't moved an inch, and raced back down to Elstree Studios for the following evening.

He looked distinctly rattled when he climbed back into the hotseat, to start from where we had left off. Meanwhile my producer had come up with a great idea. We got Catherine on the phone from her bed with a special message for Matthew: 'We all love you, all the best tonight, do your best and get back up here to the two of us as soon as you can.' It was tear-jerking stuff. Matthew looked really shaky, but his wife's voice seemed to have lent him extra courage and focus. However, he didn't have a great start.

On his very first question that evening he used up his last Lifeline:

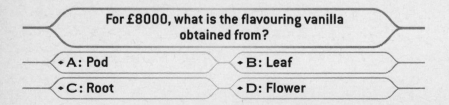

For £8000, what is the flavouring vanilla obtained from?

A: Pod
B: Leaf
C: Root
D: Flower

Matt didn't know. He asked the audience and, luckily for him, a convincing 72 per cent of them voted for 'pod'. He went along with the large majority, which took him up to eight grand.

Now for Matthew and his new family, this must have been a serious result. For a young factory worker in the north of England, I would guess that £8000 tax free would be about the bulk of one year's wages. For Matthew it was a good outcome. But good was to get even better!

He knew the answer to the next question on the SAS straight away, and for doing so he earned £16,000. For £32,000, aware that he could lose fifteen grand, he got this question:

> **On which mountain did Moses receive the Ten Commandments?**
>
> A: Ararat
>
> B: Hebron
>
> C: Sinai
>
> D: Olive

He didn't have to play the question, he knew the risk he was taking, but through closed eyes and gritted teeth, he said, 'I want to play this, Chris. I think the answer's "Sinai".' The audience yelled in delight when I told him it was the right answer. I gave him a huge bear hug and a cheque for £32,000.

By now both Matthew and his dad were ecstatic. Such money was beyond their wildest dreams and was a tremendous start for a young couple expecting a baby at any minute. With nothing to lose, Matthew had a look at the next question:

> **Which of these is the equivalent to twenty champagne bottles?**
>
> A: Jeroboam
>
> B: Rehoboam
>
> C: Nebuchadnezzar
>
> D: Belshazzar

He answered, 'Nebuchadnezzar.' The panel went to orange; he was right! I could tell that Matthew was angling to escape now, but I had to bring up the next question. Up it came, for £125,000:

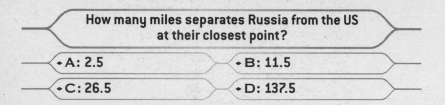

How many miles separates Russia from the US at their closest point?

| A: 2.5 | B: 11.5 |
| C: 26.5 | D: 137.5 |

As I suspected, Matthew had had enough. He didn't know, and he decided to call it a day there and then. He left with a colossal cheque for £64,000, literally racing out of the studio arm in arm with his dad, and they sped back up the motorway to Catherine and her mother. (By the way, the surprising answer was 2.5 miles.) A matter of hours later his son, Thomas, was born, weighing in at 10lb 9oz.

For the Asburys, it was the stuff of fairy tales.

Life After *Who Wants To Be A Millionaire?*

Looking back now, Matthew says the whole experience was surreal. They were able to buy a new house and have put the rest towards the kids; they now have another son, Adam, born in February 2000.

Cheryl Turner

Complete the title of this 1994 film starring Tim Allen; 'The Santa ....'

B. Clause

C. Situation

O ver the years *Who Wants To Be A Millionaire?* has made three people millionaires and dozens of others rich beyond their wildest dreams. Sometimes the tensest moments on the show are not the big winners at all, but the smaller ones. For me, one of the most unforgettable contestants was a lady called Cheryl Turner, from Dorset, who got into the chair on our first Christmas show in 1998. She had her boyfriend grinning uneasily in the audience and two very young kids at home who clearly meant the world to her. If Cheryl did win £1,000,000, which she herself said was extremely unlikely, she wanted to buy a real-life railway engine and transform it into Thomas the Tank Engine for her kids, who were huge Thomas fans. Her own dream was to get enough money together to go down in a submarine to view the remains of the *Titanic*.

But, truthfully, her mind wasn't set on the big money –

at Christmas time, especially, any money at all would clearly be a bonus for Cheryl. She looked scared to death, but she answered the first two questions correctly and with ease. All of them were Christmas-based and she got stuck on the third one:

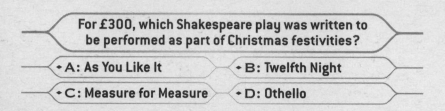

For £300, which Shakespeare play was written to be performed as part of Christmas festivities?

A: As You Like It   B: Twelfth Night

C: Measure for Measure   D: Othello

She used her first Lifeline and asked the audience. Luckily they were well clued up on their Shakespeare that night, and 93 per cent of them gave her the right answer – 'Twelfth Night'.

On £500 I thought the computer threw up a really nasty question. All right, 'they're only easy if you know the answer', but cop this for a £500 question:

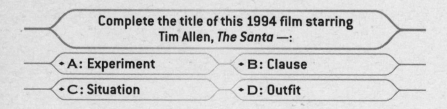

Complete the title of this 1994 film starring Tim Allen, *The Santa* —:

A: Experiment   B: Clause

C: Situation   D: Outfit

Poor Cheryl looked horrified. She used up her 50:50 and was left with 'clause' and 'situation'. Still none the wiser she phoned her friend, Zoe, who was her little boy's godmother. Luckily Zoe was on the ball (if you'll pardon the pun). And after about two seconds excitedly screamed the word 'clause' down the telephone. A hugely relieved Cheryl went with Zoe's answer and got to £500.

Poor Cheryl was looking like a girl who'd just done fifteen rounds with Lennox Lewis. She was battered and shattered, after only a matter of minutes sitting in the chair.

The £1000 question killed her off completely:

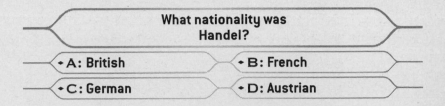

What nationality was Handel?

- A: British
- B: French
- C: German
- D: Austrian

Cheryl said she had one or two ideas but really was not at all sure and rather than risk going home with nothing, quite cheerily decided to take home £500.

Frankly, I was delighted, as we would all have been horrified if she'd left us at Christmas with nothing at all. Handel, incidentally, is German, but Cheryl clearly wasn't going to risk going to the final round. She went away absolutely delighted – she'd been on the telly, she'd done the right thing and she was £500 better off. The audience cheered her as much as if she'd won £500,000.

Fiona Wheeler

Fiona Wheeler, from Canvey Island, was one of the most hyperactive contestants who ever appeared on *Who Wants To Be A Millionaire?* She is etched on my mind, and I'm sure in the memories of all the millions who have regularly watched the show since the very beginning. She was an excitable girl, to say the least. To give you an idea of how excitable, when I called her name out as the winner of Fastest Finger First, she screamed, 'Oh my God, Chris, I've wet meself!'

She was fantastic. She hid nothing, she lay her every emotion on the line from the very first question. She was truly loveable. The audience adored her. I adored her. Luckily for her, her husband and kids obviously adored her as well. Matthew, an electrician and clearly a very patient man, sat silently in the audience, staring numbly at the developments in the studio beneath him. They had five kids, who all had very specific ideas of what they wanted from Mum's million: dirt bikes, wrestlers, a new rabbit to replace one that had died and a Chewbacca character for the bedroom. I said to her on air, 'This sounds like the house of hell' and she replied in a matter-of-fact way, 'It is, every day!'

Fiona's own dream was a simple one. All she wanted to do was lie in a bath of melted chocolate. She didn't want to lie there naked with Mel Gibson, Brad Pitt or anybody else. The only company she wanted, she said, was more chocolate, in fact all the chocolate she could eat. It sounded like a flippant sort of dream, but every time I mentioned it the glint in Fiona's eye emphasised that she was absolutely serious.

Once the game started, she was very animated – right on the edge from the very first question. She shrieked her excitement at the top of her voice when she got the £500 question right. It was about *Peter Pan*, which she said she had had to watch dozens of times with the kids. She had no problem with question five either, and having guaranteed herself and her family £1000, she roared at the ceiling and punched the air with her fists.

At this point, mercifully for Fiona and for all of us, our time that night ran out. The next evening there was a great swell of warmth from the whole studio, the audience, the crew and myself toward Fiona. She was one of those people you desperately want to win: for herself, for Matthew and for their five kids.

But the very first question on her return plunged her deep into trouble. She was asked where the film *The Piano* was set. 'I can see the piano, I can see the beach, but I haven't a clue where it was,' she said. She asked the audience: 42 per cent thought it was New Zealand, but another 33 per cent thought it was Australia. Now, still not at all convinced, she was close to tears. She used her 50:50. Sickeningly, New Zealand and Australia still remained. She took a gamble. Knowing that she was still guaranteed £1000, she went along with the audience, whispering, 'New Zealand' with no real conviction. It went to orange. She was correct. She screamed, 'Yes! Yes! Yes!' and the audience sounded as euphoric as she did.

She got to £4000 with no problem. At £8000 she screamed again, telling herself, 'Come on, come on, come on' like a tennis player in the final set. Risking losing £7000, clearly an enormous amount of money to herself and her family, she phoned Dave, her father-in-law, on this question:

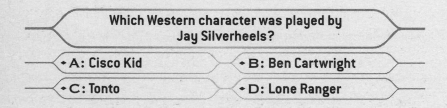

Which Western character was played by
Jay Silverheels?

A: Cisco Kid   B: Ben Cartwright

C: Tonto   D: Lone Ranger

Dave said, 'It's "Tonto"' in a matter of seconds, but even though he was her father-in-law and he sounded absolutely certain, Fiona gave him far more of a grilling than I've ever given any contestant. 'Are you sure? Definite? Honestly? Really? Do you know this?' Eventually, as convinced as she was ever likely to be, she took his answer and played it. When I told Fiona that 'Tonto' was the right answer, the whole studio erupted and she nearly leapt through the ceiling. 'I can't believe it! Sixteen grand! I can't believe it!' She had huge tears in her eyes and it seemed a good time to take a break.

After the break I was almost frightened to ask Fiona the next question. Of course, I can't influence the contestants' decisions, I can't help them, but if ever there was someone I didn't want to see lose money it was Fiona Wheeler, mother of four, from Canvey Island.

What the audience didn't know was that during the break I had given Ms Wheeler a verbal battering. I sensed she was really losing the plot; she was getting carried away. The adrenalin was beginning to take over from her own common sense and, acting like a trainer in the corner during a heavyweight boxing title fight, I urged Fiona, 'Do not lose this sum of money. This is a huge sum of money to your family. Do not lose this ******* sum of money! Watch my lips. You're not listening to me – do not lose this ******* sum of money!' It was the only way I could get it to sink into Fiona's brain. We were both still on radio mikes and the director and producer in the box were amazed at what they were hearing from me. But I make no apologies for my somewhat rough language. Fiona agreed with me afterwards that it was the only way I could have got through to her. I had said to her very, very clearly in language that she couldn't fail to understand, 'You must not go home without this money!' Sixteen thousand pounds would have made the most tremendous difference to her family; losing £15,000 would have been absolutely disastrous. She would have been gutted and so would I.

So, after the break, Fiona was ready to cut and run if she felt the slightest hint of doubt about the answer to the £32,000 question. However, something quite beautiful happened. When the question came up, in spite of her twitching lip and tearful eyes, a little smile played across her face.

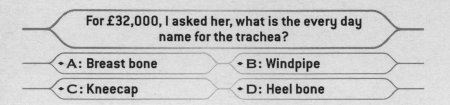

For £32,000, I asked her, what is the every day name for the trachea?

A: Breast bone   B: Windpipe

C: Kneecap   D: Heel bone

She looked at me and murmured, almost disbelieving her own words, 'I'm going to play. I know this. It's "windpipe".'

There was a gasp from the audience. 'Windpipe' went to orange and, in one of those moments that make presenting this show such a huge thrill and pleasure, I could tell her, 'It's the right answer. You've just won £32,000.' She screamed. She sobbed. She punched the air. She punched herself. More than anything, she kept shouting, 'I knew it! I knew it! I knew it!' It was raw emotional television at its absolute best.

The £64,000 question was on cricket, and Fiona got it wrong, but by now she couldn't have cared less. She had had the most fantastic night of her life and had brought joy to every single one of the millions who watched her.

Life After *Who Wants To Be A Millionaire?*

Fiona now says her two days on the show are two of the most memorable days of her life. She's managed to clear all her credit cards and will never fall back into the credit card trap again. She took her father-in-law – her Phone-A-Friend – and all the family on holiday to Kos. She treated the four kids to their first-ever white Christmas, skiing in Bulgaria, and the rest of the money has been put away. Family life is now much more comfortable.

Martin Skillings

Martin Skillings was a very gentle, quiet quantity surveyor from Norfolk. He arrived with his wife Miranda, who looked petrified throughout the entire proceedings.

They lived amid a noisy-sounding domestic menagerie, including horses, chickens, ducks, geese, a turkey called Bernard and a pigeon called Squawky. If Martin won a serious amount of money he wanted to go to the Andes for at least a month with Miranda.

Martin was extraordinarily nervous as he took the seat. In fact I'm sure he won't mind me saying he was pretty tense throughout, and Miranda seemed to be worrying as much about him as about the money they might win or lose. She hinted to me quietly before we started recording that Martin had been through a really dreadful last twelve months, but wouldn't go into any more detail. Whatever the reason, he must have felt under exceptional strain that night. He needn't have worried, though – he got up to £1000 without any problem at all, on this question:

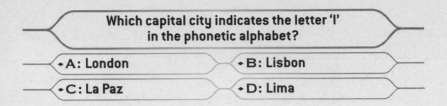

Which capital city indicates the letter 'I' in the phonetic alphabet?

A: London   B: Lisbon

C: La Paz   D: Lima

Martin knew it straight away. 'I never really use the phonetic alphabet,' he said, 'although most people seem to know it – I think they learn it from *The Bill*. But I'm pretty sure this is "Lima". Yes, "Lima" is my final answer.' He was now guaranteed £1000.

Miranda, up in the audience, let out a big sigh. She was definitely starting to look a bit better, but Martin, if anything, seemed to be worse. 'I don't believe it,' he kept saying, 'I cannot believe it.' He was clearly going through hell. He'd got as far as £2000 with all three Lifelines still intact when the klaxon sounded and he had to wait until the following night for his £4000 question.

He reappeared in the same green shirt because he thought it might be lucky, but didn't look any more confident than he had the day before. He still kept looking up to the heavens, saying, 'I don't believe this, I don't believe this.'

Fifteen minutes later he got this question for £32,000:

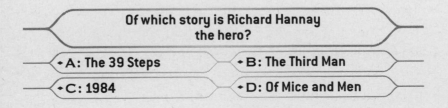

Of which story is Richard Hannay the hero?

A: The 39 Steps   B: The Third Man

C: 1984   D: Of Mice and Men

'I know this,' he said, 'it's "The 39 Steps".' 'Are you sure?' I asked him as usual. 'I was until you said that,' said Martin, 'please don't make me change my mind – final answer.' He obviously wanted to get the whole thing over with. It was the right answer, and he was now £32,000 better off. Miranda looked crazy with excitement. Martin still kept muttering, 'I don't believe it, I don't believe it.' He sounded like a kindly version of Victor Meldrew.

He raced to £64,000 with no problem, knowing that the *R101* was an airship. The next question would be for £125,000 and the great thing for Martin was that he still hadn't needed any of his Lifelines. He had all three intact. This was only our second series, and never before had anybody won £125,000.

The question for this huge sum of money was:

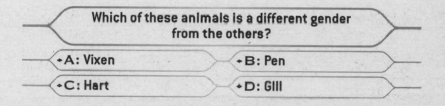

I remember thinking animal-loving Martin and Miranda, with their manic-sounding menagerie at home, might well know the answer to this question. I was right, he stared at me straight in the eye and said, 'I'll play – "C. Hart".' He looked at the heavens again but in his heart of hearts – or should that be hart of harts? – Martin knew he was right, and he was.

He had won £125,000; he was the first person in Britain ever to have answered the twelfth question correctly. Even more exciting was the fact that he *still* had all three Lifelines unused and he was only three questions away from the magic million. It was now becoming quite a responsibility if you were part of Ask the Audience or on the other end of the line as a Phone-A-Friend.

Up came the £250,000 question. I happened to look up and spot Miranda clutching a complete stranger sitting next to her in the audience for moral support. The tension was unbearable all around the studio, for the crew and for me, as much as for the audience. Martin looked as if he might go all the way.

This was the first time we had seen a £250,000 question:

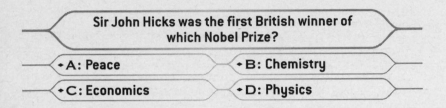

Sir John Hicks was the first British winner of which Nobel Prize?

A: Peace   B: Chemistry
C: Economics   D: Physics

Martin threw his head back in angst. After a few seconds he said, 'I'll phone Tony, please, Chris, and whatever you do, do not tell him the amount of money involved – he's an old boy like me.' We phoned Tony, but sadly he did not know the answer. Martin still had two Lifelines. He went 50:50: 'peace' and 'economics' remained. To their horror, he then decided to Ask the Audience, with £250,000 at stake. Seventy-four per cent went for 'economics', 26 per cent went for 'peace'. Martin deliberated and kept looking back to the screen but in the end the sheer amount of money involved, and the amount he could lose if he gave me a wrong answer, was too much for him. He left the studio much relieved and over the moon, clasping in his hands our first-ever cheque for £125,000.

Incidentally, the correct answer was indeed 'economics'. With tears rolling down her cheeks, Miranda came down and gave him a huge cuddle. At that moment in 1998 Martin Skillings was the biggest-ever winner on the show anywhere in the world.

Life After *Who Wants To Be A Millionaire?*

Looking back on that night now, Martin says he was utterly terrified – he is incredibly camera shy and he only rang the hotline to keep Miranda happy. He didn't expect to win Fastest Finger First and when he did he remembers hating it that the klaxon sounded, as it meant he had to come back the following day. Even though he was only on £2000 he says he just wanted to get out and go home. He has paid off his mortgage and feels as though a whole weight has been lifted off his shoulders; he is now building a new house to sell on. He and Miranda recently spent twenty-eight days in the Seychelles – their first holiday for many years. He is still working, but he says he doesn't worry about money now at all, and enjoys his life much, much more.

Ian Horsewell

We've noticed now, on *Millionaire*, that big winners are like buses. You wait ages for one and then, all of a sudden, two or three come along all at once. By sheer coincidence this is exactly what happened on the very night that Martin Skillings became the first person ever to win £125,000. There must have been something in the air, or the water that night.

Martin and Miranda left with the biggest-ever cheque we had ever written, and, with the audience still on a high, off we went again.

I read out Fastest Finger First:

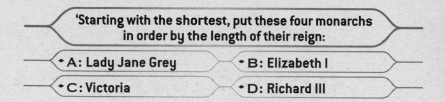

'Starting with the shortest, put these four monarchs in order by the length of their reign:

- A: Lady Jane Grey
- B: Elizabeth I
- C: Victoria
- D: Richard III

The correct order is Lady Jane Grey, who reigned as Queen for just nine days; Richard III; Queen Elizabeth I; and finally Queen Victoria, who reigned for sixty-three years. A nice little guy with a moustache, Ian Horsewell, was the fastest with the correct answer.

The whole studio was still a bit numb from the elation of Martin Skillings's big win, and Ian said he also felt drained by the evening so far.

Ian, who came from Gillingham in Dorset, answered the early questions very fast. The first time he even paused for breath was on this question for £2000:

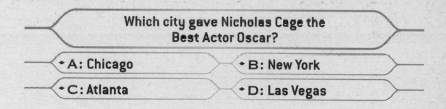

Which city gave Nicholas Cage the Best Actor Oscar?

- A: Chicago
- B: New York
- C: Atlanta
- D: Las Vegas

He looked at the screen long and hard and then said slowly, 'It's "Las Vegas". Final answer.' Right answer – he was on £2000.

It wasn't until the £8000 question that he needed any Lifelines:

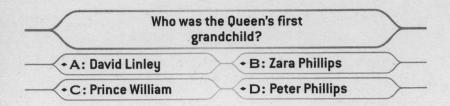

Who was the Queen's first grandchild?

A: David Linley

B: Zara Phillips

C: Prince William

D: Peter Phillips

Ian wasn't sure and used up his 50:50. 'Peter Phillips' and 'Zara Phillips' remained. 'In that case it is definitely "Peter",' said Ian, which was good thinking and put him on £8000.

A question on the triathlon that he knew straight away got him to £16,000.

For £32,000 up came a question that I knew – well, I would know this, wouldn't I? – as soon as it appeared on the screen:

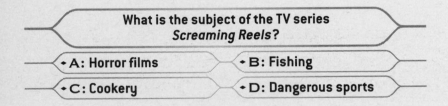

What is the subject of the TV series _Screaming Reels_?

A: Horror films

B: Fishing

C: Cookery

D: Dangerous sports

Ian wasn't at all sure and asked the audience. Eighty-two per cent of them voted for 'fishing', although, scarily, 1 per cent thought that _Screaming Reels_ was a cooking programme! Ian went with the majority and was now guaranteed £32,000. He punched the air.

After the show, in the bar, Ian said that one of the greatest adrenalin rushes he had ever experienced was when I asked him a question to which he knew the answer before the four options came up on screen. It happened several times to him that night and he said he'll never forget the tremendous buzz that it gave him.

The £64,000 question was an example of exactly that. The question was this:

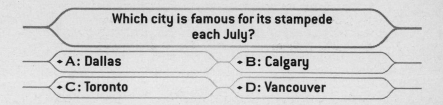

Which city is famous for its stampede each July?

A: Dallas
B: Calgary
C: Toronto
D: Vancouver

Ian threw his arms up in the air as soon as the question came up. 'I know it,' he said. 'I'm absolutely 100 per cent certain it's the Calgary stampede.' And he raced effortlessly on to £64,000.

Just minutes earlier Martin Skillings had been the first person ever to win £125,000. The next contestant, Ian Horsewell, was now on a question that could equal that:

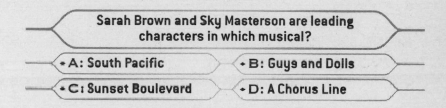

Sarah Brown and Sky Masterson are leading characters in which musical?

A: South Pacific
B: Guys and Dolls
C: Sunset Boulevard
D: A Chorus Line

'I'll phone Paul,' said Ian. 'Do you want me to tell him how much money this is for?' I asked him. 'Absolutely,' he told me. 'He won't be phased by it at all.' He wasn't either. As soon as the question came up he said to Ian, 'It's "Guys and Dolls" – I'm 900 per cent certain.' 'Can I kill you if you're wrong, Paul?' asked Ian. 'Of course you can,' said Paul amiably, knowing that he wasn't. 'Final answer,' said Ian. Paul was absolutely right and Ian Horsewell was now the second contestant to be handed a cheque for £125,000.

But he wasn't necessarily finished yet. He was now looking focused, for there was a good chance that with the right question he could take the new record up a notch by winning £250,000, or even more.

He had been pretty laid-back so far, but now, with this amount of money at stake and the potential to lose £93,000, he was looking deadly serious. As you would!

This was the question for £250,000:

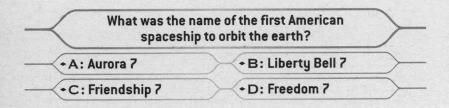

What was the name of the first American spaceship to orbit the earth?

A: Aurora ?   B: Liberty Bell ?

C: Friendship ?   D: Freedom ?

'I've absolutely no idea,' said Ian without a moment's hesitation. 'I'm out of here. Goodbye,' and he was off before I could bat an eyelid – £125,000 better off. He was only the second person ever to achieve this. Amazingly, two consecutive contestants on the same fantastic night had won £125,000. The correct answer, incidentally, was 'Friendship 7', but Ian couldn't have cared less as he raced towards the bar.

Life After *Who Wants To Be A Millionaire?*

Talking today about the difference the money has made to his life, Ian says, 'Apart from the obvious – my money worries gone – I have actually become a much nicer person. I used to be easily irritated and quite abrasive and now I'm much more laid-back and relaxed. It has made a big difference to the way I treat others. That means that my family and I have been able to enjoy far more of the good things in life.'

He gave some money to all his Phone-A-Friends – especially to Paul Moody, who gave him the £125,000 answer – has invested some and the rest of it has allowed him to finish renovating his house in one go, instead of just having to do one room at a time. He has also had an extension built, and most recently bought a plot of land in Spain to have a house built on.

Ian says he still seems to get recognised wherever he goes, and the question most asked of him in the past couple of years has been, 'What's that Chris Tarrant really like?' To which Ian always replies, 'Well, what would you think of a bloke who gives you £125,000?'

John Davidson

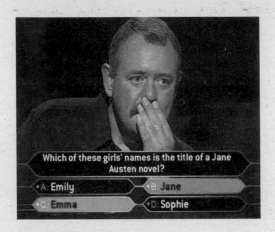

John Davidson, from Northumberland, was a big, amiable Geordie who seemed bright in rehearsal and we expected him to do well. His wife sat happily in the audience cheering his every word. He told us he had three kids, all glued to the set at home, and a trusty German shepherd, Todd, watching from his kennel.

He didn't ask for much out of life, he said, but if he did win £1,000,000 he wanted to travel the world with Sandra Bullock and Victoria Principal. So, nothing too ambitious. Even his wife, clearly a very understanding girl, seemed happy at the prospect.

He settled in and off we went, nice and easy:

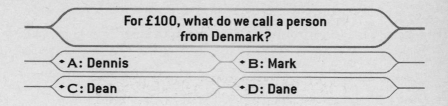

For £100, what do we call a person from Denmark?

A: Dennis   B: Mark

C: Dean   D: Dane

He went for 'Dane', of course. He got to £500 without pausing for breath. It was all proving very straightforward.

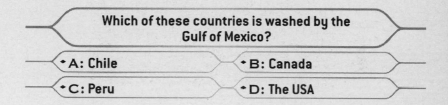

Which of these countries is washed by the Gulf of Mexico?

A: Chile   B: Canada

C: Peru   D: The USA

After barely a moment's hesitation, he said 'I know this one, Chris, it's "the USA".' And of course it is: Texas and Florida are both on the Gulf of Mexico. 'OK, John,' I said, 'let's get you to a guaranteed £1000. If you get this next question right, £1000 is the very minimum you will leave here with tonight.'

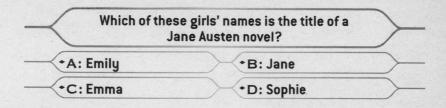

Which of these girls' names is the title of a Jane Austen novel?

A: Emily   B: Jane

C: Emma   D: Sophie

Again, this didn't faze him at all – and I knew the answer because I'd read Jane Austen during three long, dull years at university. 'Jane,' he said. A sudden panic crept into my heart. 'Absolutely certain? You've got three

Lifelines,' I reminded him. 'No,' he said, 'I'll save them for later. It's definitely "Jane". Final answer.' I was horrified. I couldn't help him. I couldn't bail him out. The audience looked uneasily at the back of his head. Even in the darkness I could see one or two of them suddenly staring sorrowfully at their feet. It was a horrible moment. 'John,' I said. 'John, I'm so sorry – it's the wrong answer. The answer is "Emma".'

For a second I don't think the penny really dropped for John. 'You're joking?' he asked, dumbfounded. 'I'm sorry, John, I'm afraid you go home with absolutely nothing.' The audience were stunned. I was stunned. 'Come on,' I said, 'let's give him a big hand. At least he got here. He got in the chair and he tried his best.' Everybody obliged me and cheered loudly, but for all of us it was sickening. He had the use of three Lifelines and I'm sure any one of them would almost certainly have swerved him away from 'Jane' to the right answer.

For this to happen is always a horrible moment but it was somehow worse for poor John Davidson, in that he was the very, very first person who had left with nothing. It is a rare occurrence – there are no trick questions on *Who Wants To Be A Millionaire?* and, usually, the first five questions are extremely straightforward, often absurdly easy. Sometimes that is the problem: they are so easy that people pause for a second in a disbelieving panic. But at the level of two or three hundred quid, if the question is, 'What is the capital of France – Paris, Düsseldorf, Wolverhampton or Toulouse', the answer really will be 'Paris'. It will not have become 'Wolverhampton' overnight.

In four years of *Millionaire*, only three people have gone home with no money at all, but poor John Davidson will always have the unwelcome distinction of being the first.

Tony Kennedy

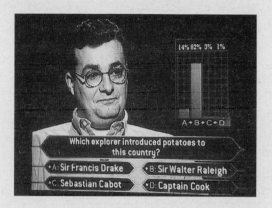

Tony Kennedy, an amiable, young warehouseman from Blackpool, was a bright lad. He was also a lucky lad, more so than he ever realised. He was very chirpy, not remotely fazed by the show, the audience or me. He told me, quite frankly, that if he won £1,000,000 he loved his job so much he would still be back in the warehouse on Monday – but only to say goodbye. He would spend his million very wisely, by buying a big new house and a swimming pool, which he would fill to the brim with malt whisky!

His wife Julie, expecting a baby in two months, sat behind him grinning uneasily throughout the show, in the way that only a woman seven months pregnant would, watching her husband, just a few yards in front of her but completely out of reach, trying to change their lives for the better in a very public arena. Julie seemed to be feeling the pressure in the early stages far more than Tony, who got off to a flying start, reaching £1000 with a question about the Millennium Bug. On £2000 we called it a night, and off he went, with all three Lifelines untouched.

The young Kennedys came back the next day with Julie looking a lot calmer and Tony in a new, bright-green shirt. Tony was unlike many other contestants, who find every second of the show an ordeal – he said to me that he was absolutely loving it. He had a twinkling smile behind his glasses, and was constantly engaging me in eyeball-to-eyeball contact, as if daring me to try to unsettle him. He was a good guy; I really liked him.

He didn't need a Lifeline until he got to £16,000:

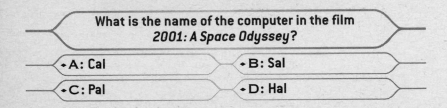

What is the name of the computer in the film
2001: A Space Odyssey?

A: Cal **B: Sal**
C: Pal **D: Hal**

He asked for his 50:50 and he was left with 'Cal' and 'Hal'. He went for 'Hal' straight away. 'I'm absolutely sure it's right,' he said. It was. He was on £16,000.

Already he had probably earned more in ten or fifteen minutes than he would in a year as a warehouseman. For £32,000 he decided to Ask the Audience this question:

Which explorer introduced potatoes into this country?

A: Sir Francis Drake **B: Sir Walter Raleigh**
C: Sebastian Cabot **D: Captain Cook**

Eighty-two per cent of the audience thought it was 'Raleigh'. I knew that from my schooldays, and that he'd also brought back tobacco. Tony started to pray. He closed his eyes and murmured, 'Don't fail me now, audience.' They didn't – he'd won £32,000. 'I love you all,' he screamed, to their delight. When he saw the cheque I had just written in his name, he said in wonder, 'That's absolutely beautiful.' Then, for £64,000, he was thrown a rather weird question:

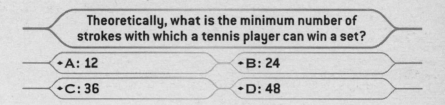

Theoretically, what is the minimum number of strokes with which a tennis player can win a set?

A: 12   B: 24
C: 36   D: 48

He grinned at me. 'I know it – it's "24",' he said, his plump little body shaking with pleasure. 'Are you sure?' I said. 'I think so,' said Tony. 'Confident?' 'Fairly confident.' 'Tennis player?' 'With this shape?' he replied. 'I've got more chance of being a tennis ball!' He was extremely entertaining. I was also pretty sure that he was right. 'Final answer?' I said. 'Absolutely,' he replied and it went to orange. The right answer came up on my screen. Four points is the minimum with which you can win a game of tennis; the points go 15, 30, 40, game; there are six games in a set, so if you won each game six-love, six fours would make twenty-four – the right answer.

'You've just won £64,000,' I told him with great pleasure. Tony fanned the air in delight and the audience clapped and stamped. This was now a very serious business. Sixty-four thousand pounds was a colossal sum of money for a young warehouseman, whose wife was expecting their first baby in a matter of weeks. Better still, he had one Lifeline remaining and was only four questions from £1,000,000. The tension was palpable on set, but still Tony remained very calm and buoyant.

This was the question for £125,000:

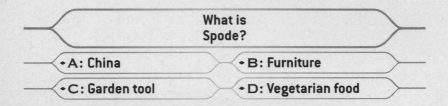

What is
Spode?

- A: China
- B: Furniture
- C: Garden tool
- D: Vegetarian food

'I'll have to Phone-A-Friend,' he said more or less straight away. 'I'm really not sure. You can tell him how much money's involved. He's called David.' I rang David, who remained impressively calm when I told him that this question was worth £125,000. 'I know the answer to this one, Tony,' said David. 'It's "china".' 'Are you sure?' asked Tony. 'Absolutely definitely,' said David. 'You'll do for me, pal,' said Tony. With £125,000 at stake, I felt the very least I could do was go for a commercial break, despite Tony's half-joking threats to kill me.

Three minutes later, possibly the longest three minutes of Tony Kennedy's young life, I told him that his mate David had just won him £125,000, at which point the cavalier, casual Tony completely lost it and yelled at the top of his voice, 'Yes! Yes! Yes!'

He was only the third person to win £125,000 since the show had started and he was certainly proving the most demonstrative. His days in the warehouse were now almost certainly over for ever. For £250,000 he got this question:

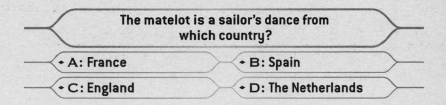

The matelot is a sailor's dance from
which country?

◆ A: France ◆ B: Spain

◆ C: England ◆ D: The Netherlands

'Give us the cheque,' he said. 'I haven't got a clue.'
'Don't you want to think about it for a little while?' I
teased. 'Are you mad?' he said. 'Lose ninety-three grand?
I've got a baby due. Come on, Chris – gimme the cheque!'
I did as I was told, and he and Julie left Elstree on cloud
nine.

By the way, the matelot is a sailor's dance from Holland.

But Tony Kennedy's *Who Wants To Be A Millionaire?*
story was not over yet. Something agonising happened
later that night. Straight after the show, we started to
receive calls saying that 'twenty-four' was the wrong
answer to the tennis question. The argument was tenuous
but we had to concede that if one player double-faults all
the way through his service games and the other player
wins all of his service games with aces, then technically it
would be possible for a game of tennis to be won in twelve
strokes, not twenty-four. I couldn't believe it. Tony and
Julie were halfway back up the motorway to Blackpool
when the calls began and I had a horrible, sick feeling,
since technically these callers were correct. It would be
the dullest game of tennis on earth; it would be like Pete
Sampras playing against my little ten-year-old son Toby.
Nonetheless, this school of thought were declaring that
Tony had given the wrong answer and that therefore his
£125,000 was null and void. How this would affect the

Kennedys was too painful even to contemplate. In my opinion the computer had said that 'twenty-four' was the right answer; we had accepted on air that 'twenty-four' was the right answer; I had told Tony on air that 'twenty-four' was the right answer. Therefore the result had to stand.

It was a horrible decision. ITV and Celador could not be seen to be paying out huge sums of money to people who'd answered a question incorrectly. I argued that it was an absurdly tenuous answer to the question but, above all, if we had told Tony he was right, then we had to face up to the consequences and pay up.

None of us slept very well that night – well, none of us, presumably, apart from Tony and Julie, who were safely tucked up in bed in Blackpool, having no idea of the drama that was being played out at ITV headquarters in London.

Mercifully, the next morning, common sense prevailed. I then explained on that night's show that the tennis question had an alternative answer, but that because the computer and I had accepted Tony Kennedy's answer the evening before, the result would stand and he would keep his £125,000. It was a huge relief to all of us. Retracting the money would have been a PR disaster for *Millionaire* and an unthinkable thing to do to the Kennedys. But Tony had had a close shave, closer than he ever realised.

Davy Young

Davy Young was a civil servant from Belfast — a sturdy Northern Irishman who had a constant twinkle in his eye. His brother-in-law James sat in the audience; his wife had wanted to come as well but she couldn't get the day off work.

Davy wanted to buy a bungalow on stilts in the Philippines if he won a million quid. Apparently he'd once visited a perfect paradise island there and he wanted to return with his family and enjoy its tranquillity for the rest of his life.

He got settled into the chair, had no problem at all up to £500 and then the klaxon went. I wished Davy good luck for the show the next night, and off he went with James for a drink or three.

He reappeared mob-handed, accompanied by not only Jim but his wife as well. Her employers, it seemed, had relented. Poor old Davy told me, 'I've already spent most of my £500 in the bar last night so, with half the family here and yesterday's bar bill, I'm running on minus!'

But he got to his guaranteed £1000 with a question about Helmut Kohl and started to feel a lot better. The first time he needed a Lifeline was on £8000, when he was thrown this question:

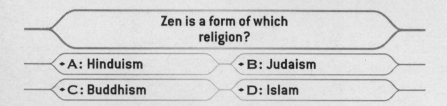

Davy said he was pretty sure, but he wanted to make double sure, which made a lot of sense. So he asked the audience and 86 per cent of them gave him the right answer – 'Buddhism'.

He looked at the £16,000 question in horror when it came up on his screen:

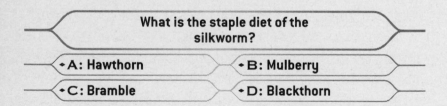

'I haven't a clue,' said Davy. 'I think I'll phone my friend Alan.' 'Does he know about silkworms?' I asked Davy. 'I hope so!' he replied with a laugh. But when he spoke to Alan, Alan wasn't particularly certain either. 'What a question,' he said. 'I'm not sure, Davy. My best guess is "mulberry", but I really don't know where it comes from.' Davy thought long and hard and said, 'I know he doesn't sound certain, but I'm going to go with him. Come on, let's risk it.' He was living dangerously, but it won him £16,000.

Davy was now starting to look very worried. He was on £16,000 but he knew that he'd been very close to losing almost all of it.

For £32,000 he got this:

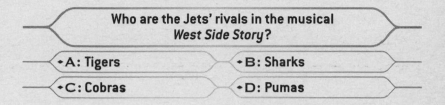

Who are the Jets' rivals in the musical *West Side Story*?

- A: Tigers
- B: Sharks
- C: Cobras
- D: Pumas

Our poor Irishman now looked as if he'd been hit between the eyes with a mallet. 'I'll go 50:50,' he eventually decided. 'Tigers' and 'Sharks' remained. One of those was the right answer; one of them would cost him £15,000.

'I really don't know,' said Davy. 'I'd probably say "Sharks" but I'm not going to risk it. I'll take the money.' Then, suddenly, he glanced at me with a slightly crazed smile on his face and said, 'Oh come on. What the hell. It's only money. I'm going with "Sharks". You're only here once. Final answer.'

Of course, this is the attitude that can lose people a lot of money, but it is also the sort of spirit that you probably need if you are going to win £1,000,000. Davy realised that this was his once-in-a-lifetime chance to be in the *Millionaire* chair, and he was going to try to make the most of it. 'I'll play,' he said. 'Final answer – "Sharks".' 'It's the right answer!' I told him. 'You're a very brave guy.' It was a fantastic moment. He'd probably gone against his better judgement, but he'd won the money. The minimum he'd go home with was £32,000 and there were tears in the eyes of Davy and his wife. 'How do you feel?' I asked him. 'I just want a huge gin and tonic,' he said.

He had no Lifelines left but he had nothing to lose by playing the next question for £64,000.

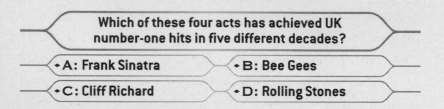

Which of these four acts has achieved UK number-one hits in five different decades?

- ◆ A: Frank Sinatra
- ◆ B: Bee Gees
- ◆ C: Cliff Richard
- ◆ D: Rolling Stones

'I might as well go for it,' he said. 'I think it's "the Rolling Stones".' 'Final answer?' I asked him. 'No,' he abruptly decided. 'Actually, let me change my mind. "Cliff Richard". Go on, "Cliff Richard". Final answer.' It went to orange and 'Cliff Richard' was the right answer. Sixty-four thousand pounds – by the skin of his teeth. Davy's courage was now earning him very serious money.

The next question was for £125,000:

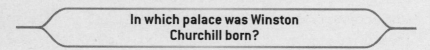

In which palace was Winston Churchill born?

I knew the answer at once, not because I'm particularly clever but because I've fished there lots of times, in the big lake in the grounds. I just hoped that Davy knew it too.

- ◆ A: Richmond
- ◆ B: Buckingham
- ◆ C: Lambeth
- ◆ D: Blenheim

'I think it's "Blenheim",' he said. 'Final answer?' I asked him, hoping it was. 'Yes,' he confirmed. 'Go for it. "Blenheim".' Again, he was spot on – he had clawed his way up to a fantastic £125,000. He started to giggle like a schoolboy when I showed him the cheque. 'This is incredible,' he said. 'I was going to run for it at sixteen grand.'

But Davy wasn't too foolhardy. He realised that he'd pushed his luck about as far as it would stretch. He didn't know, nor could he care less, about the next question – it was a very obscure one about an eighteenth-century Swedish botanist – and he took about half a second to make up his mind. 'That's it,' he said, 'It's been fantastic. I'm out of here!'

His wife, family and the entire audience stood up to cheer him all the way out of the studio.

Davy Young was a very lucky man, but sometimes you have to make your own luck. By doing so with great guts, Davy went skipping back home all the way to Northern Ireland £125,000 better off than when he had left home two days earlier.

Life After *Who Wants To Be A Millionaire?*

Davy has spent about £40,000 of the money and invested the rest for his retirement. He bought a travel caravan big enough for the entire family and a new Volvo, a car he had always wanted. He also took a wonderful three-week holiday in Disneyworld with his wife Lynn.

He says he was ready to leave on £16,000 – he couldn't feel anything in his fingers, they'd gone completely numb.

Jonathan Green

Jonathan Green was a fireman. On the night of his appearance his wife had to stay at home with their kids. One son Paul was lending support up in the audience and another twelve-year-old son was waiting on the end of the line as a Phone-A-Friend.

Perhaps it's part of his fireman's training, but Jonathan seemed very calm, very controlled. He certainly had no problem with the early questions. He thought hard about each answer before giving me very measured careful replies. He got to £1000 on this question:

What does a PhD entitle the holder of such a qualification to be called?

A: Sir

B: Your Honour

C: Doctor

D: My Lord

'Doctor' is, of course, the right answer, as Jonathan knew. He now also knew he was going back home to the wife and kids with at least £1000.

Paul clapped away enthusiastically in the audience.

Jonathan did say at this point that he was extremely wary of asking the audience anything. The previous night 55 per cent of them had been completely wrong and a contestant had lost a lot of money because of it. So Jonathan was going to be understandably cautious about asking them for help, or going with their majority answer.

It wasn't until £8000 that Jonathan started to sweat at all. The first time he looked even remotely worried was on this question:

What is the name of Chicago's
main international airport?

A: O'Donnell   B: O'Keefe
C: O'Malley   D: O'Hare

'I don't want to use a Lifeline yet,' Jonathan said, 'even though I am not at all sure of the answer. I think it's "O'Hare", but I'm not certain.' He looked at me with deep concern. But then suddenly and dramatically he fell back on his instinct. Over the years that followed, going with one's first instinct has usually been a good rule of thumb, but I have to say on the occasions when it hasn't worked, the consequences have usually been absolutely disastrous. 'It's "O'Hare,"' he said. 'Final answer.' It went to orange and my screen lit up with the magic words 'right answer'. Jonathan was now on £8000 and he'd still kept back all those Lifelines, which could be critical. However, he did need to use one on the next question, for £16,000:

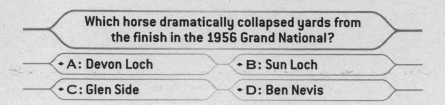

Which horse dramatically collapsed yards from the finish in the 1956 Grand National?

- A: Devon Loch
- B: Sun Loch
- C: Glen Side
- D: Ben Nevis

'I think I know the answer,' Jonathan said. 'I think it's "Devon Loch", but I'm not 100 per cent certain. I'll go 50:50.' This left 'Devon Loch' and 'Sun Loch'. 'I'll go "Devon Loch",' he said. 'Final answer,' he added, closing his eyes. 'It's the right answer,' I told him. He'd just won £16,000.

(The tragic pictures of Devon Loch have been shown on newsreel film hundreds of times over the years since 1956. The horse, owned by the Queen Mother and ridden by Dick Francis, collapsed just yards from the finishing line.)

He'd got his £16,000 but the pressure was now clearly beginning to get to Jonathan. He was closing his eyes and puffing a lot.

This question came up for £32,000:

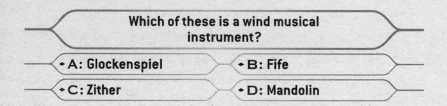

Which of these is a wind musical instrument?

- A: Glockenspiel
- B: Fife
- C: Zither
- D: Mandolin

'I'll play,' said Jonathan straight away, 'It's "Fife".' 'Why are you so certain?' I asked him. 'Because I'm sure the other three are not wind instruments,' he said. His logical thinking had doubled his money. By now Paul was jumping up and down in the audience. Dad looked very calm but admitted to me afterwards that a sort of numbness had set in.

He raced straight to £64,000 for knowing that 'agoraphobia' was a fear of open spaces. Suddenly, with two Lifelines still left, he was facing this question for £125,000:

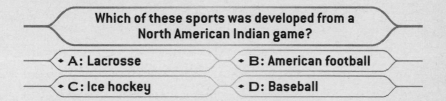

Which of these sports was developed from a North American Indian game?

A: Lacrosse

B: American football

C: Ice hockey

D: Baseball

'You've got two Lifelines,' I reminded Jonathan. 'I don't need them,' he said. 'I'll go for "A. Lacrosse". I'm sure it's the right answer.' For the first time Paul up in the audience looked really worried. He kept biting his lip and looking down at his feet. Dad was now risking losing £93,000. Paul needn't have worried. Dad was absolutely spot on and he now had £125,000 – still with two Lifelines unused. Not that his Lifelines were necessarily going to be that helpful. Not only had the audience the night before been completely wrong, but one of Jonathan's Phone-A-Friends was his own twelve-year-old son. However, as a firefighter, he was very much a nothing-ventured, nothing-gained type and took a long, hard look at this question for £250,000.

This was another potentially historic moment on *Who Wants To Be A Millionaire?* If Jonathan answered this question correctly, I reminded him, he would be the happy recipient of the largest cheque I had handed over to anybody on the show since we had started broadcasting almost a year earlier.

This was the question:

What creatures live in a formicary?

- A: Bees
- B: Fish
- C: Ants
- D: Worms

'I think I'd better Phone-A-Friend,' he decided, after a few minutes' consideration. 'I'll call Noel.' 'Hello, Noel, I've got Jonathan Green here,' I told his friend. 'He's playing for £250,000. There's probably a drink in this for you.' 'I should hope so,' said Noel. After Jonathan had asked him the question, Noel responded, 'I'm fairly certain it's "ants". From the Latin,' he added impressively. 'It's up to you, Jonathan,' I said. 'Noel wasn't 100 per cent certain and if he's wrong you lose £93,000.' 'No, Chris,' replied Jonathan, 'he sounded sure enough. I'm going to play. "Ants" – final answer.' Noel was absolutely right and had just won Jonathan Green £250,000.

He was now assured a place in TV history. He was right across the front pages of all the papers the next morning, and we had a press conference with Jonathan, his whole family and his Phone-A-Friend Noel that afternoon.

But it still wasn't over.

This was the question for £500,000 and, of course, Jonathan could still Ask the Audience he trusted so much.

> **Which of his queens did Henry VIII refer to as his 'Flanders mare'?**

Now I knew this question as soon as it came on the screen, before any of the answers were shown. From somewhere way back in the mists of time I knew at once that Henry VIII had called the hideous Anne of Cleves his 'Flanders mare'. If I'd been a Phone-A-Friend for Jonathan I would have said go with it, I am 100 per cent certain. Thinking about it after the show, I realised it was a good example of how these things get tucked away in your brain and yet are somehow there on call for the rest of your life. It happens on *Millionaire* night after night. I probably hadn't thought about Anne of Cleves since I was doing History A level in the sixth form over thirty years earlier, and yet she popped up now, and I would have staked my life on her being the right answer. We've all experienced this, but it still feels a strange phenomenon.

Up came the four alternatives:

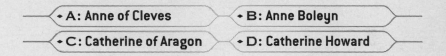

A: Anne of Cleves   B: Anne Boleyn
C: Catherine of Aragon   D: Catherine Howard

There are few things more frustrating for me, especially with this amount of money at stake, than sitting there being absolutely sure of the answer, yet not being able to communicate it to the person opposite me. Then again, Jonathan had, along the way, known two or three questions that I would really have struggled on. This time, however, he conceded, 'I just don't know. I'm going to take the money.'

'Well, out of interest,' I said, 'you might as well Ask the Audience while you are here.' 'OK,' he said, 'let's ask them.' Forty-three per cent said 'Anne of Cleves', 29 per cent said 'Anne Boleyn', 23 per cent said 'Catherine of Aragon' and 5 per cent said 'Catherine Howard'. 'It's just not conclusive enough,' said Jonathan, 'not at this level. If they are wrong I lose £218,000. I'm going to walk away.' And off he went £250,000 better off.

But, of course, if he had gone, with the majority of the audience, for 'Anne of Cleves', I would have been writing him out a cheque for half a million quid!

Sonia Davis

S onia Davis was a very excitable girl. In fact I'm sure
she won't mind me saying she was one of the most
excitable contestants we've ever seen. She screamed. She
sobbed. Her fists fanned the air. She threw her head
around, shaking her hair in manic convulsions. She went to
hell and back with every question. And that was only in
the afternoon rehearsal!

When she won Fastest Finger First on the night, she
went crazy, yelling ecstatically at the top of her voice and

grabbing and shaking me like one of the Wild Women of Wonga. To calm her down I did point out that she hadn't actually won anything yet. 'Oh, I know,' she responded. 'But it's just fantastic. I can't believe I got it right!'

Her sister Sue was sitting up in the audience, looking thoroughly embarrassed for every second that Sonia was on the screen, and her little boy was watching at home in north Devon. If she won £1,000,000, she told me, she wanted to go to Malaysia with Joanna Lumley, because she's witty, intelligent, smokes, drinks and can make a pair of shoes out of a brassière. Welcome to Planet Sonia.

She also wanted cosmetic surgery. Not to her face – Sonia was a beautiful-looking woman – but to her legs. She wanted them stretched, because they were too short. Although she was quite tall, she said, 'Most of my length is my body. My legs aren't long enough.' She was a great contestant, very articulate, very pretty, extraordinarily animated and completely potty. Once we actually started playing, she got more and more hyperactive with each question that I asked her. When she got the £200 question right, I had to gently stop her clapping herself. 'It's up to you,' I said. 'But it makes you look a bit like a sea lion! Also,' I reminded her, 'it's the sort of thing those housewives do on *Supermarket Sweep* when they get the price of a tin of peas right.' That calmed her down for a bit.

She got to the £1000 question:

> **Where were the famous Hanging Gardens, one of the Seven Wonders of the World?**
>
> A: Thebes   B: Babylon
> C: Rhodes   D: Alexandria

'I know this,' said Sonia. 'I definitely know this one. It's "Babylon".' She was absolutely right. (Babylon is in modern-day Iraq, which is probably why they don't get as many visitors to the Hanging Gardens as they used to.)

When the £2000 question came up, Sonia looked terribly worried:

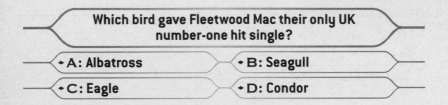

Which bird gave Fleetwood Mac their only UK number-one hit single?

◆ A: Albatross   ◆ B: Seagull

◆ C: Eagle   ◆ D: Condor

'Oh I really don't know,' she said. 'I'll have to Ask the Audience.' She assumed a look of horror at the prospect. She needn't have worried – 78 per cent of the audience knew the song was 'Albatross', although it was worrying that 3 per cent thought Fleetwood Mac had a big UK number-one hit with 'Seagull'.

'I did think it was "Albatross",' she claimed. 'I really did.' 'You're a liar,' I said to her amiably. 'You're right, I am. I didn't have a clue,' she admitted. 'I just wanted to look bright for a minute.' The audience laughed happily and Sonia was on £2000.

For £4000 she got this question:

Which successful film musical featured child stars Mark Lester and Jack Wild?

◆ A: Mary Poppins   ◆ B: The Sound of Music

◆ C: My Fair Lady   ◆ D: Oliver

'I think it's "D"', she said, '"Oliver". Oh no I don't. Yes I do. Final answer. I'm going to play "Oliver".' She looked distinctly unsure of what she'd just done.

'We'll take a break,' I said. 'You can't do that. You just can't do that!' she screamed in horror. 'Yes I can,' I answered calmly. 'I do it every night.' When we finally came back I was delighted to tell Sonia that 'Oliver' was the right answer and she'd just won £4000. She went berserk again, and this time I couldn't stop her waving her arms in the air.

For £8000 the computer asked her:

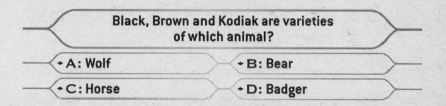

Black, Brown and Kodiak are varieties of which animal?

A: Wolf   B: Bear

C: Horse   D: Badger

'I think it's a bear,' she said. I knew she was right, but I kept the usual gormless mask on my face as best I could. 'Are you sure?' I asked her. 'No, I'm not sure at all,' she suddenly decided. 'I was confident, but now I've lost all my confidence. I'll Phone-A-Friend. I'll phone Peter.' 'Who's Peter?' I asked. 'He's a gardener,' she said. Well, he's bound to know, isn't he, I thought. But, whoever Peter was, he certainly did. As soon as she asked the question, without even hearing the alternatives, he said, 'The answer is "bear", Sonia. No problem, go for it.' Just the sort of Phone-A-Friend you need, and thanks to Peter the gardener she had now won £8000.

We moved on to question nine:

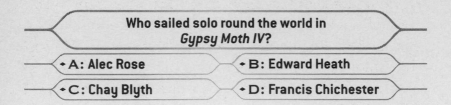

Who sailed solo round the world in
Gypsy Moth IV?

◆ A: Alec Rose   ◆ B: Edward Heath

◆ C: Chay Blyth   ◆ D: Francis Chichester

'Oh God!' Sonia moaned. 'I've never heard of at least one of them. I'll have to use my 50:50 . This is so unfair because I knew the last one!' I gently pointed out to Sonia that knowing the last one wasn't really much use on this show, you had to know each one as it came up. Her sister up in the audience was, by now, going through agonies and shaking her head nervously. It must have been a mixture of worry about how much Sonia might win or lose and a genuine fear of what her sister was going to say next. I could relate to that – I was starting to feel pretty much like it myself. But Sonia was a fantastic character.

Alec Rose and Francis Chichester were left after the 50:50 . 'I've never heard of Alec Rose,' she said. 'I bet it was him, just because I've never heard of him. Oh God, this is hopeless. I'm completely stuck! I'm going to play "Alec Rose",' she then decided. 'You're playing "Alec Rose" because you've never heard of him?' I asked. 'Yes,' she said. '"Alec Rose" – final answer,' and she put her hands over her eyes in sheer terror at the enormity of what she'd just done. She needn't have worried – it was the right answer and she'd just won £16,000. Sonia couldn't believe it. She'd got through all her Lifelines but she was just one question away from the leap to an assured £32,000.

It was this:

The spice saffron is obtained from which flower?

Sonia looked very confident. 'Do you know this?' I asked her. 'Yes, I think so,' she said delightedly.

Up came 'A: Crocus'. Sonia shook her head. Up came 'B: Tulip'. She shook her head. Up came 'C: Daffodil'. She shook her head. Finally, up came 'D: Hyacinth'. She shook her head. 'Oh dear,' she said, 'it's obviously not the one I thought at all. In fact I don't really know what I was expecting, but it's not there, whatever it was.'

'You've got £16,000,' I told her patiently. 'You really don't have to play this question. 'Yes, but I want £32,000,' said Sonia. 'Of course you do,' I said. 'But you don't know the answer.' 'Well, I might do,' she said. 'I think it might be "hyacinth". Then again, it might not.' Sonia was clearly agonising. Out of the blue she asked me, 'Do you know?' 'It doesn't matter if I know,' I told her. 'I'm not in it. It's sort of how it works every night.'

'I'm gonna play,' she eventually said. '"Hyacinth".' 'Final answer?' I asked her, trying to keep my voice even, since I secretly knew that she was completely wrong. 'No,' she said, 'Oh dear, I'm so sorry to keep you waiting,' she added very politely. 'Don't worry about it,' I said. 'You can take the money or play. There's no hurry. Take as long as you need.' 'I'm going to play,' she said positively. Then a second later she decided, equally positively, 'Oh no I'm not, I'm going to take the money.' 'Are you sure?' I asked her. 'Yes!' she shouted wildly. 'I've had enough.' So we all cheered her away, relieved she hadn't lost a possible £15,000, and that she was going home £16,000 better off.

And indeed, if she had stuck with 'hyacinth', which she very nearly did, our fears would have been realised. The right answer was 'crocus'.

Mike Cooke

Of course, I'm supposed to remain totally unbiased towards each of our contestants, but, if ever there was someone I wanted to see succeed on the show, it was Mike Cooke from Cheltenham.

He was a chirpy little guy with a lilting West Country accent, and his life must have been a real struggle, for he suffered a serious disability: he had no arms. Just watching him in rehearsal, battling with Fastest Finger First, was harrowing in itself. And yet, by putting his body through the most extraordinary contortions, he could manage to press the buttons. Knowing the right answer and inputting it at speed is a big enough problem for every contestant every night, but for Mike it was obviously a personal mountain.

So, imagine everybody's delight when he won Fastest Finger First that night on the show. He was up like a little jack-in-the-box. He had his niece Victoria in the audience, who seemed to be far more terrified by the whole thing than Mike. His wife Karen and six-year-old-son Toby were watching at home in Cheltenham. In spite of his disability, Mike had achieved so much in his life, including, he told me proudly, restoring three houses and playing percussion in a local orchestra. He was an awe-inspiring guy.

If he won £1,000,000, he wanted to saunter into a Rolls-Royce dealership wearing the scruffiest old clothes he could find, choose a car and say, 'All right, mate, I'll have that one over there, and I'll pay in cash!' He kept saying to me, 'Whatever happens, I'm loving this. I'm just so pleased to be here.' He was a great bloke and was beaming from the moment he got into the chair. His fifth question was:

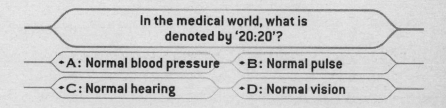

'"D",' said Mike. '"Normal vision".' 'Absolutely correct,' I said. 'You've won £1000.'

The next question was more testing for him.

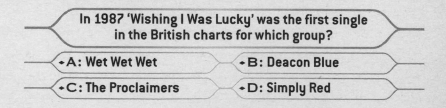

'I was dreading one of these,' said Mike. 'I'm absolutely hopeless at pop music.' 'Well, it's your choice,' I told him. 'But you could Ask the Audience. I'm pretty sure they'll know this one. It was a huge hit.' 'OK,' said Mike, 'I'll ask them, because I haven't got a clue.'

My theory was right. The audience certainly did know — a huge 93 per cent of them said 'Wet Wet Wet'. Mike looked delighted and now had £2000. He kept grinning. He was proving a real pleasure to have on the show and I desperately wanted him to do well.

For £4000 the computer asked him:

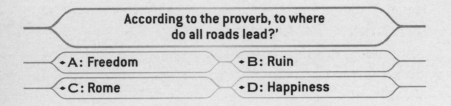

According to the proverb, to where do all roads lead?'

A: Freedom
B: Ruin
C: Rome
D: Happiness

'I've got an idea. I think it's "ruin",' said Mike. 'I'm not certain, though. I'll go 50:50 .' 'Ruin' disappeared, leaving just 'freedom' or 'Rome'. Mike cackled. 'Doesn't look like it was "ruin" then, does it, Chris?' 'No, Mike. I think you can be pretty certain that it wasn't,' I agreed. 'You've got £2000 at this moment. You can obviously take the money.' 'No,' he said. 'I think it must be "Rome".' I knew damn well it was but I had to keep my usual deadpan face. I would have loved to have given him a wink. 'Is that your final answer?' I said. 'No,' he said. 'Oh all right then, yes, go on, "Rome". Oh no! Oh I really don't know. I know, I'll Phone-A-Friend. I'll phone Sally, my sister.'

He phoned Sally, and she said 'Rome' straight away. Mike was now on £4000, but his Lifelines had all gone. I really didn't want him to lose any money. Nor did the audience. Nor did Victoria, who was looking traumatised in the audience. She kept closing her eyes and looking down at her shoes.

For £8000, with no Lifelines left, Mike got this question:

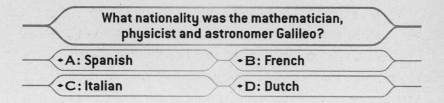

What nationality was the mathematician, physicist and astronomer Galileo?

◆A: Spanish ◆B: French
◆C: Italian ◆D: Dutch

'He's Italian,' said Mike. 'I'm absolutely sure he's Italian. Go on – I'm gonna play for £8000. "Italian" – final answer.' It was the right answer and the audience cheered him wildly.

We continued on to £16,000:

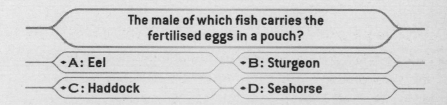

The male of which fish carries the fertilised eggs in a pouch?

◆A: Eel ◆B: Sturgeon
◆C: Haddock ◆D: Seahorse

'I think it's "sturgeon",' said Mike, 'but I'm not 100 per cent.' 'You don't have to play this, Mike,' I told him. 'You've got £8000. If you're wrong you lose £7000.' 'I think it's "sturgeon",' he said, 'but I'm just not convinced about it. No, Chris, I'm gonna cut and run. I'm going to take the money.' Thank God for that, I thought.

Then, in a moment of madness, Mike said, 'No, what the hell, I'll play. Come on, final answer – "sturgeon".' It was an awful moment. The guy had so much courage, but this time it had backfired on him. 'Sturgeon' was the wrong answer. The correct answer was 'seahorse'. 'Oh Mike, I'm so desperately sorry. You go away with £1000, of course, but you've just lost £7000.' I was really gutted. For Mike to drop £7000 was worse, for myself and I think the audience than the three occasions when somebody's gone home with nothing.

But Mike was characteristically brave, he didn't seem to care less. 'It doesn't matter,' he said. 'I've had a tremendous time. I've still got £1000. I just want to say I have enjoyed this so much,' and away he went, still grinning from ear to ear.

Even though he'd lost all that money, his good spirits were an example to us all, but, as he left, the audience, the crew and myself felt hugely disappointed for him.

Life After *Who Wants To Be A Millionaire?*

Mike says he still looks back on the show as a wonderful experience – the ultimate thrill and the ultimate scare all in one go. He still gets recognised a lot and, best of all, the travel company JMC heard that he wanted to take his son to Disneyland in Paris, and instead flew his whole family for a week's holiday in Florida.

Perry Poole

Perry Poole, from Bristol, was a very positive, attractive woman – tall and blonde. She had her husband John in the audience and her five-year-old daughter Olivia watching Mummy on TV at home, with Bonnie the fat labrador for company. Perry wore a loud, multicoloured jacket and announced to me, as soon as she got into the chair after winning Fastest Finger First, 'I'm going to go all the way, Chris. I'm here to win a million. I'm not interested in anything else. I'm not a rich woman and I just want to do it.' She seemed absolutely determined, very focused and articulate. 'Why shouldn't I? After all, it's only numbers. If I fail, I fail,' she said. 'But no half measures for me. I'm here to win the million!' She stated all this with a huge grin but she was deadly serious, and she started like a woman on a mission.

She zoomed up to £1000, and got this question:

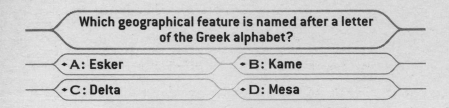

Which geographical feature is named after a letter of the Greek alphabet?

- A: Esker
- B: Kame
- C: Delta
- D: Mesa

She said, 'I'm sure it's "Delta", Chris.' Her husband and the audience all cheered, and presumably so did Olivia and Bonnie the fat labrador watching at home. Perry was on a guaranteed £1000, but she was still ten questions away from the million. Then again, in her own words, 'it's only numbers'. She carried on.

Perry knew about Culture Club for £2000 and stud poker for £4000. The first time I got her to sweat at all – sorry, that should be 'glow' – was on £8000.

Which of these is the most likely symptom of iron deficiency in humans?

- A: Scurvy
- B: Rickets
- C: Dermatitis
- D: Anaemia

I knew this one straight away, but gave her my usual non-committal blank expression. 'Chris, you are so cruel!' she said to me. I wasn't being particularly cruel, I thought – just looking my normal vacant self. Still not at all certain, Perry decided to play. 'I'm gonna go for it, Chris. I think the answer's "D: Anaemia".' It was correct. She gave me a huge beam and flexed her biceps like Lennox Lewis. She still hadn't touched a Lifeline. She was really determined to go all the way.

For £16,000, this was the next question:

'I want to ask my husband,' Perry said. 'He'll know!'
And it was clear from John's face up in the audience that
yes, he did know. Sadly, I had to remind her, there's no
Lifeline called 'Ask your Husband'. 'You can Phone-A-
Friend, though,' I said, 'but it can't be John because he's
sitting about ten yards behind you.' 'OK,' she said, 'I'll
phone my friend Lynn.' She asked Lynn the question. Lynn
wasn't at all certain, but she gave Perry her best shot: 'I
think it's "James Coburn". If I was going to guess, that's
what I'd say: "James Coburn".'

Perry looked puzzled for a few seconds and then said,
'I'm going to ignore Lynn. I'm gonna play "Charles
Bronson".' She didn't look as positive as earlier – clearly
the pressure was beginning to get to her.

'No, I'm not. I'm going to change my mind again,' she
said. 'I'm going to Ask the Audience.' The audience were
equally unhelpful. Forty-three per cent said "Charles
Bronson", 37 per cent said "James Coburn". 'I hate them!'
Perry said. 'They're no use to me at all. I'm going to go
with my gut feeling, though. "Charles Bronson",' she said.
'Come on. It's "Charles Bronson" or I go home.'

'You're absolutely right,' I said. 'It is "Charles Bronson"
or you go home.' It went to orange. 'Charles Bronson'
was the right answer. Perry was hugely excited now, still
bent on going all the way but, tactically, that was looking
less likely, since she'd used up two Lifelines. The £32,000

question was not very nice. In fact it was not very nice at all:

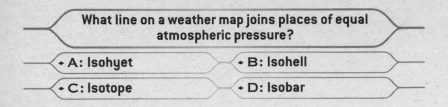

What line on a weather map joins places of equal atmospheric pressure?

- A: Isohyet
- B: Isohell
- C: Isotope
- D: Isobar

For a minute, Perry was in her own, private isohell! But then she said, 'No, I'm fairly certain on this one – I'm gonna go with "D: Isobar".' It was the right answer. John, Olivia and Bonnie the fat labrador roared their approval and Perry Poole had landed £32,000.

'Now you've got your 50:50 Lifeline,' I reminded her. 'But that's the only one left. Are you still going to go all the way?' 'Absolutely,' she said. 'That's all that I came for.' But her eyes and her voice betrayed her – I suspected she was having a secret change of heart. Very large sums of money tend to do that to people's resolve.

For £64,000, she got this question:

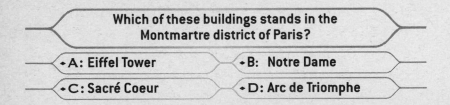

Which of these buildings stands in the Montmartre district of Paris?

- A: Eiffel Tower
- B: Notre Dame
- C: Sacré Coeur
- D: Arc de Triomphe

'I'm not sure on this one,' Perry said. 'It's one of two and I'm going to guess.' 'You could use your 50:50,' I told her. 'No,' she said. 'I'm going to save that. I want to play and I want to play "Sacré Coeur".' It was the right answer.

She was now four right answers away from her original declared target.

We were still in the pre-Judith Keppel era and I reminded her that all the winners of £125,000 or more so far had been men. 'So far,' she said, 'things might be about to change.' She said this very flippantly but she was still very determined and John, Olivia, Bonnie the fat labrador, the audience and myself were all willing her to go the full distance.

We moved onwards and upwards:

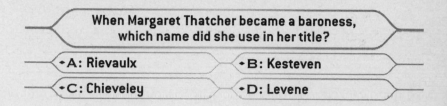

When Margaret Thatcher became a baroness, which name did she use in her title?

- A: Rievaulx
- B: Kesteven
- C: Chieveley
- D: Levene

Perry looked at me unhappily. 'I'm really not sure,' she said. 'I'm going to have to use my 50:50.' The computer took two wrong answers away and left 'Levene' or 'Kesteven'. One of those was worth £125,000. It would have been the most that any woman had won on *Who Wants To Be A Millionaire?* 'I've got to go for it,' she said, 'although I'm really not certain.' 'You don't have to, Perry,' I told her. 'You've got £64,000.' 'I know,' she said, 'but I'm not going to get to the million, am I, unless I play! And I'm going to play "Levene".' 'Is that your final answer, Perry?' I asked. 'No,' she said, 'I'll take the money! I've had enough. I want to go home.' She had suddenly cracked. Sheer common sense had prevailed. Sixty-four grand was a magnificent night's work by any standards.

'No,' she said. 'I'm going to change my mind again. It's "Levene". Go on, "Levene".'

'You don't have to play this, Perry,' I told her, quite concerned. 'No, come on,' she said, "Levene". 'Are you sure?' I said. 'Chris, don't do this. Stop now,' she instructed me. 'Well, it's your call,' I said. 'Is that your final answer?' 'Yes,' she said. 'Come on. Final answer. Final answer!' It went to orange. I looked down at my screen. Agonisingly, it was the wrong answer. Perry looked crestfallen for about a quarter of a second and then said, 'Oh well, I gave it my best shot.' And she certainly had.

She went away £32,000 the richer. She was a great player with a terrific attitude and was still far better off than when she came into the studio. Bonnie the fat labrador must have been very proud.

Life After *Who Wants To Be A Millionaire?*

Perry says she is relieved she got the question wrong because she would have just kept gambling and it was easier to drop back to £32,000 at that level. She says it was the most memorable day of her life, and compares the experience to giving birth. She used to earn money by ironing for five hours a day; in one night on the show she earned eight years' salary. However, she has now gone back to work – having spent all the money!

Sylvia Nixon

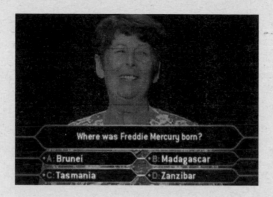

Where was Freddie Mercury born?

A: Brunei   B: Madagascar
C: Tasmania   D: Zanzibar

Christmas Eve 1999 was one of our most memorable early shows. It's always a nice time to give people money and Sylvia Nixon was certainly a deserving case. She was quite a woman: a small, feisty lady with a huge smile. She was a taxi driver. She had brought her son Richard with her, on his first-ever trip to London; he looked absolutely terrified throughout the entire proceedings. Her husband Ian and the two other kids were watching at home. She told me in all seriousness that if she won lots of money she wanted 'a uniform like Sean Bean wore in the *Sharpe* series and a rifle like his as well'. Weird or what?

For £100, which in itself would have been a handy Christmas present, we set off with this question:

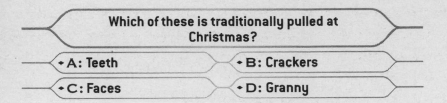

Which of these is traditionally pulled at Christmas?

◆ A: Teeth   ◆ B: Crackers

◆ C: Faces   ◆ D: Granny

Sylvia resisted the temptation to tell me it was 'granny'. The right answer, of course, was 'crackers', and she was £100 better off.

She had told me she was very nervous, though at this stage she didn't seem to be. 'Are you calmer?' I asked her once she'd got over the £100 hurdle. 'No,' she said, 'I'm actually getting worse by the second.' She needn't have worried, for she was very bright and, at least outwardly, appeared to be thoroughly enjoying the limelight. She got to £1000 with a question about New Scotland Yard. For £2000 she was asked:

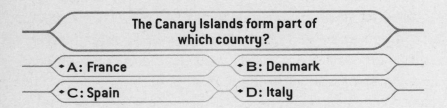

The Canary Islands form part of which country?

◆ A: France   ◆ B: Denmark

◆ C: Spain   ◆ D: Italy

'I'm pretty sure it's "Spain",' she said. 'But I don't want to waste a Lifeline yet.' So she decided not to and offered "Spain" as her final answer. She'd won £2000 and she went racing on. Her general knowledge was very varied – she knew that G Men came from the FBI and that Joan of Arc was the Maid of Orleans. In fact the first time she hesitated at all was on the £32,000 question:

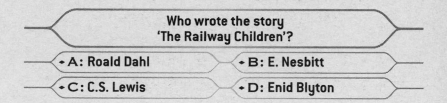

**Who wrote the story
'The Railway Children'?**

A: Roald Dahl   B: E. Nesbitt

C: C.S. Lewis   D: Enid Blyton

'I'm really not sure,' she told me – 'I want to Phone-A-Friend of mine, Doctor O'Messi.' Doctor O'Messi was read the question and said 'Nesbitt' more or less at once. 'I'm fairly confident Sylvia, go with "Nesbitt". Good luck!' Sylvia thought this was great. 'He's a very, very, nice man,' she told me. 'Well, he is if he's right,' I said. And he was. 'The Railway Children' was indeed written by E. Nesbitt. Sylvia and her son Richard in the audience punched the air in unison.

By now our time was up, and Sylvia returned home that night guaranteed to come back in time for the Christmas Day show with £32,000. She reappeared in a splendid multicoloured dress. 'I've now decided,' she told me, 'that if I get my million pounds I want to go to the Ukraine with Sean Bean.' I'm sure Sean would have had a blast with Sylvia – she was a terrific character and quite a wealthy lady now. She was also just five questions away from becoming a millionaire. 'This is turning into the best Christmas of my life,' she said.

For £64,000 she got this question:

**Fiorello LaGuardia was a popular mayor
of which city?**

A: Chicago   B: Los Angeles

C: New York   D: Dallas

Sylvia looked at it, puzzled. 'I think there's a LaGuardia airport in New York,' she said. 'I'm not sure, but I reckon if there's an airport of that name, it'll be in memory of him. I'm gonna play "New York".'

It was wonderful to be able to tell her that it was the right answer. She screamed with delight; she was almost sobbing. 'I really wasn't sure.' Sure or not, Sylvia was correct, and now had £64,000.

The next question was for £125,000:

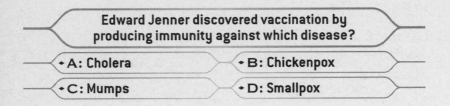

'I think it's "smallpox",' she whispered in a frightened voice, and the audience gasped. 'Let me go 50:50, please, Chris.' She used her 50:50 – 'chickenpox' and 'smallpox' remained. 'I'm gonna play,' she said. 'I think it's "smallpox".'

'You don't have to play this,' I told her. 'I know I don't,' she said, 'but I want to. Final answer – "smallpox".' It went to orange, and I saw 'right answer' flash up on the screen. She'd just won £125,000. Richard went wild. Sylvia went wild. I think I went wild, grabbing her in a bear hug. 'I don't believe it!' she said. 'It's fantastic. I am so excited!' This was the highest amount any woman had ever won on any game show anywhere in the world. Don't forget these were early days and Judith Keppel was still many months away.

The next question was for £250,000 and Sylvia had preserved one Lifeline. 'This is where I start getting serious,' she said jokingly. This was the question:

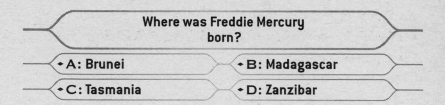

Where was Freddie Mercury born?

- A: Brunei
- B: Madagascar
- C: Tasmania
- D: Zanzibar

From years of playing Queen records on the radio, I knew this. But Sylvia sadly said, 'I haven't a clue. But I've still got my Lifeline. I'll Ask the Audience anyway.'

'OK, audience,' I said. 'I think we need a huge majority here to make Sylvia gamble on this. Let's see what happens.' Fifty-two per cent said 'Zanzibar'. It was a majority but, with a possible loss of £93,000 if they were wrong, not a big enough majority. Sylvia couldn't risk ruining her Christmas. 'I applied to the show for a laugh,' she said. 'I came for the enjoyment and if you knew how much I've been risking it along the way with some of my answers you wouldn't believe me. I've had a fantastic time. This is the best Christmas of my life. I'm gonna take the money, please.'

So away went Sylvia Nixon in her taxi back to her family, no doubt intending to go straight out and buy a Sharpe outfit, plus authentic rifle, with some of her £125,000.

She was a lovely woman and it was a real pleasure to hand her the cheque. Whether she ever went to the Ukraine with Sean Bean, I'll never know, but I suspect husband Ian might have had something to say about that. Although I'm not so sure that Ian would argue with his wife in full uniform and loaded rifle.

Incidentally, I can tell you that 52 per cent of the audience were absolutely right – Freddie Mercury was born in

Zanzibar. Sadly, it wasn't a convincing enough majority for Sylvia. Who can blame her, when she was already *Who Wants To Be A Millionaire?*'s biggest-ever lady winner.

Life After *Who Wants To Be A Millionaire?*

Since she came on the show, Sylvia says she has managed to fulfil both of her lifetime dreams. A lady from the Sharpe Appreciation Society contacted her shortly after her appearance, and Sylvia has now joined the Society and owns not only the uniform but also the gun. Another great dream, she told us afterwards, was to be in the audience at the Eurovision Song Contest. She got to attend the show, as well as the after-show party. She's been on a cruise with her husband, their first holiday since their honeymoon twenty-one years ago. She's helped her kids out financially and is still a celebrity in her hometown in Jersey.

Gerry Lennon

Gerry Lennon was a prison officer from Yorkshire. He didn't go into details but I got the impression that the prison was a tough one. Nevertheless, he said to me cheerily as he settled into the chair, 'This show is very popular inside,' which was quite a strange thought. Clearly, we literally had what is meant by a captive audience. Not that any of the inmates would be allowed to take part – one of the strict rules of *Who Wants To Be A Millionaire?* excludes anyone with a criminal record. It's caused one or two problems over the years. In any case, it was unlikely that a prison governor, however lenient, would allow one of his charges out for the evening to appear on a game show in London.

Gerry was an amiable, quietly spoken man who wanted to do the best that he could and hopefully take a decent amount of money home to his wife, who was watching the show back in Yorkshire with their three little daughters. I don't know what they pay prison officers, but I bet it's not a lot – almost certainly not enough for what must be a difficult, demanding and at times dangerous job.

Gerry had a big, open face. He read each question carefully and was very slow and deliberate about his answers. Before the klaxon went he had reached £1000 with a question about Boris Yeltsin, as well as a particularly daft one about Tom Tom the Piper's Son – who, as you may recall, 'stole a pig and away he run'.

He came back on the second night with three Lifelines still intact. The next few questions didn't worry him unduly, and got this for £16,000:

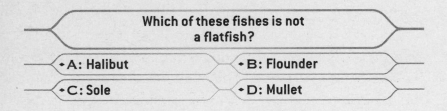

Which of these fishes is not a flatfish?

A: Halibut   B: Flounder
C: Sole   D: Mullet

'It's "mullet",' he said. 'That's definitely not a flatfish. All the other three are.' It was the right answer.

For £32,000 I asked him:

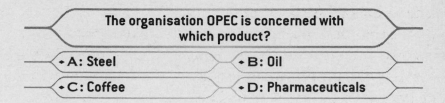

The organisation OPEC is concerned with
which product?

A: Steel	B: Oil
C: Coffee	D: Pharmaceuticals

"It's "oil",' said Gerry. 'Final answer?' 'Absolutely –
final answer.' It was the right answer. Gerry Lennon was
now on a guaranteed £32,000 and he still hadn't used a
single Lifeline. At this point I'm sure Daddy was a very
popular man with his three little girls. I bet they were
already compiling their shopping list for his return.

To double his money, he had to answer this:

Which of these sports is played
on a rink?

A: Badminton	B: Bowls
C: Rounders	D: Shinty

'I'll play,' he said very positively, without a moment's
hesitation. 'It's "bowls".' 'It's the right answer.' I told him.
The audience screamed their delight. Gerry was on
£64,000 and still he hadn't touched a single Lifeline.

I asked him to have a look at the next question, worth
£125,000:

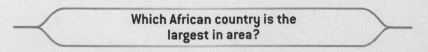

Which African country is the
largest in area?

Gerry looked at me with a strange grin. 'I think I know
this,' he said. 'What do you think it is?' I asked him. 'I

think it's Sudan,' he said. Up came the four possible answers:

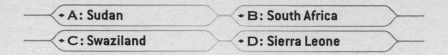

‘It's "Sudan",’ said Gerry. ‘Definitely.’ ‘You've just won £125,000,’ I told him. He jumped from the chair in excitement. I pumped him by the hand and hugged him – I was thrilled for him. ‘I've never seen £125,000 in my life,’ he told me delightedly. ‘Well, you will now,’ I said, ‘and at this moment you can walk away. But this next question is worth £250,000, a quarter of a million, and still you have 50:50, Phone-A-Friend and Ask the Audience untouched.’ We weren't finished yet.

This was the question for £250,000, and it stopped Gerry in his tracks:

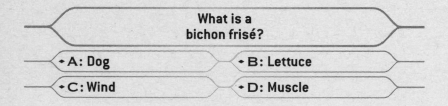

‘I've never heard of it,’ said Gerry, and the audience gasped. ‘I'd better start using my Lifelines. I don't want to risk this amount of money. I'll Ask the Audience.’ With £250,000 at stake, the audience was amazingly positive. Ninety-three per cent – a massive majority – voted for ‘dog’. ‘That's spooky,’ said Gerry. ‘Ninety-three per cent. Because if they're wrong I lose £93,000!’ It was a sobering thought but, even at this level, it was such a huge percentage that I assumed Gerry would go for it.

But Gerry decided to go 50:50 first. 'Lettuce' and 'muscle' disappeared, which left 'dog' and 'wind'. This would have been enough for most contestants, but the sheer amount of money involved was now getting to Gerry. 'You can walk away,' I told him, 'with £125,000, but 93 per cent of the audience are saying a bichon frisé is a dog and "dog" and "wind" are the only two remaining.'

Gerry still looked unhappy. 'I'm going to Phone-A-Friend,' he said. 'I'll phone Harry, my brother.' Harry wasn't at all certain. He said, 'I don't know for sure, Gerry, but I think it's a dog. That would be a guess, though,' he emphasised. 'It's your call, Gerry,' I said. 'You don't need to play this question, but 93 per cent of the audience are certain that "dog" is the right answer. Your 50:50 still left "dog" and your brother thinks, of the two possibilities, it's probably "dog". It's your call. It's worth £250,000.'

Gerry looked at me long and hard and said, 'I'm going to take the money.' The audience groaned, but he was adamant. I reminded him once more that if he answered this question correctly, he would win £250,000, but Gerry had had enough. 'No, I'm going to take the money and run,' he repeated.

The audience was amazed. But they all cheered him, of course, and before he left I was able to confirm that "dog" was indeed the right answer.

I had a long chat with Gerry in the bar afterwards. 'Any regrets?' I asked him. 'None at all,' he said. 'How can I have regrets about coming down here and leaving with £125,000? It's more money than I've ever seen in my life and there is absolutely no way I would have risked losing it. It's a fantastic result and I'm absolutely delighted.'

Of course, Gerry's right. If 93 per cent of the audience had been wrong all the offices and pubs the next day would have been full of, 'Did you see that thick audience on *Millionaire* last night? Ninety-three per cent of them gave that poor geezer the wrong answer.' The audience would have been the talking point but Gerry would have been the fall guy. For a prison officer, £125,000 would take many years to earn the hard way and Gerry was not going to gamble it for himself or his young family.

So Gerry Lennon went back to Yorkshire a conquering hero to his kids, and with great respect from all of us on *Millionaire*.

Life After *Who Wants To Be A Millionaire?*

Gerry says the day between the first and second show was the longest day of his life. The money has made a huge difference, allowing him to pay off his debts and his mortgage, and to save for his kids' future. He did splash out on a holiday home on the east coast and has since enjoyed trips to Singapore and Australia. He has no regrets at all.

Peter Lee

The night that Peter Lee came on the show was quite a night. We still hadn't seen our first £1,000,000 winner, but the guy immediately before Peter, David Neale, had been the second person ever to win £250,000 on the show. The first thing Peter Lee said when he sat down was, 'I really thought tonight we were going to be able to say, "We were on the show the night it had its first £1,000,000 winner."' Strange that Peter should say that, considering what happened during his stint in the chair.

Peter was a really amenable guy. He described *Who Wants To Be A Millionaire?* as the 'holy grail of game shows' and said it was the most exciting competition he'd ever seen.

Little did he know how much he was going to add to that excitement himself over the next couple of evenings.

Peter came from Cardigan, in Wales, but he had been in the Navy for twenty-five years, so he had seen a lot of the world, which is often useful on this kind of show. His wife Sue was stuck at home looking after their menagerie of pets, and his son, who lived in the USA, was rooting for Dad from there. Peter said if he did win lots of money his main aim was to bring one of his grandsons, who was now ten, back to the UK so he could become affiliated to a football club and get into their training scheme. Apparently the boy had tremendous potential but it was not being realised in the States.

Although Peter kept grinning and was obviously thoroughly enjoying his appearance on the show, he did also look incredibly nervous, particularly early on, staring down at the computer as if it was full of demons, and biting his lip hard. He needn't have worried. For a man who spent twenty-five years in the Navy the question to get him to £1000 couldn't have been more friendly:

> **Which word means a person who has little or no experience at sea?**
>
> ◆ A: Landlady   ◆ B: Landholder
> ◆ C: Landowner   ◆ D: Landlubber

I think if Peter had got this one wrong he would have been keelhauled by all his old mates in the Navy, but, of course, he didn't. 'Landlubber' got him to a guaranteed £1000.

I asked Peter what his goal for the evening was. He was refreshingly modest: 'I've just bought a car for £4000, which I can't really afford. If I could win four grand tonight that would be a real result and a load off my mind.'

The £4000 question, though, proved a bit of a stumbling block for Peter:

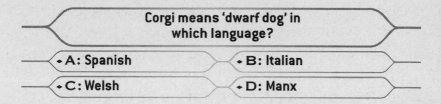

Corgi means 'dwarf dog' in which language?

A: Spanish   B: Italian
C: Welsh   D: Manx

Peter looked really stuck. 'I can't think where they come from,' he said. 'I'd better Ask the Audience.' The audience's answer was not totally conclusive, but 48 per cent said they thought corgis were Welsh. Now, bearing in mind that Peter came from Cardigan, if he had got this one wrong he'd probably have been pelted with rotten fruit or put in the village stocks when he crawled shamefacedly back home. 'I've just realised,' he said. 'Welsh corgis. Corgis come from Wales, which is where I live. How embarrassing! "Welsh" is my final answer.' It was the right answer.

Now Peter could pay off the HP for the car he'd just bought. He got to £8000 with a straightforward question about the last governor of Hong Kong being Chris Patten and then the klaxon sounded for the end of the show.

Peter came back the following night, a lot more composed, with Alison and Nicola, the daughters of two of his Phone-A-Friends, looking thoroughly self-conscious up in the audience. He confided that if he won a lot of money he'd like to go to the States for himself and visit his two grandchildren – as yet he'd never set eyes on them. He'd also like to have his garden landscaped by Charlie Dimmock. Dirty little devil!

The question that welcomed him back for £16,000 was this:

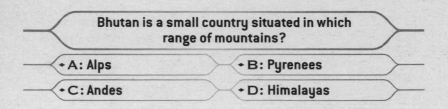

Bhutan is a small country situated in which range of mountains?

- A: Alps
- B: Pyrenees
- C: Andes
- D: Himalayas

Peter knew straight away it was the Himalayas. He then proceeded to £32,000, knowing that pastrami was made from beef.

Our sailor now began to get understandably tense and bit his lip harder than ever. This was the £64,000 question:

Which of these actresses has not appeared in *Coronation Street*?

- A: Patricia Routledge
- B: Maureen Lipman
- C: Prunella Scales
- D: Joanna Lumley

Peter was instantly sure that the answer was 'Maureen Lipman'. 'I definitely remember Joanna Lumley being in it, as somebody's girlfriend,' he said. 'Patricia Routledge has been in it, so has Prunella Scales, it must be "Maureen Lipman".' Absolutely correct! I wrote him out a cheque for £64,000 with the date – 18 January 2000.

Bearing in mind we'd come on air in September 1998, I still find it amazing that we'd gone this long without a £1,000,000 winner. But tonight, like the previous evening, we seemed to be getting closer. Peter was now on £64,000 with two Lifelines still intact. This was the next question:

> **Which John Osborne play features the character Archie Rice?**

As soon as he saw this, Peter grinned at me. 'You know it, do you?' I said. 'I do,' he replied, 'It's "The Entertainer".' Up they came in order, 'The Entertainer' the first to appear, to a cheer from the audience. These were the four possibilities:

| A: The Entertainer | B: West of Suez |
| C: Look Back in Anger | D: Time Present |

Peter was right — it was the classic role portrayed by the late Sir Laurence Olivier. As I handed him a cheque he was visibly shaking. 'I've never seen one that big before,' he said. The next question was for £250,000:

> **Which French Impressionist painter had a son who became a successful film director?**

| A: Pissarro | B: Degas |
| C: Sisley | D: Renoir |

Understandably, Peter looked very worried. We were now playing for enormously high stakes. He used his 50:50, leaving him 'Pissarro' and 'Renoir'. 'I think it might be "Renoir",' he said. 'I'm a bit of a film fan and it seems to ring a bell, but I think I'd better Phone-A-Friend. He announced that he was going to phone Derek, who was the father of one of the young girls in the audience. She immediately went bright red and started shaking her head, mouthing, 'Oh my God, they're going to ring Daddy!'

This was an important phone call – it was worth £250,000, and Peter asked me to tell Derek this. Considering how much money was involved, they were both very laid-back. Peter called Derek 'Delboy' and 'Delboy' called him 'Peterkin'. 'I'm not sure on this one,' said Delboy. 'I do know there is a film director called Renoir, but I've never heard of one called Pissarro.' 'That's what I was thinking,' said Peterkin, as the phone hung up. 'I'm going to go for it. Final answer – "Renoir".' Once 'D' had gone to orange he realised the enormity of what he'd done and sat staring at me with one eye open, one eye closed. He needn't have worried, his instincts were spot on. It was the right answer – he'd just won £250,000.

Peter punched the air with his fists. So did Nicola and Alison up in the audience, and they looked a lot less embarrassed to be there now. The next question, for £500,000, would have stopped most people in their tracks:

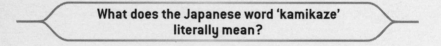

What does the Japanese word 'kamikaze' literally mean?

Peter grinned at me again as the options came up:

A: Sacred venture
B: Divine wind
C: Self destruction
D: Final attack

I knew it was the word for Japanese suicide missions in World War II. I don't think I'd have risked it for this amount of money, but if I'd had to go for one I would almost certainly have chosen 'self destruction' or 'final attack'.

'It's "divine wind",' said Peter and the audience gasped loudly, in unison. 'Why are you so sure?' I asked him. 'Japan's one of my favourite countries,' he told me. 'I have been there a few times and picked up the odd Japanese phrase. I think "kamikaze" translates literally as "divine wind". I started out last night with nothing,' he rationalised. 'If I go with £32,000 that would be fantastic, but I'm sure I know this.'

This was a big moment – nobody had ever won more than £250,000 before on the show. The crowd cheered his bravery. 'Let's go for it,' said Peter. 'Final answer,' and this time he closed both his eyes, as did almost everybody in the audience. The panel went to orange and I was able to tell him that he'd just won a record-breaking £500,000. His win also meant that, for the first time ever on *Who Wants To Be A Millionaire?*, we were going to see a £1,000,000 question.

There were tears in Peter's eyes and the whole studio was buzzing. I don't know how often we'd planned this in rehearsals, but it was the first time I was finally able to utter the words, 'The next question is number fifteen of a possible fifteen. It's worth £1,000,000 if you give me the right answer. If you give me the wrong answer, you lose £468,000.' I've still only said that a few times over the past four years, but on each occasion I've done so, I've always noticed the contestant's eyes glaze over when they hear, 'You lose £468,000.' Even if you're Paul McCartney or Richard Branson, that's a pretty sobering thought.

Up came the question:

Which county cricket side is based at Chester-le-Street?

- ◆ A: Warwickshire
- ◆ B: Durham
- ◆ C: Northamptonshire
- ◆ D: Leicestershire

By the standards of £1,000,000 questions, it wasn't that difficult. Dozens of people have come up to me since to say, 'I was screaming the right answer at the screen when Peter Lee got that question.' An enormous number of people, sports fans or not, knew the answer – obviously the whole population of Chester-le-Street for starters. But I ask all of them, 'I bet you didn't know "Divine wind", did you?' And nearly every single one admits, 'No, I certainly didn't.'

It's the perfect example of our catchphrase 'they're only easy if you know the answer'. And Peter Lee did not know the answer. He told me, 'I really haven't got a clue. I think it might be Leicestershire but I'm certainly not going to risk it.'

So, regrettably, we waved goodbye to the first person ever to win £500,000 on the show. For Peter Lee it had been a truly fantastic night; for everybody who's ever watched cricket at Chester-le-Street, it was rather a frustrating anticlimax. Then again, if Peter had gone for 'Leicestershire', he would have had to have lived with losing £468,000. 'Durham' was the right answer.

Life After *Who Wants To Be A Millionaire?*

Peter says both nights went like a flash. He describes them as 'life-changing moments that seemed to come and go in a second'. The money has totally changed his life. His wife gave up work within three weeks of his appearing on the show, and he was able to pay to put his daughter through veterinary college. He has visited his children in America and paid for them to visit England. He says he has spent about a third of the money and invested the rest, although he suspects that if he had won the money when he was in his twenties, it would all have gone by now.

Margaret Whitaker

A loveable teddy bear of a lady from Wokingham, Berkshire, Margaret Whitaker had trained as a nurse, but was not working in the profession when she came on the show. Her daughter Joanna was up in the audience and her sons Paul and Jack were watching at home. Mum's first priority, according to Joanna, was to win her £400 for a school-choir trip to Paris. Margaret was a single parent and I sensed that life was tough for her and her young family.

She certainly didn't seem to be in the mood for risking

losing any money, and fortunately she couldn't have had a much gentler start:

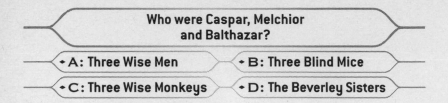

Who were Caspar, Melchior and Balthazar?

A: Three Wise Men   B: Three Blind Mice

C: Three Wise Monkeys   D: The Beverley Sisters

Margaret knew, of course, that the right answer was 'Three Wise Men'. She had made £100. 'If I do win a lot of money,' she told me, 'eventually all of it will go to the kids. I'm going to sit on my hands and leave it well alone.' Margaret was careful and deliberate in her manner right through the show, thinking very methodically about each answer before she delivered it. She got through the first nine questions without any real problems and, for £32,000, she got this:

In which county is Stonehenge?

A: Wiltshire   B: Cornwall

C: Dorset   D: Hampshire

Slowly she looked up and said to me, 'It's "Wiltshire", Chris.' This was the right answer and she'd won £32,000. Amazingly, she had still not used a single Lifeline.

The first time she needed a Lifeline was on the question for £64,000:

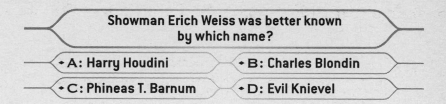

Showman Erich Weiss was better known by which name?

- A: Harry Houdini
- B: Charles Blondin
- C: Phineas T. Barnum
- D: Evil Knievel

She weighed up her options. 'I'm going to have to use a Lifeline,' she decided, 'because I really don't have a clue. But which Lifeline should I use?' Joanna looked pale and drawn in the audience. Margaret decided to Ask the Audience first, to see what they thought. Sixty per cent of the audience said 'Houdini' and 27 per cent thought 'Evil Knievel'. 'Sixty per cent is a pretty good percentage,' said Margaret. 'I'm going to go with this audience, I trust them. You have to put your trust in people sometimes,' she said. 'I'll play "Harry Houdini".' The audience cheered as loud as she did when I told her it was the right answer. She said 'When I came on to the show I never dreamed even for a second that I'd be sitting here with a cheque for £64,000. This is fantastic!'

She still had two Lifelines, though, and the next question was for £125,000. Margaret looked genuinely afraid – the enormity of the amount of money was suddenly sinking in. This was the question:

What is the specific name for an angler's basket for carrying his catch?

She smiled as soon as it came up and when I asked her why, she replied, 'Because I know that you're a fisherman and you will know this answer, and I don't.' Sadly, there isn't a Lifeline called 'Ask Chris'.

These were the four possibilities:

A: Trug   B: Creel
C: Skip   D: Pannier

'I'll go 50:50 ,' said Margaret. It left her 'trug' and 'creel'. She suddenly brightened visibly. 'The answer is "creel",' she said, 'because a trug is something a gardener uses. I'll play. Final answer – "creel".' 'You lose £32,000 if you're wrong,' I told her. 'I'm not wrong,' she said, to the amusement of the audience. It was the right answer. She'd won a huge £125,000.

This was the most that any woman had won on the show since we'd begun broadcasting in September 1998. 'It's absolutely indescribable,' she said. 'As a single mum, life is just one long struggle from day to day. This is beyond my wildest dreams.' But Margaret Whitaker was not finished yet.

This was the question for £250,000, although clearly she did not have to play it:

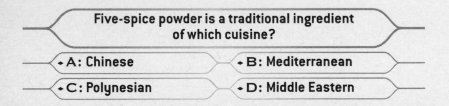

Five-spice powder is a traditional ingredient of which cuisine?

A: Chinese   B: Mediterranean
C: Polynesian   D: Middle Eastern

Margaret didn't know this, and understandably looked very worried. 'I'll Phone-A-Friend,' she said. 'I'll phone my friend Rhonda. She might know, but please, please do not tell her how much money is involved.' 'OK,' I said, noticing that Joanna was looking as white as a sheet. If

Rhonda gave the wrong answer now and Margaret went with it, she would lose £93,000. Unthinkable.

Margaret asked Rhonda the question characteristically carefully, her friend blissfully unaware of just how much money was involved. 'It's Chinese,' Rhonda told her, sounding positive. Margaret turned to me and said, 'I'll play, Chris. "Chinese".' It was an agonising moment. Up in the audience Joanna looked like she was praying hard. 'Do you trust Rhonda that much?' I asked Margaret. 'If she wasn't sure,' said Margaret, 'she would have told me. I'll play. "Chinese".'

It was an incredibly tense moment but Rhonda was right and her answer, combined with Margaret's courage, had won Margaret £250,000 — at that point the most ever won by any woman on *Who Wants To Be A Millionaire?* For the first time, Margaret really cracked. She screamed out at the top of her voice, and up in the audience Joanna was crying her eyes out.

As we approached the £500,000 question, Margaret said to me very clearly and slowly, 'There is no way I'm going to lose this amount of money. No way, José.' Up came the question:

> **Who was the US President at the outbreak of World War I?**
>
> ◆ A: Calvin Coolidge   ◆ B: Herbert Hoover
> ◆ C: William Taft   ◆ D: Woodrow Wilson

Margaret looked at me with a twinkle in her eye and said, 'I don't have a clue. I'm going to take the money and run!' The answer was actually 'Woodrow Wilson', but Margaret couldn't have cared less. She was cheered loudly as she left the studio and she had big tears in her eyes as she waved to her kids on the way out.

After the show she told me that most of the money would be earmarked for her young family. But £250,000 would also allow her to get back to doing what she wanted to do more than anything in her life – nursing. She had kept it very quiet but financial problems had meant that for the past few months she'd had to resort to stacking shelves in a supermarket to make ends meet. As Margaret herself said, 'How ridiculous that I can make more shelf-stacking than working as a nurse, and only by winning an enormous amount of money like this can I actually afford to go back and do the vital job that I trained to do.'

Margaret is quite right – it is ridiculous, completely absurd, that the luxury she could afford from her win on *Who Wants To Be A Millionaire?* was to go back into nursing.

Paddy Spooner

Paddy Spooner arrived fresh from Australia with his girlfriend Jane, who confidently took her place in the audience. He'd won Fastest Finger First all three times in rehearsals, and he got the important one right first go on the show. This sounds fairly predictable, but in fact it doesn't happen often: frequently people who do well in rehearsal blow it when they get on the show. Perhaps they peak too soon, or perhaps the rest start getting the hang of it.

Paddy described his home as 'occasionally Hampshire', but basically he's a backpacker. He'd just flown in from Down Under, where, in a blaze of publicity, he'd won 250,000 Australian dollars on their *Who Wants To Be A Millionaire?* He'd been back in the UK for about ten days and he'd been on the phone non-stop to the show ever since – presumably using some of his Australian winnings. So, here he was now, on the rather more lucrative UK version.

He said, 'Ideally I want to be a hemispherical commuter. I want to spend six months in the northern hemisphere, six months in the south. As soon as it gets cold, I'll move up or down and never see a winter again. Above all,' he said, 'I've really got a taste now for the money.' He was an unusual guy and certainly a challenge. He's probably the most determined player I've ever met and I really enjoyed the direct eye contact. I noticed that he had a nose that looks like it's been broken at least once, and damaged knuckles. So I think our Paddy had literally fought his way through life, or at least some of it. He was clearly very competitive, but also very intelligent.

There were very few jokes to be had with Paddy. When we knew he'd got a place, we'd spoken to our mates who work on the show in Oz, and they told us, 'He's quite a bloke. You're about to have "the Spooner experience"!' I must admit I thoroughly enjoyed 'the Spooner experience'; it was fun trying to rattle him and once or twice I actually managed it.

When question number four came up, for £500, Paddy couldn't believe his luck. Bearing in mind where he'd just been, this was certainly a nice question:

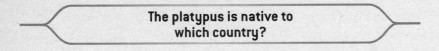

The platypus is native to which country?

Paddy nearly allowed himself to break into a grin, as the options were:

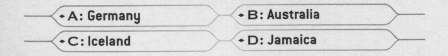

- A: Germany
- B: Australia
- C: Iceland
- D: Jamaica

Of course, it was 'Australia'. I asked Paddy what his expectations were from the show. He said, 'My goal here realistically is £125,000 sterling. The odds at that point are very good. It would be well worth playing if I get there. Everything is calculated.' See what I mean? Very methodical.

I soldiered on — there was little small talk, but I was relishing the contest. For £8000 we saw this question:

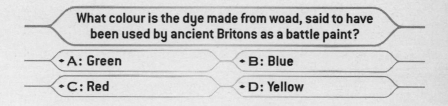

What colour is the dye made from woad, said to have been used by ancient Britons as a battle paint?

- ◆ A: Green
- ◆ B: Blue
- ◆ C: Red
- ◆ D: Yellow

I was surprised that anyone as competitive as Paddy called for a Lifeline on this question. 'I'm 95 per cent certain of the right answer,' he said, 'but I'll Ask the Audience.' This was interesting, even with a percentage as high as 95, Paddy Spooner was clearly leaving nothing to chance. Fifty-five per cent of the audience said 'blue' and the next biggest vote was 18 per cent for 'red'. 'Lock in "blue", please,' said Paddy. 'Lock in' is apparently the Australian equivalent of 'final answer'.

So dutifully we locked it in. I paused for a while — to be truthful, just to make him sweat a bit — and suddenly he didn't look so confident. 'You're OK,' I said eventually. 'It's the right answer.'

The question for £16,000, though, did stop him completely in his tracks:

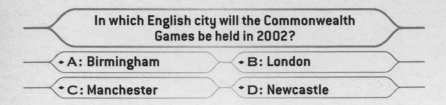

In which English city will the Commonwealth Games be held in 2002?

A: Birmingham

B: London

C: Manchester

D: Newcastle

For the first time Paddy went completely silent, and there was a very long pause. It was probably only thirty seconds but it felt like several minutes. 'I know Manchester applied for the Olympic Games and lost,' he said, 'but I don't know about the Commonwealth Games. I'll Phone-A-Friend, please. I'll phone Nick.'

Typically, Paddy didn't even bother about 'London' or 'Newcastle' when he phoned his friend Nick — that's how much of a gamesman he was. He simply asked him, 'In which English city will the Commonwealth Games be held in 2002 — is it "Birmingham" or "Manchester"?' 'I think it's "Manchester",' said Nick. 'So do I,' said Paddy. 'Lock it in.'

I stared him in the face again, and at that moment he looked genuinely worried. I think he thought his friend Nick had let him down and he'd blown it. Imagine his horror if it had been 'London' or 'Newcastle'. But he needn't have worried — 'Manchester' was the right answer and he was now on £16,000.

He was frowning, though. When I asked him why he informed me, 'I am annoyed with myself for losing my Lifeline.' 'That's what they're for,' I reminded him, but Paddy was having none of that.

For £32,000 this was question number ten:

Who composed the theme for the film
The Pink Panther?

Paddy smiled happily.

- A: Marvin Hamlisch
- B: John Williams
- C: Henry Mancini
- D: Bert Bacarach

He said to me instantly, 'Lock in "C", please – "Henry Mancini".' He knew it was right, and he was now on £32,000. His girlfriend Jane in the audience looked down, clearly pleased but strangely dispassionate – the majority of partners go through the studio roof with relief at this point. I showed Paddy the £64,000 question and again, almost in spite of himself, he gave me a big smile.

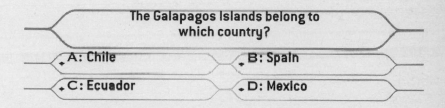

The Galapagos Islands belong to
which country?

- A: Chile
- B: Spain
- C: Ecuador
- D: Mexico

'It's "Ecuador",' he said at once. 'I'm absolutely certain.' I looked at him. 'There's really no point stringing you out on this, is there? You know it, you're spot on, the right answer is "Ecuador" – you've just won £64,000.' Paddy was now in very good shape. He was four questions away from £1,000,000 sterling, and he still had one Lifeline left.

For £125,000 Paddy the backpacker was asked:

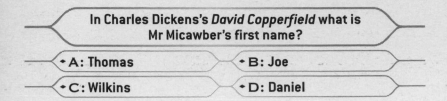

In Charles Dickens's *David Copperfield* what is Mr Micawber's first name?

• A: Thomas   • B: Joe

• C: Wilkins   • D: Daniel

He looked at me in alarm. 'I've really no idea,' he said. 'I'll go 50:50.' 'Thomas' and 'Daniel' went, 'Wilkins' and 'Joe' remained. Paddy stared at me long and hard and suddenly pronounced, 'There's a character called Joe Gargery in one of them, so I'm going to have to go for "Wilkins".' 'You don't have to do anything,' I reminded him. 'I do,' he assured me. '"Wilkins" – lock it in.'

It was his final answer. The panel went to orange. Paddy seemed to be having doubts as he glanced up at me. I suspect the Australian host probably hadn't made him sweat quite so much. I hope not, I was thoroughly enjoying it. In a perverse sort of way, I'm sure he was as well.

'It's the right answer,' I said. 'Mr Wilkins Micawber.' I showed Paddy the cheque for £125,000. 'It's a lovely one,' he said.

'Well, you won 250,000 Australian dollars,' I told him. 'This is for £250,000 sterling.' His eyes lit up at the prospect.

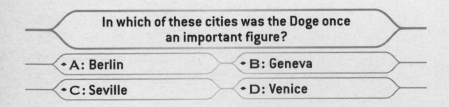

In which of these cities was the Doge once an important figure?

• A: Berlin   • B: Geneva

• C: Seville   • D: Venice

'Lock in "D: Venice",' he said at once. He was absolutely right. He'd now won £250,000. Jane at last became emotional; her lip was trembling. It was getting deadly serious.

Paddy had no Lifelines left but for £500,000 he got this question:

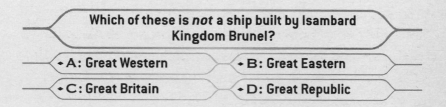

Which of these is *not* a ship built by Isambard Kingdom Brunel?

- A: Great Western
- B: Great Eastern
- C: Great Britain
- D: Great Republic

He looked at the monitor dispassionately. 'I know "Great Eastern" was built by Brunel,' he said, 'and I know "Great Britain" was as well. But I'm going to take the money. Nothing you say will make me change my mind, Chris Tarrant. There are a lot of other countries broadcasting *Who Wants To Be A Millionaire?* – I'm going to have to go and learn a few more languages.'

So Paddy Spooner left us £250,000 better off, free to continue on his worldwide travels of *Millionaire* shows. 'Just out of interest,' I asked him, 'which option would you have gone for?' 'I'm pretty sure I would have gone for "Great Western",' he said. 'That would have been a shame,' I told him, 'because that would have lost you £218,000. The right answer was "Great Republic".'

I had a drink with Paddy and Jane in the bar afterwards. They were an amazing couple. Paddy had so many theories about *Who Wants To Be A Millionaire?*, he could have studied for a degree in it. He knew far more about the show – the odds, the likely and less likely outcomes – than I or probably the rest of our production team did. We've had a couple of players since who've used Paddy as one of their Phone-A-Friends – he is, of course, on a percentage of their winnings.

Amazingly, Jane seemed almost disappointed with his huge win. 'C'mon,' I said, 'the guy's won £250,000!' 'No, it's not that,' she told me. 'Of course we're delighted with a quarter of a million, it's fantastic. But he has gone through so much preparation for this show, I honestly thought he'd get to a million. Even in the small hours of this morning we were lying in bed together practising Fastest Finger First . . .' There's no answer to that!

Life After *Who Wants To Be A Millionaire?*

Paddy's winnings from the show enabled him to continue his backpacking adventures. In June 2002 he returned from a ten-week trip to South America, where he trekked the Inca Trail.

In March 2002 Paddy appeared on his third *Millionaire*, in Dublin. Unable to name Piers Brosnan's youngest son for 4,000 euros, he tossed an old Irish punt, which came up tails. Unfortunately the answer (Paris) coincided with heads – sadly this time the luck of the Irish wasn't with Paddy! Not that this has deterred him, he says that he hopes to enter the South African version of the show in the next few years, and any profit he makes from doing so will go to charity. Look out, world – 'the Spooner experience' is coming your way!

Graham Hickin

Graham Hickin worked as a civil servant in Pontefract. He had a strong northern accent and like a lot of Yorkshiremen was, outwardly at least, unemotional. But he was very funny. He had his mate Jim in the audience, while at home were Leslie, Clare, Martin and Jamie. He loved American football and was obsessed with Bugs Bunny: he had Bugs Bunny key rings, pens, even Bugs Bunny boxer shorts. He commented, 'Mentally, I am thirty-nine going on three.' He appeared on the show with one arm lost from view inside his shirt. I asked him why and he replied, 'It's a very cheap shirt and it's only got one sleeve.' I must have looked bemused, as you would be, and he let up: 'Oh, all right then,' he said. 'I fell off a motorbike and broke my arm and collar bone.' Quite how he had managed to win Fastest Finger First, I'm not sure, but he had, and now, with his Bugs Bunny socks and an arm in a sling, he was playing for as much money as he could take back home to his family.

It soon became obvious that, underneath the reserved Yorkshire façade, this was a guy with a considerable range of general knowledge. He reached £1000 with a question about Tchaikovsky and the ballet, and still hadn't used any Lifelines when he got to this question for £8000:

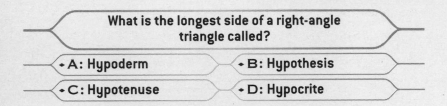

What is the longest side of a right-angle triangle called?

A: Hypoderm   B: Hypothesis
C: Hypotenuse   D: Hypocrite

Graham grinned at me, 'I had a maths master when I was about fourteen who swamped me with this and I think if I got it wrong he'd come out of this audience and brain me with a mallet. It's "hypotenuse".' He said this with total confidence. It was the right answer.

At this £8000 point, Jim, who had been smiling happily in the audience, started looking very worried. The pressure of the money that his mate was now playing for was clearly beginning to get to him. He needn't have worried. Graham was settled in for a while yet.

This was the question for £16,000:

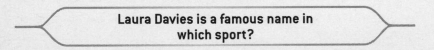

Laura Davies is a famous name in which sport?

Graham started to grin again. 'She's a lady golfer,' he answered, with no hesitation at all.

Up came the four possibilities:

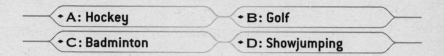

A: Hockey **B: Golf**
C: Badminton **D: Showjumping**

'I told you,' he said. 'It's "golf" – no question.' He was now on £32,000. But then the klaxon sounded the end of the show and Graham and Jim went off for a few well-deserved pints.

He came back the next day, still wearing the same pair of lucky Bugs Bunny socks, in the nice position of knowing that he would be going back to the family in Pontefract with at least £32,000.

He was faced with this next question, for £64,000:

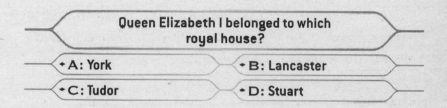

Queen Elizabeth I belonged to which royal house?

A: York **B: Lancaster**
C: Tudor **D: Stuart**

Quite often we've found that when people return on the second night the first question stops them in their tracks, but this didn't faze Graham at all. He smiled as soon as it came up, slapped his knee and said, 'She's a Tudor.' 'Why are you so sure she's a Tudor?' I asked him. 'She just is,' said Graham. And, of course, she just was.

He was now on £64,000. He had all three Lifelines and four questions between him and a million quid, tax free. If the pressure of the situation was beginning to get to Graham Hickin he certainly didn't show it.

This was the question for £125,000:

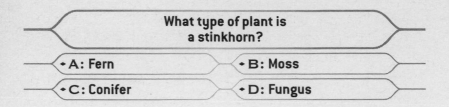

**What type of plant is
a stinkhorn?**

A: Fern   **B: Moss**

C: Conifer   **D: Fungus**

'I've got a feeling it's a fungus,' he said. 'Let's go 50:50.'
With £125,000 at stake this was the first Lifeline he'd used.
'Fungus' and 'fern' remained. 'It's a fungus,' he said, for
the first time not daring to look up or look me in the eye.
He stared down at the screen and just kept repeating, 'It's
a fungus, it's a fungus, it's a fungus,' as it went to orange.

'You've just won £125,000!' I was delighted to tell him.
For the first time he showed real emotion and let out a
huge whoop. I wrote out the cheque for £125,000, but he
wouldn't look at it. 'Show *them*,' he said, waving vaguely
towards the audience with his one working arm. 'Not me.'

For £250,000, with two Lifelines remaining, I asked
Graham:

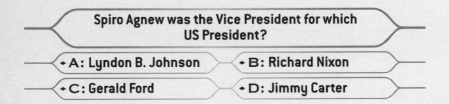

**Spiro Agnew was the Vice President for which
US President?**

A: Lyndon B. Johnson   **B: Richard Nixon**

C: Gerald Ford   **D: Jimmy Carter**

Graham paused. 'Let's ask this lot,' he said, suddenly
pointing at the audience all around him. We asked them.
Thirty-seven per cent said 'Nixon', 26 per cent 'Johnson'.
'I'll phone Geezer,' he decided. 'Graham, who's Geezer?'
I asked him. 'He's my mate Gary,' he told me. So I duti-
fully rang Gary. 'Hello, Gary,' I said, 'I've got Graham

Hickin here.' 'Who's he?' Gary joked, and Graham let out a great snort. They were obviously the best of mates. 'OK, Geezer, here's the question,' Graham said, and told him the four possibilities.

'I think it's "Nixon",' said Geezer, 'but I'm not completely sure.' 'You're a diamond geezer,' said Graham. 'Come on, Chris, let's play. Final answer – "Richard Nixon".' As the computer accepted his answer, the enormity of what he had done suddenly sank in. 'I'm not confident at all. I swore I was not going to do this. I shouldn't have risked this,' he was muttering with the orange already locked into our screens. He needn't have worried. I told him, 'You've just won £250,000.' 'Yes,' he screamed. 'Yes! Yes! Yes!'

'What does this amount of money mean to you?' I asked, and Graham suddenly revealed a side of his life that you'd never have guessed at. 'I'll tell you what it means,' he told me. 'You see that little number five down there [£1000],' he said, 'that's about all the money I've ever had in the world. My little lad Martin has got cerebral palsy – he's in a wheelchair and that's why I'm here.' For just a few seconds, and I suspect for one of the very few times in his life, there were tears in Graham's eyes. It was a wonderful warm moment, but we were not finished yet.

For £500,000 this was question number fourteen:

Which of these Russian names means 'fellow traveller'?	
A: Sputnik	B: Vostok
C: Soyuz	D: Voskhod

Graham immediately looked up at me, pointed to the

'Exit' sign in the studio and said without a second thought, 'I'm going that way, give us the cheque.' Just before he went, I asked him what he thought the answer would be. He said to me, 'I am absolutely not going to play this, but I think it's probably "Vostok".' 'Lucky you didn't play it,' I told Graham. 'Your instincts have been great all night, but in this case they were completely wrong. If you'd said to me "Vostok" you would have lost £218,000 – the right answer was "Sputnik".'

Ann Stanley

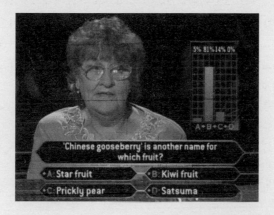

5% 81% 14% 0%

A • B • C • D

'Chinese gooseberry' is another name for
which fruit?

A: Star fruit B: Kiwi fruit

C: Prickly pear D: Satsuma

I have very fond memories of our hundredth show at
Elstree Studios. It was quite an evening. There is still a
real bond between myself and the contestants who appear
on the programme, on what many of them openly call the
most unforgettable night of their life, and that night there
were some good old familiar faces dating back from show
one. The audience was made up entirely of some of our
favourite winners, along with their partners, families and
friends. The atmosphere both during filming and in the bar
afterwards was brilliant. It was a very good night for
asking the audience — it was probably our most intelligent
ever.

A very nice lady called Ann Stanley came on our hundredth show. She was from Rugeley and had a nice, soft
Staffordshire accent. Her hubby Arthur was sitting in the
audience looking very proud; their sons Mark and David

were watching at home, along with Ann's five grandchildren, who called her 'Supergran'.

'Most of the money I win tonight will go towards my family,' she told me, 'but I'll keep a bit back for an operation I need to have.' At this point she wouldn't give me any more details about it.

Although Ann was quite nervous she was doing just fine until she got to question number five. For £1000 the computer threw up this:

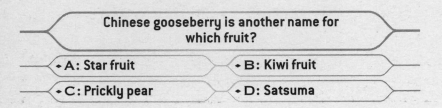

Chinese gooseberry is another name for which fruit?

A: Star fruit

B: Kiwi fruit

C: Prickly pear

D: Satsuma

'I think I know the answer to this,' said Ann, 'but I don't want to risk going home with nothing, I'm going to Ask the Audience.' Eighty-one per cent of our previous winners and their families knew that the right answer was 'kiwi fruit', guaranteeing Ann at least £1000. Arthur cheered in the audience, but then the klaxon signalled the end of our hundredth show.

When Ann returned the following evening she asked if we minded putting her into the hotseat from the top of the show, as she found walking and standing quite difficult. This was no problem for us, of course, and the floor manager and I gently lifted her into place, before the show began. That night Ann told me in more detail about the operation at which she had hinted darkly. It turned out that she was on an absurdly long waiting list for a hip replacement, probably something like a couple of years. But if she could only get to £8000 she could have a new hip fitted tomorrow as a private patient. It was an absurd situation and a terrible indictment on the state of the health service in this country. Many of the audience looked horrified when she told us all this, but Ann herself was very pragmatic about it. 'I'll just have to get on and win £8000,' she said.

Supergran was clearly quite a girl. She had ridden on elephants in Thailand, she had gone scuba-diving and she had climbed a fifteen-hundred-foot waterfall in Burma. If she could only have a new hip Ann would have a new lease of life – there was no question that, mentally, she was as bright as a button.

At the post-show party the night before, she'd swapped one of her Phone-A-Friends for Peter Lee, the man who a few weeks earlier had walked away with a massive cheque for £500,000 – at this stage the biggest winner on the show. There's nothing in the rules forbidding this, and it seemed a very enterprising idea.

We got Ann comfy, on a great big cushion on the chair, and started again from £1000.

She reached the £8000 question with few problems but this was, of course, the big one. If she answered this correctly she could have a hip replacement immediately:

What was Genevieve in the 1953 film?

A grin spread across Ann's face even before the options were shown. 'It's a car,' she said immediately. 'I've seen the film, I know it's a car.'

Up came the four possibilities:

A: Train   B: Bus
C: Bicycle   D: Car

She shouted, '"Car!"' at the top of her voice. It was the right answer, and Ann had enough money for a new hip. 'Whatever you do,' I told her, 'do not lose this amount of money – do not get carried away now.'

For £16,000 this question was brought up on the screen:

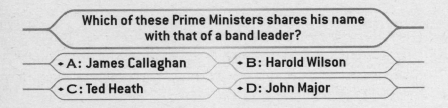

Which of these Prime Ministers shares his name with that of a band leader?

A: James Callaghan   B: Harold Wilson
C: Ted Heath   D: John Major

If anything, the grin on Ann's face was wider than before. 'It's "Ted Heath",' she said to me, 'I used to dance to Ted Heath and his band with Arthur when we were much younger.' Arthur, up in the audience, looked suitably embarrassed. We all laughed. Ann was now on £16,000.

The next question was for £32,000. I felt as though I was feeling the pressure more than Ann. I know how carried away some people can get when they feel on a winning streak on *Millionaire*, and if Ann did so and gave me a wrong answer, she would lose £15,000, which would mean no hip operation after all.

For £32,000 I asked her this question:

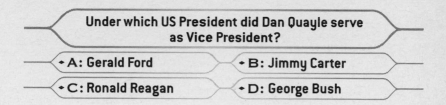

Under which US President did Dan Quayle serve as Vice President?

◆ A: Gerald Ford
◆ B: Jimmy Carter
◆ C: Ronald Reagan
◆ D: George Bush

'I think I know this,' she said, 'I think it's "Reagan".' I had to maintain the inscrutable mask on my face but it was an awful moment because I knew that 'Reagan' was wrong. 'I'll go 50:50,' she said. 'Reagan' and 'Bush' remained. I groaned inwardly. Luckily, Ann still wasn't entirely convinced and the realisation that she could lose such a vital sum of money was weighing heavily on her. 'I'll Phone-A-Friend,' she said. 'It's too much money to risk. I'll phone Peter Lee.'

'I'm fairly sure it was George Bush,' said Peter, 'but I must say I am not 100 per cent certain.' Mentally, I heaved a sigh of relief. 'I think it must be "Bush" now as well,' Ann told me. 'Hang on,' I said to her, 'you thought it was "Ronald Reagan".' 'No I'm going to go with Peter,' she said, 'I think it's "Bush". Come on Peter,' she urged him out loud, 'do the works for me. I'm going with Peter. Final answer – "George Bush".' This was probably the biggest risk Ann had ever taken in her life.

It had a happy ending, thank goodness. 'Bush' was correct: Ann had won a guaranteed £32,000. Up in the audience, Arthur looked absolutely wrecked at his wife's close shave. But she now could not lose the money for her operation.

For £64,000 she got this question:

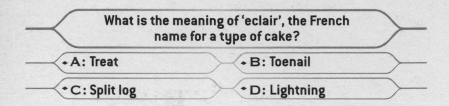

What is the meaning of 'eclair', the French
name for a type of cake?

A: Treat

B: Toenail

C: Split log

D: Lightning

'I can't lose on this question,' she said, 'can I?' 'No,' I replied, 'you might as well play.' Ann considered it. 'I'm really not sure, but I think it's "split log". I've made some chocolate eclairs and you sort of split the pastry to put the chocolate in.' It was a good theory but, unfortunately, it was completely wrong – the correct answer, bizarrely enough, is 'lightning'. Ann didn't care one bit, as she was off with Arthur to enjoy a healthier and happier life. We were all delighted for her – she was a lovely lady.

Life After *Who Wants To Be A Millionaire?*

Ann has told me since that her favourite memory of her second night on the show was being hoisted up into the chair by me and 'the very handsome floor manager'. (God knows which one that was!) She says she no longer wants for anything in life and always has a 'lovely comfortable feeling'. Of course, she had the operation straight away. She gave her sons £8000 each and invested the rest. She has been to Tenerife and Skiathos with Arthur since the show, and they are planning another adventure, to Crete, soon.

Bav Patel

Bav Patel was from Brighton. He worked in insurance. His partner Nicki was rooting for him in the audience, although she didn't look very keen on the prospect of Bav sitting in the hotseat. He told me he had a dream about the show the night before: he had got to £1000 and lost it, but, being in a very good mood, I'd given him another go. We laughed but I had to remind him that it had been a dream. Sadly, no matter how good my mood, I don't do 'second go's'.

From the beginning Bav looked tense. He was really going through it and was very hesitant about everything on the way up to £1000. On question number five he got completely stuck and seemed to be facing the possibility of returning home with no money at all. The question causing the trouble was:

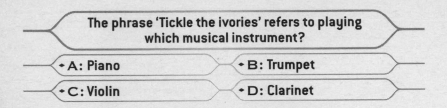

The phrase 'Tickle the ivories' refers to playing which musical instrument?

A: Piano   B: Trumpet

C: Violin   D: Clarinet

'I've not a clue,' said Bav, nervously taking a huge gulp of water. 'I've never heard of this. I'll have to Ask the Audience.'

Luckily, the audience had heard of it and 90 per cent gave him the right answer – 'piano', of course. Looking a bit better, he said, 'I've now got £1000. I came with nothing, so I'm really happy.'

For £2000 he got this question:

Who plays Q's assistant R in the James Bond film *The World Is Not Enough*?

A: Rowan Atkinson   B: John Cleese

C: Mel Smith   D: Richard Briers

'I've got an inkling it's "Mel Smith",' said Bav, 'but I'm not absolutely certain. I think I'll Phone-A-Friend. I think I'll phone Debbie.' Apparently Debbie was his boss in Brighton. 'I'm pretty sure it's "John Cleese",' she said, when Bav asked her the question. Now he looked more worried than ever. 'I'm going to go with Debbie,' he finally decided. '"John Cleese".' It was the right answer.

He was now on £2000. So much for his inkling about Mel Smith.

Bav was riding his luck all the way. He'd hardly been sure about a single answer but the audience were loving him for his sheer courage – or was it sheer madness?

For £4000 this came up:

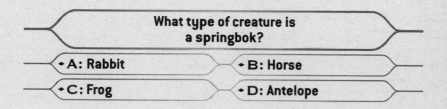

What type of creature is a springbok?

A: Rabbit
B: Horse
C: Frog
D: Antelope

I thought Bav would probably know this one, but again he shook his head. 'I think it's probably "horse",' he said, at which point millions must have been yelling obscenities at their television sets all over the country. Any visiting South Africans would have been absolutely horrified. 'I'm just not certain,' he said. 'I'll go 50:50.' Terrifyingly, 'horse' remained, along with 'antelope'. 'I think it's "horse",' said Bav, still not very certain of anything, adding, after a long pause, 'But then again it could be "antelope".' Another long pause. 'I'm going to play,' he said. '"Antelope". Final answer – "antelope".' 'Why are you going for "antelope"?' I asked, mystified but relieved. 'I don't know,' he said, 'I just like the sound of it. It sounds better than "horse". I'm going to risk it – I'm going for "antelope".'

He closed his eyes when it went to orange, and then beat the air frantically with his fists when I told him he had just won £4000. By now Nicki was a nervous wreck, and so was I.

For £8000 Bav got this question:

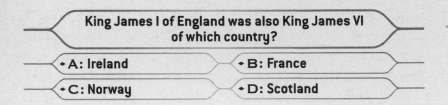

King James I of England was also King James VI of which country?

- A: Ireland
- B: France
- C: Norway
- D: Scotland

'I really don't know,' he said. 'You haven't really known anything,' I said, 'but somehow you're still getting there.' 'I think it's probably Scotland,' he said. 'Let's play for it, let's go for it — "Scotland".'

Extraordinary — it was right! He'd staggered up to £8000.

Bav screamed at the top of his voice. Nicki screamed at the top of her voice. 'You're frightening me to death,' I told him. 'Come on, ask me another,' he urged me, 'I feel lucky.'

The next question was for £16,000:

A chukka is a period of playing time in which sport?

- A: Badminton
- B: Volleyball
- C: Polo
- D: Hockey

It looked like Bav's luck was finally going to run out. 'I haven't got the foggiest,' he said slowly, and I assumed he was about to take the money. 'It's only money, though, isn't it?' he suddenly added brightly. '"Polo" looks good. Oh no, cor blimey, come to think about it, so does "badminton". But "polo" looks sort of mintier, know what I mean, Chris?' I must say, I didn't really know what he meant: for the last ten minutes his reasoning had been very mysterious. Nicki was white. 'What the heck, eh?' Bav continued. 'Let's go for it. Final answer.' 'Are you sure?' I asked. There was a short pause. 'No,' Bav now decided. 'I'm going to take the money.' Then he broke off. 'Actually, no I'm not. I hope Nicki doesn't kill me . . .' He stopped himself again. 'No, I'm going to take the money. That's it, I'm going to take the money.' I was just about to open my mouth when Bav interrupted me again. 'No! I'm going to play, I'm going to play, "polo" – final answer – quick, quick, quick, quick, quick.' Almost speechless by now, as quickly as I could I accepted his answer. 'Polo' went to orange. Somehow Bav Patel had earned himself £16,000.

I now gave him some advice I've never given to any other contestant, 'Bav, you have somehow got to £16,000 – you've known absolutely nothing – please, please, do not play any more, please just go.' Understandably, though, he had to have a look at the £32,000 question before he left us. He had no Lifelines. This was his next question:

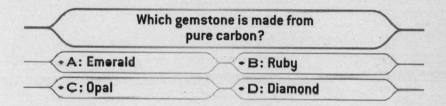

Which gemstone is made from pure carbon?

A: Emerald   B: Ruby

C: Opal   D: Diamond

'I think it's "diamond",' he announced immediately, sounding far more sure than he had all night. He looked at me for a second. 'But,' he concluded, 'I'm not going to risk it, I don't want to push my luck. It is a lot of money. I'm going to take £16,000.'

'Thank God for that,' I said. Bav had managed to guess his way to a fabulous £16,000. The twist in the tale was that he'd quit on the first question that he actually appeared to know, and he'd been right – diamond is indeed made from pure carbon.

Duncan Bickley

Duncan Bickley was a helicopter instructor. Now, this is a strange thing, but over four years on *Millionaire* we've always found that people who fly do rather well. We've had pilots, flying instructors and air traffic controllers on the show and they've all been reasonably successful. They're probably used to living on the edge of their nerves and handling pressure; they also must need to be quite intelligent to pass the written exams they have to take. Whatever the reason, they tend to win some big money, certainly a lot more than, say, teachers, who, with one notable exception, have done really rather badly.

Anyway, Duncan was a bright, outgoing sort of bloke who had his sister Gillian sitting in the audience for comfort and moral support. He said he'd never taken her flying as she'd be far too nervous, and he went on to be very amusing about the terrors of teaching people to fly. Although it's obviously in his financial interests to take on as many pupils as possible, he said to me, 'I'm afraid there are some people who should just never, ever be allowed near the controls of a plane.'

If he won lots of money on the show, he said, he was quite happy to carry on messing around in helicopters for a living as he thoroughly enjoyed it, but he did have a great fantasy: to go on a scuba-diving holiday with Anna Kournikova.

Duncan had no problem with the early questions and the first milestone for him came at £2000 – which he said would be enough money to pay off his phone bill. This was the question:

> **In which European country does over half the population live on reclaimed land?**
>
> A: Belgium
> B: The Netherlands
> C: Luxembourg
> D: Liechtenstein

He knew at once that it was 'the Netherlands'. For £8000 he was asked something which certainly would have stopped a lot of men in their tracks:

> **Which nuts are traditionally used to decorate Dundee cake?**
>
> A: Walnuts
> B: Hazelnuts
> C: Brazil nuts
> D: Almonds

But Duncan was unruffled; he smiled at me happily. 'I've never made one,' he said, 'but I've seen a picture of them on the top of tins.' 'So you're risking £7000,' I asked him, 'on a vague memory of an image on the top of a cake tin?' 'That's right,' he said. 'It's almonds.' And indeed his memory had served him well.

For £16,000, the computer threw up this:

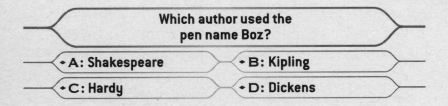

Which author used the
pen name Boz?

A: Shakespeare   B: Kipling

C: Hardy   D: Dickens

'I'm fairly sure it's Charles Dickens,' said Duncan. 'But do I use a Lifeline to be sure?' 'It's your choice, Duncan,' I reminded him. 'Yes, go on,' he said. 'I'll Phone-A-Friend. I'm going to phone Tim, he's a mate of mine from down the pub.' Tim from down the pub was just the sort of Phone-A-Friend you need, as he knew the answer before any of the possibilities even came up on the screen. 'It's Charles Dickens,' he said after less than two seconds, and Duncan was now on £16,000.

Duncan was still pretty unfazed. He'd probably sat through a lot worse nightmares trying to teach people to fly helicopters.

Question number ten, for £32,000, was:

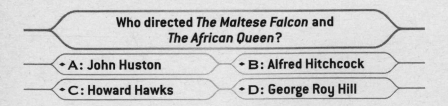

Who directed *The Maltese Falcon* and
The African Queen?

A: John Huston   B: Alfred Hitchcock

C: Howard Hawks   D: George Roy Hill

Duncan wasn't at all sure, so he asked the audience. Sixty-three per cent said 'John Huston' and 20 per cent thought it was 'Alfred Hitchcock'. 'I'm still not certain,' said Duncan. He thought long and hard about his situation. 'Oh, go on,' he eventually relented. 'I'll go with the audience. "Huston". Final answer.' Mercifully, it was correct, and he was now guaranteed to take home at least thirty-two grand.

'Thank God!' he yelled in triumph: it was the first time he had shown real emotion. The enormity of the amounts of money that were now achievable was beginning to sink in, which often happens at this stage. People are very glad to reach £32,000 but they then glimpse the potential of how much they might win. Duncan was only five right answers away from £1,000,000 and he still had one Lifeline remaining. He was a very intelligent man and was looking ever more focused.

He answered a question about cochineal with no problem for £64,000, and suddenly we were at the £125,000 mark:

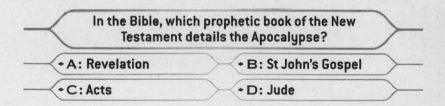

In the Bible, which prophetic book of the New Testament details the Apocalypse?

A: Revelation

B: St John's Gospel

C: Acts

D: Jude

Duncan smiled at me — that familiar, relieved smile of someone who knows the answer. 'It's "Revelation",' he said. 'Have you ever read it?' I asked him. 'I have actually,' he said. 'It's very weird. It's all that stuff about the Whore of Babylon, 666, horsemen, et cetera.' He was, of course, absolutely right and had won £125,000.

The audience cheered, beginning to sense that Duncan just might go all the way. 'I'm absolutely speechless,' he said. It was getting better all the time. With the next question it got better still.

For £250,000 I asked him:

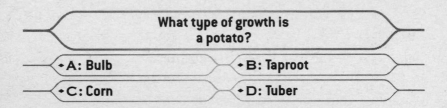

What type of growth is a potato?

- A: Bulb
- B: Taproot
- C: Corn
- D: Tuber

'It's a tuber,' he shot back at me immediately. '"Tuber", "tuber", "tuber". Final answer. No question. "Tuber", "tuber", "tuber".' He had now won £250,000.

He looked at me with a huge grin. 'Good 'ere, innit?' he said. He was two away from a million, with one Lifeline remaining, and this was the question for £500,000. Bearing in mind he was a pilot, this one looked like manna from heaven:

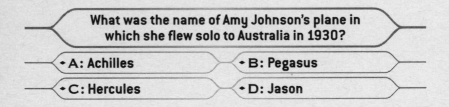

What was the name of Amy Johnson's plane in which she flew solo to Australia in 1930?

- A: Achilles
- B: Pegasus
- C: Hercules
- D: Jason

I told Duncan that if he answered this correctly to win £500,000 it would be the most that anybody had ever won since the show started transmission. 'It's a huge amount of money to lose,' he said, 'but it's got to be "Pegasus", surely. You know what I'm thinking? Pegasus, wings, winged horse, et cetera. It's not "Achilles" or "Hercules", and "Jason" has nothing whatsoever to do with flying.' To make sure, double sure, he used his 50:50 and "Pegasus" and "Jason" remained. Deep inside me, I was pretty sure that he was right. 'If you go for this and give me a right answer, Duncan, you'll have won the most of anyone on *Who Wants To Be A Millionaire?* in the UK. I suppose I should also mention that if you're wrong you'll have lost the highest amount ever.' Even though he was pretty sure of his answer, Duncan looked seriously stressed. 'It's such a big risk,' he said. 'Then again, what the hell, it's only money, innit?'

'I'm sure it's got to be "Pegasus". Final answer.' It went to orange, the audience held their breath and on my screen, to my horror, up came 'wrong answer'. I gulped inwardly and broke the news to Duncan. The audience gasped, horrified. None of us could believe it. Duncan muttered quietly, 'I'm absolutely gutted.' He went away having lost £218,000 – I think it still remains the highest sum that anyone's ever lost on the show anywhere in the world.

It turned out later that Jason was the name of one of Amy Johnson's sons.

Kate Heusser

As has happened on several occasions with some of our most memorable contestants, on the night Kate Heusser was on *Millionaire*, she was the only one who got the Fastest Finger First question right and she raced into the hotseat happy, but with no real expectation of winning very big money.

Her husband Peter was sitting proudly in the audience, and they had two sons at home, Edward and Gregory. Kate's was a complicated career story. She had been a solicitor for years, but was currently about to start work as a postwoman since she wanted to be a writer and to begin her first book she needed time that working in the legal profession just didn't give her. Delivering the local mail would mean she would have to get up early and try to avoid mad dogs, but would then have the rest of the day to sit at her word processor.

She looked very nervous at the beginning. 'It's all a bit of a shock to be here, to be truthful,' she said. But it certainly didn't show in the way she disposed of the early questions.

Right at the end of the show that night she got this question for £4000:

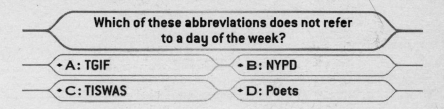

Which of these abbreviations does not refer to a day of the week?

- A: TGIF
- B: NYPD
- C: TISWAS
- D: Poets

For the only time that first evening Kate was hesitant. 'I think it is "NYPD",' she said. 'In fact I'm pretty sure it is "NYPD", but I really never knew what "TISWAS" stood for.' This was one of those silly moments when it was pretty obvious to both of us that I would know the answer but equally obvious that I was quite unable to help her. Luckily she went for "NYPD" anyway, which are the initials of the New York Police Department. 'TISWAS', incidentally, stood for 'Today Is Saturday Watch And Smile'.

She was on £4000, and the klaxon sounded for the end of the show. She looked very relieved and went off to join Peter.

Kate was supposed to have begun her new job the following morning, but, rather embarrassingly, now had to ask for time off before she had even started since, as she

put it, 'I'm on *Who Wants To Be A Millionaire?*'
Apparently her boss at the post office had been very rea-
sonable about this. 'It's an excuse I've never heard before –
it must be true,' he said. It was, of course, but I began to
suspect that Kate might never see her first early morning
on the post round.

She told me she was writing a novel about the TV
industry, but after her experiences of the day before she
said she was now going to make a few changes. I didn't
quite know what she meant – it sounded rather ominous.

With three Lifelines still available, she started all over
again with the £8000 question:

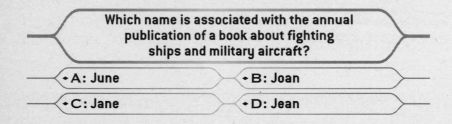

Which name is associated with the annual publication of a book about fighting ships and military aircraft?

- **A: June**
- **B: Joan**
- **C: Jane**
- **D: Jean**

'I know this,' she said straight away. 'It's "Jane".' And
she was quite right.

I couldn't resist asking her, 'At what point would you
stop even thinking about becoming a postwoman?' 'I'm
not going to tell you,' she replied. 'Let's see the next question!'

For £16,000, the screen threw up this:

Calvados is a type of brandy made with which fruit?

- **A: Plums**
- **B: Cherries**
- **C: Oranges**
- **D: Apples**

'I think it's "apples",' she said, but with less certainty than she had been displaying previously. 'I'm going to play – it's not "plums", it's not "cherries", it's not "oranges". I'm going to play. Please forgive me if I'm wrong, Peter,' she said, with a silent prayer towards the ceiling. Peter was nodding. I think he knew she was right. I knew she was right. She had just won £32,000.

The early-morning alarm calls for her new job were looking less and less likely. She still had all three Lifelines and she was guaranteed £32,000.

But at £64,000, for the first time, she stuck solid.

This was the question:

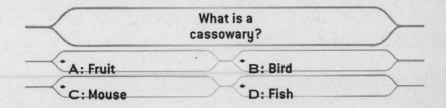

What is a cassowary?

A: Fruit   B: Bird

C: Mouse   D: Fish

'I've not got a clue,' said Kate. 'I'll phone Ian.' Ian was a very good choice. 'I'm 99.9 per cent certain it is a bird,' he told her. 'Bless you,' said Kate, 'Let's play – "bird".' It was correct.

For £125,000 this question appeared on her screen and she started nodding:

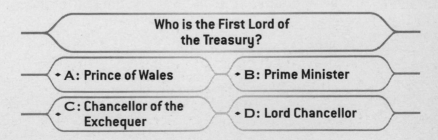

Who is the First Lord of the Treasury?

A: Prince of Wales   B: Prime Minister

C: Chancellor of the Exchequer   D: Lord Chancellor

'Why are you nodding?' I asked her. 'I'm nodding because I know it,' she said, 'but I'm too scared to say it out loud.' There was a long pause. 'It's the Prime Minister,' she said. Right answer – £125,000. Peter, in the audience, looked elated, and rather shell-shocked.

This was the £250,000 question:

In mythology who was the twin
of Castor?

Kate grinned and said, '"Pollux".' There was huge laughter from the audience. 'With a "p",' she emphasised. '"Pollux", "Pollux".' 'OK,' I said, 'let's see what comes up on the screen. These are the four possible answers:'

• A: Endymion	• B: Achilles
• C: Leander	• D: Pollux

'"Pollux!"' She said it again at the top of her voice with enormous enthusiasm. She knew that Castor and Pollux were the heavenly twins, and it won her £250,000.

She still had two Lifelines left and was just two right answers away from £1,000,000. 'I think you are probably very unlikely to ever start work now as a postwoman, aren't you?' I asked her. She grinned at me, but still admitted nothing.

This was question number fourteen:

New Sarum is the former name
of which city?

A: Salisbury   B: Stoke-on-Trent
C: Shrewsbury   D: Sheffield

Kate became very tense. 'I'll go 50:50, please,' she said. 'Salisbury' and 'Shrewsbury' remained. She was still not certain. 'How would the audience feel if I asked them with £500,000 at stake?' She asked me. 'Absolutely terrified, I would think,' I replied. But she did it anyway.

Seventy per cent of the audience thought it was 'Salisbury', 30 per cent 'Shrewsbury'. 'I was thinking "Salisbury" already,' she said. 'It's not their responsibility. I'm going to play.' There was a gasp all round the studio. 'It's my final answer – "Salisbury".' Kate had just won £500,000.

There were scenes of frantic rejoicing in the audience. Peter was almost beside himself with joy. Kate looked absolutely stunned at the enormity of what had just happened. Unless she was mad enough to take the most absurd gamble on the final question her career as a postwoman looked like a non-starter. So, beyond her wildest expectations, Kate Heusser, along with Peter and the rest of the United Kingdom, was about to view a £1,000,000 question. She said to me, 'I don't even want to look at the next one.' 'Peter, how's she doing?' I asked her husband. 'Not bad,' he said, a huge grin on his face.

'Kate, you can obviously walk away with this amount of money.'

'I'm planning to,' said Kate.

'If you give me a wrong answer you lose £468,000, but this is question number fifteen – it's worth £1,000,000:'

Which monarch was known as 'the wisest fool in Christendom'?

As soon as it came on the screen she beamed at me. The options were:

• A: James I   **• B: Charles I**

• C: Edward I   **• D: Henry I**

For a second I thought she was grinning because she knew the answer, but she said, 'I'm delighted to say that I have absolutely no idea. I am so relieved.'

We had seen this before several times at these extraordinary moments when the stakes are so high. The contestant realises that at last all the pressure is off. They haven't a clue, there's no question of them risking an answer and they are going home with an enormous cheque intact. This was exactly what Kate was doing. She went back to West Sussex on a wonderful high, but still feeling numb from the whole experience.

Incidentally, 'the wisest fool in Christendom' was James I.

Life After *Who Wants To Be A Millionaire?*

Kate never did take up her job as a postwoman! She and Peter gave away some of the money, spent a little more – they bought their house outright and now have two apartments in Tenerife to rent out – and invested the remainder. The money has enabled Kate to spend far more time at home, and she has opted to educate their children there.

166

Judith Keppel

To be honest, when I first met Judith Keppel I didn't think she seemed likely to get very far. Although she was clearly a very articulate, intelligent lady, she appeared to have no confidence at all and, at the end of rehearsal when we ask if any of the contestants have any questions, she asked me an unusual question: 'Do you ever stop filming during the show?' I told her, 'We stop for each round of Fastest Finger First for a minute or two, but otherwise, unless there's a computer breakdown, we tend to just keep recording.' 'But what if something happens?' Judith enquired. 'Such as?' I asked. 'Well, what if I faint?' I have to say I'd never been asked this before by any contestant. I reassured her that it was surely very unlikely that she would faint but, if it was any comfort, yes, we probably would stop recording as it wouldn't be much of a show if I was asking the questions to a body lying on the studio floor.

Anyway, Judith didn't faint on the night, and she was the only contestant who got her particular Fastest Finger First question right. She did so in a comparatively slow time — just over eight seconds — but often accuracy wins over speed. Judith had her daughter Rosie beaming in the audience, and two other older kids and two grandchildren watching. She told me that if she won a lot of money, her dream was to let Alan Titchmarsh mess about in her shrubbery. She confided that she'd been having nightmares about coming on the show and had been waking up in the night pressing imaginary buttons on her pillow, as she practised Fastest Finger First in her sleep.

But once we got down to business she had a nice, clear voice, read each question carefully and got to £1000 on a pretty straightforward one:

In which sport do two teams pull at either end of a rope?

◆ A: Tug of war   ◆ B: Basketball
◆ C: Ice hockey   ◆ D: Polo

Judith, of course, knew that it was 'tug of war'. She said, 'I now feel very relieved,' but at £8000 she admitted to me, 'I seem to be getting more nervous all the time, rather than less.' However, she kept on coming up with the right answers.

For £8000 she got this:

Sherpas and Gurkhas are native to which country?

◆ A: Russia   ◆ B: Ecuador
◆ C: Nepal   ◆ D: Morocco

She had no problem with this at all – she knew it was 'Nepal'. She'd said she loved travelling and I asked her if she ever wanted to go to a country as exciting as Nepal. 'Absolutely not!' she exclaimed. Judith suffers from vertigo. 'No,' I agreed. 'In that case, you probably wouldn't like Nepal very much.'

For £16,000 she got this question:

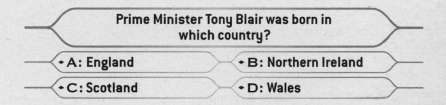

Prime Minister Tony Blair was born in which country?

A: England   B: Northern Ireland

C: Scotland   D: Wales

'I know he went to school in Scotland,' she remembered. 'But was he born there?' I looked at her with my customary deadpan expression. 'I'll Ask the Audience,' she said, taking advantage of her first Lifeline. Fifty-three per cent said 'Scotland'; only 19 per cent thought Tony Blair was born in England.

'I just don't know what to do,' Judith said, apparently worried. 'Oh, I'd better go for "Scotland", I suppose. Final answer. Come on,' she pleaded, when I paused, 'please don't tease. Just tell me.' After another even longer pause I took pity on her, delighted to inform her that she'd won £16,000. I gave her a big smacker on the cheeks, a gesture the editor of the *Daily Telegraph* was later to compare to 'the indignity of being licked by a great big labrador'.

Then the klaxon went: Judith had lived to fight another day. After the show, she told me later, her kids had thanked her for not embarrassing them and, remarkably, the next day, at the end of his Sunday morning sermon, her local vicar had announced, 'Before we leave our church today, let us all pray for easy questions for dear Judith on tonight's *Who Wants To Be A Millionaire?*

The following evening she informed me, 'I feel less nervous but the game is affecting my whole life. I seem to look at everything in multiple choices. I was getting on a bus at lunchtime and I found myself thinking 'Which is the bus that goes to Piccadilly non-stop. Is it "A: The 75", "B: The 37" . . .' Nonetheless, she was perfectly ready to get down to the serious business of answering some more questions.

Judith's first one that night was for £32,000:

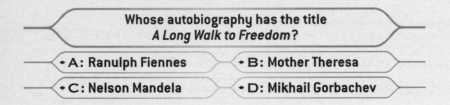

**Whose autobiography has the title
A Long Walk to Freedom?**

◆ A: Ranulph Fiennes   ◆ B: Mother Theresa
◆ C: Nelson Mandela   ◆ D: Mikhail Gorbachev

She looked at me and said cautiously, 'It's "Nelson Mandela". Hang on, can I think for one second, please . . .? Yes, it's Nelson Mandela.' I was delighted to tell her she'd just won £32,000 and, for the first of several times that evening, Judith exclaimed, 'Wow!'

I wrote her out a cheque and then snatched it out of her hand, doing my 'but we don't want to give you that' routine, which made her jump in fright. When she'd calmed down, I offered her this question, for £64,000:

**Duffel coats are named after a town in
which country?**

◆ A: Belgium   ◆ B: The Netherlands
◆ C: Germany   ◆ D: Austria

'Oh dear,' she said. 'I really have no idea. It sounds sort of Frenchy, so I suppose it could be "Belgium". I really can't think of any Phone-A-Friend who'd know.' She decided to use her 50:50, which left 'Belgium' or 'The Netherlands.

'It's so funny for Belgium to have a coat,' she said. 'You just don't think of the Belgians as the sort of people who'd invent a coat.' 'These really aren't the easy questions that the vicar prayed for, are they?' I joked to her. 'No, they're not,' she said. 'The vicar hasn't done very well at all.' 'You can still Phone-A-Friend,' I reminded her. 'I really don't think there's any point,' she said sadly. 'I'll just have to save it and hope that I'm still here to use it later.' This turned out to be a critical decision. 'I'll play,' she said. 'I'll play "Belgium", although I'm not in the least bit sure.'

I looked at my monitor and announced, 'You've just won £64,000!' She smiled widely and said, 'Wow!' again, at the top of her voice.

The next question was for £125,000:

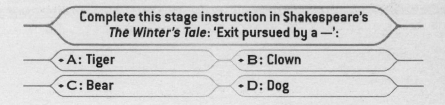

Complete this stage instruction in Shakespeare's *The Winter's Tale*: 'Exit pursued by a —':

- A: Tiger
- B: Clown
- C: Bear
- D: Dog

I have to say that I knew this at once, from years and years of studying Shakespeare, at O level, at university, *ad nauseam*, but Judith declared quite openly, 'I really haven't a clue. I'll phone Jillie and yes, you can tell her how much money's involved.' Nothing like £125,000 between friends to sharpen the concentration.

Jillie had obviously been to as many Shakespearian

classes as I had because as soon as Judith read her the question, she said, 'It's a bear, darling. I'm absolutely certain. One hundred per cent. The answer's "bear".' 'Oh bless you, Jillie,' said Judith excitedly. 'It is the sort of thing she would definitely get right,' she told me. And she had. Judith now had £125,000, but that was her last Lifeline.

'I've gone completely blank,' she said. 'But that is a wonderful amount of money. There are so many things I can do with it.' However, she hadn't quite finished.

For £250,000 she got this question:

> ## The young of which creature is known as a squab?

'I know this one,' she said. 'It's a pigeon. You eat them in America. Squabs are definitely baby pigeons.' 'Pigeon' was quite right: Judith Keppel was now on £250,000. Rosie was looking almost apoplectic in the audience.

Compared to her daughter, Judith seemed to be an oasis of calm. 'I'm not really,' she said and looked hard at the screen, waiting for the next question. This was for £500,000. Only Peter Lee and Kate Heusser had ever won this amount of money before.

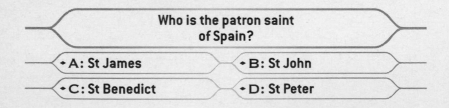

> ## Who is the patron saint of Spain?
>
> | ◆ A: St James | ◆ B: St John |
> |---|---|
> | ◆ C: St Benedict | ◆ D: St Peter |

Judith immediately stated, 'I think it's "James",' and the audience gasped. 'I'm really sorry,' she said, 'but I think it's "James".' 'Don't be sorry,' I said. 'There's no need to apologise. If you're right it's great.' 'Yes,' she replied, 'but I'm frightened of being wrong. No, I'm sure it's "James". Final answer.'

She had just won £500,000.

'Wow!' she repeated for the umpteenth time that evening. 'I've been very lucky.' 'No you haven't,' I told her. 'You've had some seriously hard questions. You've been absolutely brilliant.' But there was still a chance for her to lose the great bulk of it.

'This next question is for £1,000,000,' I said for only the third time in my life. I reminded her that if she did give me a wrong answer she would lose £468,000. When I spelt this out to Peter and Kate, it had the most sobering effect on them, and Judith's reaction was no different. 'Gosh!' she said, and looked at me in horror as if this was all new information.

This was question number fifteen:

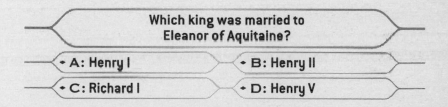

Which king was married to
Eleanor of Aquitaine?

A: Henry I   B: Henry II

C: Richard I   D: Henry V

'I think it's "Henry II",' she said at once, and there was an involuntary shriek from somebody in the audience. Rosie looked as if she wanted the earth to swallow her up. 'I'm sure it's "Henry II",' she said. 'I saw Eleanor of Aquitaine's tomb in France this summer.' 'Yes, but what did it say?' I asked her. 'It's rather important!'

'Well, I hope it said she was married to Henry II,' she rambled on. The studio atmosphere was almost unbearable. 'I said I wasn't going to gamble,' said Judith, 'but I sort of can't resist it. I studied History at school for A levels . . . Thirty-two thousand pounds is still very nice. Ooh, my heart! I'm fairly sure, though . . . I think it's worth going for,' and, at that moment, for the first time ever on a £1,000,000 question, Judith Keppel uttered the fateful words 'final answer'. It went to orange; she was at the point of no return. The adrenalin rush that came over me when I saw, spelt out on my monitor, the enormous implication of what had just happened was a feeling I'll never forget.

In the long wait of over two years for our first £1,000,000 winner, I often wondered if I'd be brave enough to go to the commercial break at this moment. I thought I'd probably bottle out. But somehow, that night, I felt it just had to be done! 'We'll take a break,' I said, hardly believing myself. 'Oh, Chris,' Judith said in absolute horror, and the audience screamed abuse.

There was a day between the recording of the Judith Keppel show and the actual transmission, so we were terrified that somebody in the audience would sell the big secret to the tabloids, and I'm afraid that's what happened. It did mean, however, that this particular ad break must have been one of the most lucrative in commercial television history.

We got back on air and Judith looked drained and scared. I told her it was the right answer. She'd just won £1,000,000.

'I can't believe it, I really can't believe it,' she repeated over and over. She kept insisting, 'I was very, very lucky with the questions.' But Judith Keppel did not win £1,000,000 through luck. I've spent a lot of time on various chat shows with Judith since and she is an extraordinary woman – very calm, quite shy, and obviously super-intelligent. Rosie came down to join Mum in a far worse state, sobbing her eyes out, while Judith comforted her, tenderly dabbing her daughter's cheeks.

The audience all stood on their seats screaming and cheering her as she left the studio clutching her cheque for £1,000,000. And the first word the crew and I exchanged after the show was 'Wow!'

Life After *Who Wants To Be A Millionaire?*

Judith's memories of the show are very confused, but she still remembers that commercial break as the longest three minutes of her life. Just before we went on air, she saw me round the back of the set jumping up and down and waving my arms manically to get myself loosened up. She said she tried it and felt like an idiot.

She's bought a new car and redecorated her house. She says her win has made a colossal difference to her life in all sorts of ways. As well as being £1,000,000 richer, she has now been offered all sorts of exciting media opportunities, such as columns to write and TV and radio appearances. She also became interested in the preservation of tigers in India, and gave some money to a reserve there. Recently she and Rosie flew over to visit the sanctuary. Judith said it was a tremendous thrill to see the animals and know she'd been able to contribute to their well-being in a small way.

Judith is recognised everywhere she goes in the UK and says that people are always incredibly friendly when they meet her — some even want to touch her for luck. She says the whole experience has been fantastic.

Chris Elliot

The contestant who had to follow the first £1,000,000 winner on *Who Wants To Be A Millionaire?* was never going to have an easy time of it. Here in the UK Chris Elliot ended up in this unenviable position. First, he'd had to sit through an exceptionally dramatic show, with its twists and turns, agonising as to whether he was even going to get the chance to play Fastest Finger First; secondly, he knew when he'd won it that his appearance was bound to be a bit of an anticlimax.

Chris Elliot was a really nice lad. He was a teaching assistant from Castleford in Yorkshire. Sally, his girlfriend, was sitting in the audience, looking numb. Chris admitted that he had found the tension of watching Judith almost unbearable. He also confessed that he wouldn't have been able to answer many of her questions. 'But,' he said, 'Just one tenth of her money would be very nice.' And, of course, £100,000 would be rather handy for a young teaching assistant. His dream, he said, was to cook Cameron Diaz a beach barbecue.

So we started all over again. From the dizzy heights of the £1,000,000 question, we were now back down to question one, for £100:

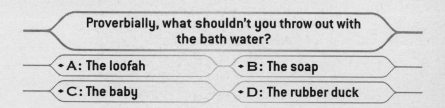

Proverbially, what shouldn't you throw out with the bath water?

A: The loofah   B: The soap

C: The baby   D: The rubber duck

To my horror, Chris looked at me blankly and said, 'I've never, ever heard of this saying before in my life.' There was a gasp from the audience. 'I can't believe that this could happen,' I blurted out. 'One person has just left with £1,000,000; the next might go with nothing!' 'I know, but I really have never heard of it,' Chris replied. He looked hard at the possible answers. 'It must be "baby",' he suddenly realised. 'Please, God, it's got to be "baby".' Before he could say another word, I yelled out, 'It's the right answer!' 'Thank God,' sighed Chris. But understandably this, combined with the timing of his appearance, had really unsettled him and he began to look very ill at ease. Mercifully, though, he got to £1000 with all three Lifelines intact and he, Sally and I all breathed a sigh of relief. The first time he needed any help was on the £4000 question:

Which member of the Freud family is a former MP?

A: Sigmund   B: Lucian

C: Emma   D: Clement

Chris wasn't sure, so he asked the audience. Three per cent, rather alarmingly, thought Emma Freud was a former MP. Eighty-three per cent had the good sense to say it was Clement, a former Liberal MP.

For £8000 he got this question:

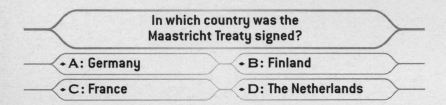

In which country was the
Maastricht Treaty signed?

A: Germany

B: Finland

C: France

D: The Netherlands

Chris looked at me for an age but then said fairly positively, 'It's "the Netherlands", Chris – final answer.' It was the right answer. After a horribly shaky start things were improving.

For £32,000 he got this question:

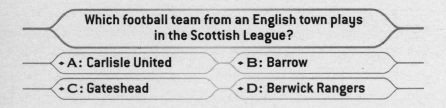

Which football team from an English town plays
in the Scottish League?

A: Carlisle United

B: Barrow

C: Gateshead

D: Berwick Rangers

Chris's face broke into a huge grin. He was clearly well up on his northern football and told me that 'Berwick' was the answer, guaranteeing himself £32,000. For the umpteenth time that night the crowd broke into spontaneous cheering. 'This is a massive amount of money,' said Chris, with a disbelieving look in his eyes.

For £64,000 the question was:

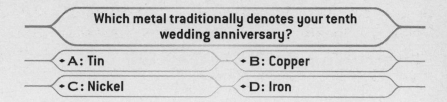

Which metal traditionally denotes your tenth wedding anniversary?

◆ A: Tin

◆ B: Copper

◆ C: Nickel

◆ D: Iron

Chris had no idea – not that many young lads would. 'I'll have to Phone-A-Friend,' he said. I gave him a piece of advice: 'Trust me on this, Chris – if you're going to Phone-A-Friend, phone a woman.' 'OK,' he agreed, 'good thinking. I'll phone my mum Pat, but please don't let her know how much money this question is worth or it will throw her completely.'

We phoned Pat, who was very excited that her boy was in the chair that night – not that she'd know the half of it until she saw the whole show the following evening. 'I'm really not sure,' Pat told her son, having heard the question. 'But I think it could be "tin".' We hung up and Chris decided immediately, 'I'm going to go with it. I've got nothing to lose – I might as well play this one, I'm going with Mum. "Tin" – final answer.' 'Your mum has just won you £64,000,' I told him, delighted, shaking him warmly by the hand. 'How long would it take you to earn £64,000?' I asked him. 'Seriously,' he said to me, 'it would take me most of my life and the next. It means the world.' I suspect maths was not Chris's strong point, but I got his drift. 'OK,' I told him, 'so whatever you do, do not lose it now. You've got one Lifeline left and this is your £125,000 question:'

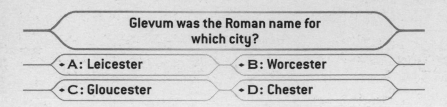

Glevum was the Roman name for
which city?

A: Leicester   B: Worcester

C: Gloucester   D: Chester

'I'm not sure,' Chris said, staring at the screen in front of
him, 'but I think it's "Gloucester".' There was a groan
from the audience. 'You don't have to play this question,'
I reminded him. He went 50:50 and 'Gloucester' remained.
'I'm still tempted by "Gloucester",' he told me. 'I'm sure
the "cester" bit means "city". I'm going to play. Glevum is
"Gloucester" – final answer.' He was right. The audience
had groaned in pure alarm – nothing more – and Chris
had won £125,000.

Then the klaxon sounded and we all crawled away to the
bar absolutely exhausted. It had been an extraordinary
show. Since we had come on air an hour earlier, we had
given away a staggering £1,125,000.

Chris Elliot came back the next day with Sally, who was
clearly very proud of him. He had no Lifelines left but I
showed him the question for £250,000:

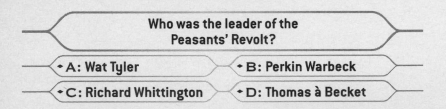

Who was the leader of the
Peasants' Revolt?

A: Wat Tyler   B: Perkin Warbeck

C: Richard Whittington   D: Thomas à Becket

He looked at me. 'It's not "à Becket",' he said, 'and I'm
sure "Richard Whittington" is Dick Whittington, the Lord
Mayor of London. I think it's Wat Tyler, in fact I'm almost

sure it's "Wat Tyler". Then again, it's just a vague idea coming from the back of my brain somewhere.' He thought for a while, then shook his head regretfully. 'It's just too much money to risk. I've got £125,000, which will completely change my life. It's just not worth risking it – I'm going to take the money.' He grinned at me from ear to ear.

Considering Chris had nearly been eliminated on question one, just seconds after another contestant had won £1,000,000 before his eyes, he had fought back with real guts. If he'd answered 'Wat Tyler' he would have doubled his money, but I honestly don't think he cared. He was pretty triumphant to be out of that chair with £125,000, and he was probably now the richest teaching assistant in Britain.

John Randall

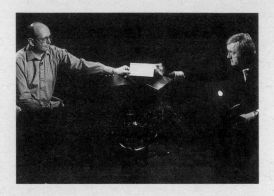

John Randall is a horse-racing statistician from Beckenham in Kent. He compiles a daily list of information about jockeys and horses for the *Racing Post*, but told me he didn't believe in betting himself. He wisely counselled that it was a lot safer to keep your money in your pocket. If he won enough money on the show, he said, he would like to buy three racehorses, which he would call 'Fastest', 'Finger' and 'First'. Not a man to mince his words, John also confided a desire to take Hugh Grant to Antarctica and bury him under the snow. His dear old mum Betty was sitting up in the audience thoroughly enjoying it, although she did admit that she'd seen the show for the first time only a couple of nights before, just to check up on what on earth her son was getting into. She also added that if John did win enough money for a racehorse, or racehorses, he'd have to keep them in his bedroom. The mind boggles. John had one final ambition: to take Betty bungy-jumping. Funny family the Randalls!

With John's attitude to betting and playing it safe, I didn't think he would be staying in the chair any longer than necessary. I expected him to cut and run at the first opportunity.

He looked unsettled by the first five questions, but got to £1000 easily enough and actually managed a smile when this question came up for £2000:

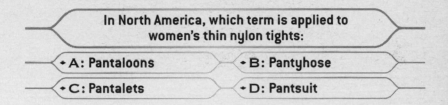

In North America, which term is applied to women's thin nylon tights:

- A: Pantaloons
- B: Pantyhose
- C: Pantalets
- D: Pantsuit

'It's "pantyhose",' said John, with a smirk coming at me from behind his spectacles. 'How do you know?' I asked him. 'I couldn't begin to tell you,' said John. 'But it's definitely "pantyhose".' He was right. He got £2000.

Betty looked down unimpressed from the audience as the £8000 question flashed up:

Which island in the British Isles has a parliament called the Tynwald?

- A: Jersey
- B: Holy Island
- C: St Michael's Mount
- D: Isle of Man

'I know this,' said John. 'It's "the Isle of Man". I've never been there, but I've read about it. Final answer – "Isle of Man".' He was right. Betty remained unmoved in the audience.

Up came John's first five-figure question:

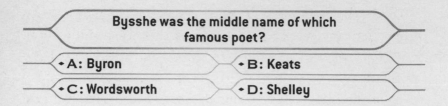

Bysshe was the middle name of which famous poet?

A: Byron

B: Keats

C: Wordsworth

D: Shelley

'It's "Shelley,"' he said. 'Final answer.' Again, he was spot on. He still hadn't used a Lifeline and he was on £16,000. John had been very nervous from the moment he sat down, hardly looking up at me at all; staring at the screen as if it was some kind of monster. And yet he was quietly doing rather well. Betty still sat silently in the audience. It was going to take a lot more money yet to impress Mum.

For £32,000, John got this:

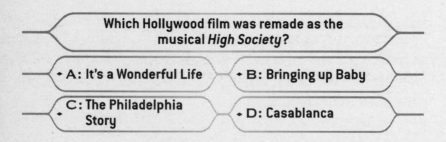

Which Hollywood film was remade as the musical _High Society_?

A: It's a Wonderful Life

B: Bringing up Baby

C: The Philadelphia Story

D: Casablanca

It's "The Philadelphia Story",' he said straight away. He'd had a fairly hard set of questions and he'd said himself from watching other people lose lots of money betting he wasn't going to take any risks, but he'd managed to race to £32,000 while preserving all three of his Lifelines. He was just five away from the magic million.

At this point, sickeningly, the klaxon went for the end of our half hour. But this gave John the chance for a breather, and he went home to Kent with Betty, who commented

that *Millionaire* was all right but she'd have much pre-
ferred a 'good historical show'.

When they returned the next evening, Betty got herself
comfy again in the audience and John climbed in the chair,
admitting to feeling queasy. He said he wanted to get the
whole thing over and done with. Now that he was guaranteed
to go home with at least £32,000, Betty had put in a request
for a brand-new chairlift. She still wasn't very keen on the
show, she told me quite openly, but she'd enjoyed coming
back because she rather liked the food in the Elstree canteen.

For £64,000, we continued:

> **Who was British Prime Minister at the end of World War I?**
>
> • A: Herbert Asquith   • B: David Lloyd George
> • C: Andrew Bonar Law   • D: Stanley Baldwin

'I know this one,' said John. 'I'm 100 per cent confident
it's "David Lloyd George".' It was the right answer. This
was getting serious. He was on £64,000, his Lifelines still
there for the taking.

On question number twelve, for £125,000, John said,
'This is the one I've been dreading!' I was intrigued, but he
didn't volunteer an explanation, so I got the question up as
soon as possible:

> **The wine tokay originated in which country?**
>
> • A: Germany   • B: Hungary
> • C: Japan   • D: Bulgaria

John looked perplexed. He decided to use his first Lifeline and asked the audience. The audience, as is so often the case at this level, were worse than useless. Five per cent said 'Germany', but 34 per cent said 'Hungary', 32 per cent 'Japan' and 29 per cent 'Bulgaria'.

Not at all what John needed with this amount of money involved, I thought. However, he saw it differently. He said, 'I was thinking "Hungary" in the first place, but in any case' – and this is a horse-racing statistician talking – 'the upside is £61,000, the downside is £32,000. So to a racing man you're virtually getting odds of two to one, for an even-money chance, which is fairly good odds.' Puzzled? Don't worry – so was I. And, looking around me, so it seemed, was the audience.

John continued, 'On the strength of my own gut feeling and the slightly larger percentage of this audience, I'm gonna play "Hungary". Final answer.'

It was the right answer! Even Betty was impressed. Her son had just won £125,000.

If anything, John was now calmer than when he'd sat down in the chair at the very top of the show the night before. Win or lose, he was starting to thoroughly enjoy the contest. So was Betty. She suddenly announced to the camera that it was now her favourite TV show in the world, even though she'd only seen it twice.

For a quarter of a million, John got this question:

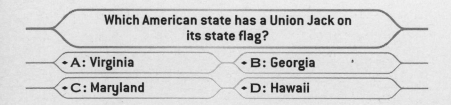

Which American state has a Union Jack on its state flag?

- A: Virginia
- B: Georgia
- C: Maryland
- D: Hawaii

John looked up at me slowly. He had a manic glint in his eye, and said, 'I've seen this – it's something to do with Captain Cook when he discovered Hawaii in the eighteenth century. I know I wasn't going to take any risk, but I'm sure it's something to do with him.' He looked tense as he very deliberately told me, '"Hawaii" is my final answer.' John knew his stuff, and for doing so, he was now £250,000 better off and two right answers away from £1,000,000, with his Phone-A-Friend and 50:50 still available to him.

Bear in mind that this was only seven days after Judith Keppel had won our first-ever £1,000,000. John had been so unflappable throughout, and had demonstrated such a wide range of general knowledge, that it looked odds on that he could be our second millionaire in a week, and the first man to win this vast sum. The hairs on the back of my neck were starting to stand out and my mouth was getting very dry. The producer afterwards told me that he had the same sort of feeling, as did most of the crew and the audience.

At such moments, as host of *Who Wants To Be A Millionaire?*, I give myself a mental talking to, reminding myself to keep my diction precise and clearly worded so that there can be absolutely no misunderstanding of the question. There are also certain camera moves that we rehearse for the moment when somebody wins £1,000,000: special effects with glitter coming down from the ceiling and a crescendo of dramatic music. So all this flashes through my mind, the director's and the whole crew's as we get ready for a potential £1,000,000 winner.

Fears of a mispronunciation aren't helped when you get a question like this for £500,000:

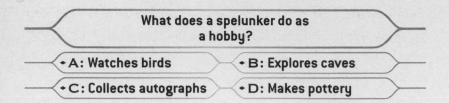

What does a spelunker do as a hobby?

A: Watches birds

B: Explores caves

C: Collects autographs

D: Makes pottery

I read the question very carefully to John. He stared at it for what seemed an age before admitting, 'I have heard of this. I do have some idea of what I think is the right answer. I've got a gut feeling but I don't want to tell you what it is yet. I want to go 50:50.' Two wrong answers were removed, leaving 'explores caves' or 'makes pottery'. 'The one I thought it was is still there,' said John. The audience were absolutely silent. You could have heard a pin drop. 'I think it's "explores caves".' 'It's your call,' I said to John. 'You lose £218,000 if you're wrong. You still have a Phone-A-Friend.' 'I'm sure it's right,' said John blankly. 'It's my final answer.'

He had won £500,000! The crowd cheered and cheered, John looked thrilled, even Betty looked excited. If John gave me the right answer to the next question, he would become the second person in the UK ever to win £1,000,000 on a game show. If he gave me the wrong answer he would lose £468,000, a prospect to restrain even the most confident contestant.

This was the £1,000,000 question:

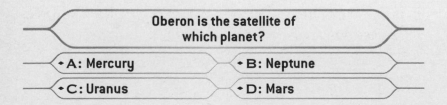

Oberon is the satellite of which planet?

A: Mercury

B: Neptune

C: Uranus

D: Mars

'I'm going to Phone-A-Friend,' said John immediately. 'I want to phone Richard. 'Do you want me to tell him how much money is involved?' I asked him, intrigued to know how he would play such a vital call. John smiled, 'I think not! Don't you?'

'OK,' I said, 'it's entirely your choice.' Richard answered the phone and I explained to him that John was on the show, he was doing 'quite well' – what an understatement that was! – and John, surprisingly calmly, read him the question and its four possible answers.

'It's not "Mercury" or "Mars",' said Richard, 'but I'm just not sure which of the other two it is. I'm really not sure. Sorry, mate.' 'OK,' said John. He looked long and hard at the screen one more time and said, 'I'm really not sure either. I really don't know. I'm going to take the half a million.'

The audience all let out a disappointed 'Aaahhh!', and I had to gently but firmly tell them all off. 'For God's sake, you lot, what do you mean "Aaahhh!" – if he's wrong he loses £468,000. Are you all mad?' They laughed, suitably chastised.

So John Randall left us with a cheque for £500,000. His mate Richard was absolutely right – Oberon isn't a satellite of Mercury or Mars (neither planet has any satellites, in fact). The right answer is 'Uranus'. I wonder how he would have reacted if we'd told Richard just how much money the question was worth. When people volunteer to be a Phone-A-Friend on the show, just for a laugh, I doubt if they imagine that one day they might be asked to answer the question worth £1,000,000.

Looking back, John says the pressure of being on the show blotted everything else out of his mind. All the money has been invested — he hasn't spent a penny of it. He lives in the house in which he's lived for forty years and has the same job he's had for sixteen years. He says he was already very happy with his life and didn't want anything about it to change.

Betty has been won over by the show and hasn't missed a single episode since.

Laraine and Russell Thomas

Our couples shows have been a mixed success. In theory they seem like a good idea and, with double the general knowledge, a couple playing *Who Wants To Be A Millionaire?* should do extremely well. But, unfortunately, in the main, the pairs tend to work against each other: where one wants to play on and go for the big sums, the other frequently becomes extra cautious and wants to take the money and run. It's happened time and time again. Also, couples who are loving and affectionate at £100 become fighting, spitting cats and dogs at £1000.

The compatibility or otherwise of the couples can be very entertaining. For starters, I frequently find myself sitting in front of two people thinking, what on earth are you doing with him? Or, why has a bloke like you married a woman like that? I don't ask them this out loud – that would be rather rude. But it's sometimes hard not to, as I sit there trying to maintain the usual inscrutable mask on my face. And I'm sure that people watching at home are thinking exactly the same.

But we have had some very nice couples on the show. Laraine and Russell Thomas from Sutton Coldfield, in the West Midlands, were great fun. They'd lived together for thirty years and now they also worked together. Their sons Nicholas and Christopher were watching at home, and their advice to Mum was to keep cool – apparently she had a tendency to get carried away.

Laraine, by her own admission, was very hyper. In fact she was potty! Russell had that glazed look men get when they've lived for a long time with an excitable woman. I have the same look myself, after years of living with the completely big Ingrid from the fiords!

Theirs was quite a love story. They'd met when Laraine was thirteen and a half and Russell was sixteen – he'd helped her with her homework. He said that his wife lived life to the full, and she said that her husband kept her on an even keel as best he could. And that's exactly how they worked together on the show.

Laraine said when she first met Russell he was an Adonis. Russell was certainly a very nice guy, very calm, gently amused by his wife, and the more steady of the two. But, I'm not sure I'd have rated him as an Adonis. Then again, in fairness, that *was* thirty years ago.

The Thomases got to £1000 easily enough, and now they began to relax and enjoy themselves. I asked them how the money was going to be handled when they got home and Laraine said, 'I'll bank it . . . and spend it!' Russell nodded amiably. It seemed that his main purpose was to enable her to do that by providing lots of right answers.

The questions were fairly straightforward until they got to £4000:

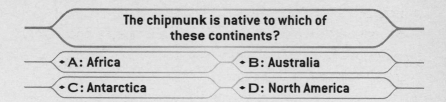

The chipmunk is native to which of these continents?

A: Africa

B: Australia

C: Antarctica

D: North America

Russell looked puzzled. Laraine looked aghast. 'I think it's "North America",' said Russell. 'I don't,' said Laraine. 'I think it's "Australia".' But, of course, couples have to agree on their final answer. 'You'll have to convince me,' said Laraine. 'Well, I've seen quite a few programmes about chipmunks,' Russell told her, 'nature programmes, and I'm sure they're all set in the USA.' 'All right then,' said Laraine, 'I'll go with "North America".' 'Well, we don't have to hurry this,' said Russell, very calmly. 'We can use one of our Lifelines.' 'No, no,' said Laraine, 'let's go for it.'

'He's very good at tactics,' I said to Laraine. 'Yes, he is,' she said to me openly, 'but he's getting on my nerves now.' Russell just carried on smiling patiently. 'Come on!' Laraine said to him. 'Be forceful.' 'OK,' he said, 'Let's play. "North America".' Mercifully, it was the right answer. They'd reached £4000.

The next question appeared:

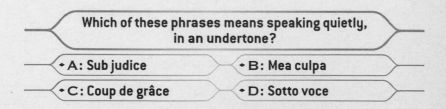

Which of these phrases means speaking quietly, in an undertone?

A: Sub judice

B: Mea culpa

C: Coup de grâce

D: Sotto voce

'This isn't one of my strong points,' giggled Laraine, and Russell nodded emphatically. 'No, I don't suppose you've ever done this in your life,' I said to her. 'No,' she agreed. 'I don't really do speaking quietly!' Luckily for her, Russell knew it was 'sotto voce', and they won £8000.

For £16,000, I asked them:

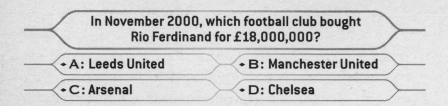

In November 2000, which football club bought Rio Ferdinand for £18,000,000?

A: Leeds United   B: Manchester United

C: Arsenal   D: Chelsea

'I haven't got a clue,' said Laraine. 'Are you a football fan?' I asked Russell. 'Well, I *am*,' he said, 'although you can't really be a football fan and support Birmingham City!'

Laraine turned to him. 'Will you get on with it?' she demanded. 'Give us the answer. Stop faffing around!' So Russell quietly told us the answer was "Leeds United". It was correct – Rio had gone there for a record transfer fee. The Thomases were on £16,000. Laraine gave her husband a hug and a great soppy kiss on the top of his head. Thirty years on, he was still clearly her Adonis.

They had to get one more question right to be guaranteed £32,000:

What would you be ordering if you asked for poussin in a restaurant?

A: Lobster   B: Chicken

C: Mussels   D: Quail

Russell and Laraine both looked fairly alarmed. 'Well, it's not "lobster",' said Laraine, 'and it's not "mussels". So it'll be one of the other ones.' 'My guess is "chicken",' said Russell. 'But a quail's like a chicken, isn't it? A sort of bird,' he added. 'He doesn't do a lot of cooking,' explained Laraine patiently. 'Come on then,' said Russell. 'This is your department, food.' 'I think we'll Ask the Audience,' said Laraine. 'Are you sure?' asked Russell. 'Yes, come on. I'm in charge,' his wife replied positively. 'Let's Ask the Audience.'

Seventy-four per cent of the audience said "chicken", 19 per cent "quail". 'There you are,' said Laraine. 'That proves it. I'm right.' 'Not necessarily,' I pointed out. 'If they're wrong and you go with them you've lost £15,000.' 'We'll play. "Chicken",' said Russell patiently. 'Final answer.' Laraine put both hands over her ears and closed her eyes, so it seemed a good idea for me to go to the break. That wasn't too popular with Laraine, as you can imagine.

When we came back from the ads Laraine and Russell had lost all confidence in 'chicken' and were absolutely convinced that the audience had messed up and that the right answer was 'quail'. Laraine was unusually quiet and subdued, her eyes still shut. When I told them 'chicken' had won them £32,000, she went berserk, grabbed Russell in another huge bear hug and slobbered all over his head like a demented St Bernard. 'Russell, you're still an Adonis,' I reminded him. 'Apparently,' he agreed, looking thoroughly battered. 'It's so different when you're here,' said Laraine, echoing the words of hundreds of contestants since September 1998. 'At home we're always shouting, "Go on, go for it! Go for it! It's 'B'!" But,' she added, 'a huge amount of doubt creeps in when you're sat here. It's like a different planet to watching it at home.'

With £32,000 guaranteed and two Lifelines left, they got this question for £64,000:

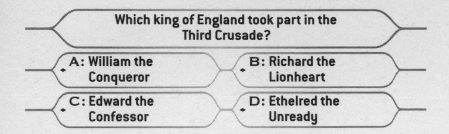

Which king of England took part in the Third Crusade?

A: William the Conqueror

B: Richard the Lionheart

C: Edward the Confessor

D: Ethelred the Unready

Laraine started to recite something under her breath. Russell looked puzzled by his wife, not for the first time that evening. 'What are you doing?' I asked her. 'I'm reciting the kings of England,' she said. '"Willy, Willy, Harry, Steve, Harry, Dick and John".' 'So where on earth does that lead us?' I asked her. 'To Dick,' she informed me. 'It's "Richard".' 'How does that make it the Third Crusade?' asked Russell patiently. 'Who were the first two?' 'Willy, Willy,' said Laraine, in a matter-of-fact way. 'I'm sure it's "Richard",' she told Russell. 'Just a minute,' he said. 'Let's think it through. I think it might be "Edward the Confessor".' 'No, no,' Laraine repeated. 'This is the rhyme – "Willy, Willy, Harry, Steve, Harry, Dick and John." They were the ones who went on the Crusades. It's "Richard the Lionheart".'

Russell didn't seem overly convinced, but he went with her anyway. Somehow Laraine's 'Willy, Willy' poem had got them to £64,000. Now it was Russell's turn to give Laraine a great big kiss – we were climbing to the giddy heights of serious money. 'This will make a huge difference,' said Russell. 'The last five years really have been tough with the business. We've had a lot of problems. This is fantastic.'

Up came the £125,000 question, and they still had two Lifelines left – 50:50 and Phone-A-Friend.

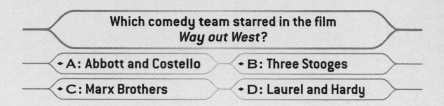

Which comedy team starred in the film
Way out West?

◆ A: Abbott and Costello	◆ B: Three Stooges
◆ C: Marx Brothers	◆ D: Laurel and Hardy

'I've got absolutely no idea,' said Russell. 'Nor have I,' said Laraine. 'We have to Phone-A-Friend.' 'Should we use 50:50,' wondered Russell, 'and make it easier for them? Then again, do we want to waste both Lifelines?' 'We'll go 50:50 — let's get rid of two of them,' Laraine decided for both of them, as she had done for most of the night.

'Abbott and Costello' and 'Laurel and Hardy' were left. 'I think it's going to be "Abbott and Costello",' said Laraine. 'Yes, but remember that song,' Russell reminded her – "The blue, blue mountains of something-or-other." I'll bet you that song comes from that Laurel and Hardy film. I bet that's the answer. God, I don't want to lose this money.'

'OK, we'll phone Ian,' said Laraine. When Laraine asked their friend Ian from Stafford the question he calmly informed them, 'It's "Laurel and Hardy".' 'How sure are you?' asked Laraine, with real agony in her voice. 'A hundred per cent,' said Ian. Laraine gasped. 'Thank you, Ian. Thank you!' 'He's my best friend now,' said Russell. It was the right answer and, thanks to Ian, Russell and Laraine, now screaming like lunatics, were £125,000 better off.

The next question was an absolute killer:

Which American First Lady wrote the book
It Takes the Village?

◆ A: Rosalyn Carter	◆ B: Nancy Reagan
◆ C: Barbara Bush	◆ D: Hillary Clinton

'I haven't got a clue,' said Russell. 'Nor have I,' said Laraine. 'But for some reason I think it's "Hillary Clinton". Go on, let's play!' 'Don't be mad!' said Russell. 'We've got no Lifelines, you really haven't the foggiest idea why you think it's "Hillary Clinton". We're out of here!' 'You've got no sense of adventure,' said Laraine. 'Not with this amount of money at stake!' replied Russell. 'We're off, back up the M1.' There was no way he was going to be persuaded, so in the end even Laraine admitted defeat and they quit while they were ahead. I wrote them a cheque for £125,000, and off they went, with the applause of the audience ringing in their ears.

However, I had to tell them before they climbed down from their hotseats, that if Laraine had persuaded her Adonis to go along with 'Hillary Clinton', their cheque would have been worth £250,000. Ouch!

Life After *Who Wants To Be A Millionaire?*

Laraine and Russell say they are both still constantly recognised and Laraine is often asked to speak at functions about her experience on the show. They have invested some of the money and spent the rest – they gave some to Ian for being such a good Phone-A-Friend.

Laraine's abiding memory of the show is how cross she was with Russell when they came off the set. She says that she has put a picture of Hillary Clinton in the toilet, to annoy him whenever he goes in there. Apparently, a week after the show was aired, football manager Ron Atkinson came up to her in a club and told her that if he'd been in her shoes, he would have killed Russell for not letting her go with her instincts.

John and Karen Hannaford

J ohn and Karen Hannaford, from Cornwall, were not, by
their own admission, the most romantic of couples. They
couldn't even remember where, when or how they'd first
met. They just seemed to have ended up getting married.
John was a policeman, Karen a psychology student. They
had two kids, Tony and Ryan, watching at home. John
described Karen as 'extremely loud when she gets excited
and nervous' and they said the secret of their marriage was
that she does her own thing and John does what he's told.

Karen told us that when they watched the show at home,
John tended to know more answers than her but every
once in a while she had 'inklings'. 'It's weird,' she added.
'Sometimes there's no rhyme or reason to them at all, but
my inklings do tend to be correct!' John looked worried.
Understandably. It would be very difficult to just go along
with an inkling, with the amounts of money that are
frequently involved on this show.

Anyway, they made a confident, amicable start and got to £1000 easily enough with this question:

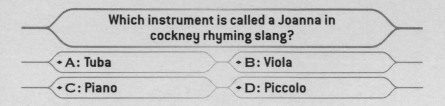

Which instrument is called a Joanna in cockney rhyming slang?

◆ A: Tuba   ◆ B: Viola

◆ C: Piano   ◆ D: Piccolo

The right answer, they said in unison, is 'piano', and they had £1000 guaranteed. The first Lifeline they needed was on £16,000:

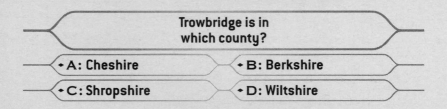

Trowbridge is in which county?

◆ A: Cheshire   ◆ B: Berkshire

◆ C: Shropshire   ◆ D: Wiltshire

'We could Phone-A-Friend,' suggested John hesitantly. 'No, let's Ask the Audience,' said Karen confidently. Fifty-two per cent of the audience said "Wiltshire". Bewilderingly, a high 34 per cent thought "Shropshire"; 3 per cent even thought Trowbridge was right up in Cheshire. 'I didn't think it was in Wiltshire,' said John. 'Nor did I,' said Karen. 'I don't really know where it is.' 'I thought it was in Cheshire or Shropshire,' said John. 'I'm fairly sure it's not in Berkshire.' 'We'll go with the audience,' said Karen. 'Come on, final answer.' The audience were right, or at least 52 per cent of them were, and they'd got to £16,000.

We were still waiting for one of Karen's inklings. The next question was for £32,000. Question number ten was this:

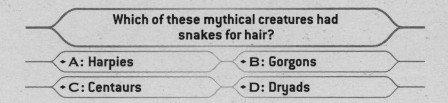

Which of these mythical creatures had snakes for hair?

◆ A: Harpies ◆ B: Gorgons

◆ C: Centaurs ◆ D: Dryads

'I thought I knew the answer to this,' said Karen, 'but the one I thought it was isn't there!' 'I was thinking of Medusas,' said John, 'but they haven't come up.' 'We could really do with one of my inklings here,' said Karen. 'We certainly could,' said John. But no inkling came and they decided to Phone-A-Friend called Frazer. 'I think it's "Gorgons",' said Frazer. 'I'm about 90 per cent sure.' 'That sounds like good odds,' said John. 'Yep, we'll go with Frazer,' said Karen. 'Gorgons' was the right answer and they were on £32,000.

The next question was for £64,000:

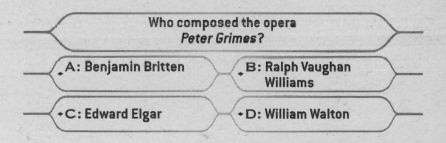

Who composed the opera *Peter Grimes*?

◆ A: Benjamin Britten ◆ B: Ralph Vaughan Williams

◆ C: Edward Elgar ◆ D: William Walton

'I've got an inkling!' said Karen. At last, one of her inklings. 'I think it's "Edward Elgar".' 'Why do you think it's him?' asked John, looking concerned. 'I don't know,' said Karen. 'I've just got an inkling. I think it's "Edward Elgar".'

'I've never heard of William Walton,' said John, 'so it's probably him.' It was a strange kind of logic. 'Let's go

50:50,' they agreed. "William Walton" disappeared, along with "Edward Elgar". So much for Karen's inklings, the first one she had turned out to be a dud. 'We've got nothing to lose,' said John. 'Let's go for "Benjamin Britten".' I don't know how they got to that conclusion, nor did they seem to, but it won them £64,000. Luckily, they'd chosen to ignore Karen's inkling, otherwise they'd already be on the bus back home.

Karen and John now looked really tense. Question number twelve was for £125,000:

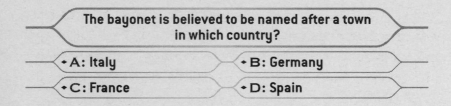

The bayonet is believed to be named after a town in which country?

A: Italy   B: Germany
C: France   D: Spain

Initially I thought it was "France",' said John, 'but now I'm not so sure.' 'I thought that as well,' said Karen. 'Who's the gambler of the two of you?' I asked them. 'Absolutely, definitely Karen,' said John. 'If you gamble and get it wrong, you'll be kicking yourself for ever.' 'But you'll be kicking yourself if "France" is the right answer and we don't get to £125,000,' said Karen. 'But you could be kicking yourself with £64,000 in your pocket,' said John. 'We'll go "France",' said Karen, with a mad glint in her eye. 'Final answer. Come on, let's do it. We're only here once!' 'All right,' said John. 'If somebody had said to us we could leave here tonight with £32,000 we'd be very happy, so come on – final answer.'

I very slowly took the cheque out of John's pocket and tore it in half. They had just won £125,000.

The next question provoked a few moments I shall

never forget. Karen was looking absolutely distraught. This was the question for £250,000:

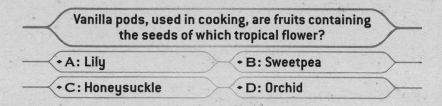

Vanilla pods, used in cooking, are fruits containing the seeds of which tropical flower?

A: Lily

B: Sweetpea

C: Honeysuckle

D: Orchid

'I haven't a clue,' said John. 'It's "orchid",' stated Karen. 'I was hoping you were going to say, "I don't know,"' said John. 'How do you know? What on earth makes you think it's "orchid"?' he asked, clearly in agony. 'It's an inkling!' said Karen. 'But it's more than an inkling. I'm sure it's "orchid".' John was looking understandably terrified. 'I'd be quite happy to take the money,' he said, 'even if I get kicked all the way home! Your last inkling, "Edward Elgar", was completely wrong.' 'I'd beat myself up all the way home,' said Karen. 'I'd be thinking, why the hell did I let him persuade me not to go for it. I'm sure it's "orchid".'

'We've got £125,000,' said John. 'Why on earth would we risk this amount of money on your whim that it might be "orchid"? Whose idea was it to bring couples on?' he asked. 'This is impossible.' 'If I was playing on my own,' argued Karen, 'I would go "orchid".' 'If I was playing on my own,' John retorted, 'I would take the money. No question – £125,000 is far more than we ever thought we'd get.' 'I still think it's "orchid",' said Karen.

'I still think we should take the money,' said John.

This was now a serious impasse and they were all but having a row on the set. 'All right then,' said Karen finally, 'let's take the money. Go on. Take the money. Take the money.' 'Oh God, I'm in trouble now,' John realised. 'I can't win on this.' 'Go on, take the money,' said Karen, 'if that's what *you* want to do.' 'You can clout me afterwards,' said John. 'I *will*,' said Karen. 'We're going to take the money,' John announced. Karen begrudgingly agreed. 'Final answer,' she said, looking distinctly unhappy for someone £125,000 better off.

I was then able to reveal that "orchid" was the right answer. If looks could have killed, John would have been dead on the spot.

I would have loved to have been a fly on the wall in their dressing room.

Life After *Who Wants To Be A Millionaire?*

John's lasting memory of the show is the look that Karen gave him when they found out her answer to the final question was correct. He says she has still not forgiven him for not going for it. He had to compensate his wife with the Audi A6 that she always wanted. They have also bought a house in Florida and Karen is setting up her own travel agency.

Steve Devlin

Steve Devlin came from a fairly hard part of Belfast. He had brought along his Northern Irish mate Big Joe to lend him support. In fact Joe was there for rather more than support – he was needed to stop Steve literally doing a runner!

Steve had been selected to appear on the show about eighteen months earlier. He had arrived at the studios in the morning, and was greeted by the production girls, who look after the contestants throughout the day. But, during the course of that day, he began to slowly lose his bottle. He became more and more nervous, saying to the team, 'I can't go ahead with this,' until, unbeknown to any of us, he snuck out of the dressing room, paid for his own taxi back to Heathrow and got the first flight back to Belfast.

We have two standby contestants ready for each show, so this was a lucky day for one of them. Before we'd even started recording that night, Steve Devlin was back in

Belfast, in the pub, trying to explain to his mates quite what had brought on such a panic attack and feeling remorseful and absolutely devastated at what he'd done. In his own words, 'I reacted out of blind terror. It just wasn't an environment that I could feel at ease in. Nobody could have been kinder to me at the studio, but I had a total panic attack. Once it sunk in, I couldn't believe what I'd done and I spent the next eighteen months on the phone desperately trying to get on a second time.'

So, when Steve climbed into the chair that night, it was as if he had finally laid low all the demons of the last couple of years. Playing *Millionaire* was no longer about the money for him. He just had to prove to himself that he could conquer his own nerves. It was an amazing story of courage and perseverance and I was delighted when he won Fastest Finger First.

Everybody on the team was rooting for Steve: we never let him out of our sight for a second and Joe was on constant watch. Big Joe was large, but Steve wasn't exactly tiny himself. He was a broad man with a strong Northern Irish accent. I suspected life for him had been tough. He was currently unemployed, although he did say rather colourfully that most of his recent work had been down the Belfast sewers, working 'mainly with a shovel'.

It left nothing to the imagination.

It could not have been the most rewarding or remunerative way of earning a living, even when he could get work. Steve is quite shy and modest for a big man and his accent takes a bit of getting used to, so I think we all thought if he got a couple of thousand pounds that would be a great night's work for him. Which was true. But as it turned out, Mr Devlin did rather better than anybody expected, including himself.

Assuming Steve had not travelled much, his knowledge, even at an early stage, was quite wide. He answered questions on Ruby Wax, Soho, fabric and cider to reach £500, and this was for £1000:

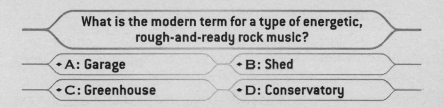

What is the modern term for a type of energetic, rough-and-ready rock music?

A: Garage

B: Shed

C: Greenhouse

D: Conservatory

I suspect a lot of people of his generation would have had absolutely no idea. But Steve said, straight away 'It's garage music, Chris.' He was now sure of a hero's welcome in Belfast. He looked delighted and Joe clapped wildly. Steve had conquered his nerves and he was guaranteed to go home with at least £1000. I asked him, as I often do, 'When you're playing this at home, obviously it's very different, but how do you normally get on?' And Steve said to me, in all seriousness, 'Well, not always, but I frequently get up to at least a quarter of a million.' The audience gasped and, inwardly, so did I. Steve was turning out to be a complex and fascinating character. He also drank more water than any contestant we've ever had on the show. After just four questions he'd already gulped down his entire glass and I had to top him up with mine.

For £2000, he got this question, which would have stumped a lot of people:

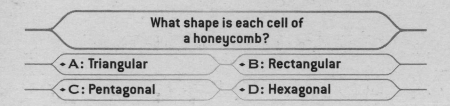

What shape is each cell of a honeycomb?

A: Triangular
B: Rectangular
C: Pentagonal
D: Hexagonal

Steve had no problem at all. '"Hexagonal",' he said straight away, and it was the right answer. Suddenly the idea of him getting to a quarter of a million didn't sound the pipe dream it had just a few minutes ago.

The first time Steve needed a Lifeline was for £8000:

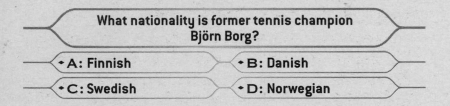

What nationality is former tennis champion Björn Borg?

A: Finnish
B: Danish
C: Swedish
D: Norwegian

Steve wasn't sure and opted to Ask the Audience. It seemed a surprising question for someone as bright as he was to get stuck on, but 'they're only easy if you know the answer'. The audience had no problem with it. Ninety per cent went for 'Swedish' and Steve trusted them, getting himself up to £8000.

The smile on Joe's face in the audience was getting wider and wider. It was turning into a great night. Steve carried on drinking water at a rate of knots, but he did admit that he was starting to feel really good, that the apprehension was far worse than the reality of the show, and he now realised, 'It could really change a person's life.' It was about to change Steve's, because he hadn't quite finished yet.

For £32,000 he got this question:

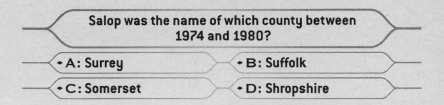

Salop was the name of which county between 1974 and 1980?

◆ A: Surrey   ◆ B: Suffolk

◆ C: Somerset   ◆ D: Shropshire

He looked puzzled, thought for a while, and then said, 'I think Surrey has always been called Surrey. The same with Suffolk and the same with Somerset. So I think it must be "Shropshire".' For an unemployed sewage worker this really was a tough decision. If he was wrong he would lose £15,000, which would probably be a lot more than a year's wage packet, not that he was even working at the moment. 'I'm going to play,' he said. 'I'm sure it must be "Shropshire".' It was the right answer. We were all absolutely thrilled for him. At that moment every pub in Northern Ireland must have erupted. Steve was guaranteed to come home with £32,000.

But we didn't want to give him thirty-two grand. He still had two Lifelines and this came up for £64,000:

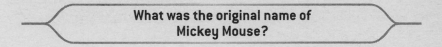

What was the original name of Mickey Mouse?

As soon as it came up, Steve started nodding. I said to him, 'You know this, don't you? What do you think it is?' 'It's "Mortimer", Chris,' he replied. We had a look.

◆ A: Marlon   ◆ B: Marvin

◆ C: Mortimer   ◆ D: Montague

Steve grinned happily. '"Mortimer" — final answer.'

He'd just won £64,000. Our unemployed sewage labourer, who worked 'mainly with the shovel', was now four questions away from a million, with two Lifelines left.

This came up for £125,000:

> **What is the substance that causes the irritation of a sting by a nettle or an ant?**
>
> • A: Formic acid   • B: Oxalic acid
>
> • C: Ascorbic acid   • D: Folic acid

Steve looked at it very hard and said to me very slowly and deliberately, 'It's "formic acid", Chris.' The audience gasped. It was his final answer. It was the right answer.

For the big man from Belfast, who'd been too nervous to even come into the studio eighteen months ago, this was an amazing turnaround. Everybody suddenly realised that Steve Devlin might just become our first unemployed millionaire. You could have heard a pin drop.

Steve got this for £250,000, and he still had two Lifelines left:

> **Which Charles Dickens novel features the sisters Charity and Mercy Pecksniff?**
>
> • A: Bleak House   • B: Martin Chuzzlewit
>
> • C: David Copperfield   • D: Hard Times

Steve looked at it hard. So did I. I read Dickens at university as part of my English degree and I still have trouble remembering which character is in which of his books. They all sound horribly similar, and no doubt this

210

was going through Steve's head, only it was rather more of a dilemma for him, with £250,000 at stake.

'I'll Phone-A-Friend,' he announced after a bit of thinking. 'I'll phone Jim.' 'Do you want me to tell Jim the amount of money involved?' I asked. Steve thought about it for a couple of seconds and then said, 'Yes' with a mischievous grin. The idea of his mate back home getting a call worth a quarter of a million greatly amused him. Jim would no doubt be surprised and pleased to hear that Steve had managed to get into the studio without doing a runner, let alone be told that he was this close to winning a million quid.

When I told Jim that Steve was in the chair and doing 'rather well', he said, 'I'm pleased to hear that.' When I said, 'In fact he's doing very well, he's on a quarter of a million,' Jim said, 'My God!' with a mixture of amazement and terror in his voice. This was a huge responsibility for any Phone-A-Friend.

Steve read out the question and its four possible answers but, sadly, Jim didn't manage to give him any sort of answer in the thirty seconds, even though he read it twice. 'I might as well use my 50:50,' Steve decided. It left him 'Martin Chuzzlewit' or 'David Copperfield'. One was worth a quarter of a million. One would cost him £93,000.

Joe, up in the audience, looked grey as a ghost. He kept shuffling and looking down at his feet really hard. I'm sure he badly wanted Steve to take £125,000 and get the hell out of that chair. But Steve hadn't finished yet. 'I'll play,' he said, to the amazement of everyone. 'I want to go for "Martin Chuzzlewit".' I asked him why and he said, 'I do have vague memories of reading *David Copperfield* when I was much younger and I don't remember Charity and Mercy Pecksniff in it. Final answer.' I have to say I was fairly sure Steve was right, but I wasn't certain, and I was terrified that he might be about to lose £93,000, so it was a huge relief to see 'right answer' appear on my screen. I grabbed him and hugged him. Joe went berserk and the roof nearly came off the studio. It was a fantastic moment. I asked him how he was feeling and Steve, the master of understatement, said, 'Pretty happy.'

The next question, I told him, was worth £500,000, and he laughed like a maniac. 'Why are you laughing, Steve?' I asked him. 'Because it's just getting silly now,' he said. 'Unless I'm absolutely certain of the next question, there is absolutely no way that I'm going to risk this amount of money. There was a huge cheer and a cry of relief from Joe in the audience, drowning out everybody else. Steve had done what he said he'd done frequently at home and got up to question thirteen – to £250,000. But this was not at home in Belfast – this was real money in the *Millionaire* studio – so Joe and I were terrified in case it slipped away from him.

Unless Steve Devlin now took a ridiculous gamble, his life would never be the same. Thirty-two thousand pounds would have been a great result (well, I'd thought that £1000 would have been a great result at the top of the show) but to have £250,000 in his bank account tomorrow would mean an extraordinary change for the better for the rest of Steve's life. I assumed, and I think Steve assumed, that he would have a quick look at the £500,000 question, say a very happy goodnight and be out of that chair like a scalded bunny, heading straight for the nearest bar, with Joe in hot pursuit.

However, things don't always go according to plan on

Who Wants To Be A Millionaire? This was the question Steve had to answer for £500,000:

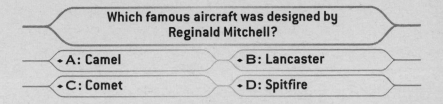

Which famous aircraft was designed by Reginald Mitchell?

A: Camel	B: Lancaster
C: Comet	D: Spitfire

When Steve looked at me with a grin of wonderment on his face, I didn't know whether to laugh or cry. He nodded his head and said 'I know it. It's "D". It's "the Spitfire".' 'If you're wrong, you lose £218,000,' I reminded him nervously. 'That's all I'm going to say to you.' 'I know that, Chris,' he said. 'But I know I'm right. It's "D. Spitfire".'

People in the audience were clutching themselves. Joe was looking petrified – I think he was convinced that Steve had completely lost his marbles. But Steve was adamant. 'I want to play,' he said. 'Mitchell was definitely the Spitfire man. Final answer.'

It was one of the moments I'll remember for the rest of my life. I looked down at my screen and saw that 'Spitfire' was correct. When I told Steve he'd just won half a million you could have heard the roar from Elstree to Belfast. What a result!

Steve was one question away from £1,000,000, but of all the moments for this to happen, the klaxon sounded for the end of the show. Agonisingly, we had run out of time. The whole place was aghast and Steve was going to have to come back the following evening knowing that he would be faced with a question worth £1,000,000.

I don't think Steve or Joe got much sleep that night and

I know that I didn't. It was one of the longest twenty-four hours I can remember. When the two lads returned the next day (with Joe looking far more worried about the situation than Steve) our sewage worker told me, 'I'm not going to guess anything, but if I know the answer I'm gonna go for it.'

Steve Devlin was about to be the fifth person to see a £1,000,000 question since we had broadcast our first show in September 1998. I asked him if he'd known the answers to any of the other £1,000,000 questions. He looked at me and said, 'I don't think I did. If I'm truthful, no.' This was actually quite surprising because his general knowledge was extraordinarily wide. We were all twitching to get on with it.

Steve had no Lifelines left and tonight would only answer one question. This was it, for £1,000,000:

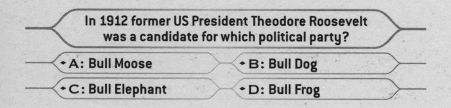

In 1912 former US President Theodore Roosevelt was a candidate for which political party?

A: Bull Moose **B: Bull Dog**
C: Bull Elephant **D: Bull Frog**

Steve looked at it long and hard. The tension in the studio was almost unbearable and then, in his very slow, deliberate way, he said 'I think I know this.' There was a gasp from within the studio. 'If you're wrong you lose £468,000,' I told him. 'But it's worth a million.' 'The more I look the more sure I am,' said Steve. 'I think it's "Bull Moose".' Up in the audience, Joe had his eyes completely closed. I think he was praying! Inwardly, so was I. Steve kept looking hard at the question. He was drinking huge gulps of water. At one point he even drank my glass by mistake.

'The more I look the more certain I am,' Steve repeated. 'I'll play,' he said. '"Bull Moose".' 'Is that your final answer?' I said. 'You can walk away with £500,000 right now if you want to.' The first seeds of doubt began to creep into Steve's mind. 'It's a huge amount of money,' he said. 'Thirty-two thousand pounds is obviously very nice, but I could do so much with half a million. I think I'm going to change my mind and take the money, even though I'm pretty sure it's "Bull Moose".' 'It's up to you,' I said. 'I can't influence your judgement at this point.' 'No,' he said. 'It's just too much money. I'm going to take the £500,000.' There was a huge cheer of relief from the whole audience, with nobody cheering louder than Joe.

Steve Devlin, the guy who'd been too terrified to even set foot in the studio less than two years ago, was going back to Belfast, the hero of all Northern Ireland, with half a million quid.

Incredibly, if Steve had gone for 'Bull Moose', in that instant he would have become a millionaire. And I'm absolutely convinced that if the klaxon hadn't gone the night before, he would have gone for that fifteenth question.

Steve Devlin is certainly one of my all-time favourite contestants. What an amazing human being.

Michelle Simmons

Michelle Simmons was very bright and bubbly in rehearsal in the afternoon, a lot of fun, and we expected her to do pretty well.

She was working as a hotel administrator in Luton and her husband Andrew was up in the audience. They had no kids but they had two goldfish called Ferrari and Porsche, presumably watching at home from their little bowl. Michelle confided to me that she's not normally very lucky in competitions. She once won a hammock, which was a bit of a shame, as it was a very nice hammock but she had no garden. And perhaps this next event was ominous. 'This morning when we arrived and were shown into our dressing room, I spotted a money spider on the floor by the door,' said Michelle, 'but then Andy trod on it by mistake!'

She confessed, 'I'm not at all confident, but I've had a fun day and if I get even a couple of thousand pounds that'd be great. Apparently I'm related to Turner by the way,' she added, as an aside. 'The painter, that is, not Anthea.'

For £100, this was her starter question:

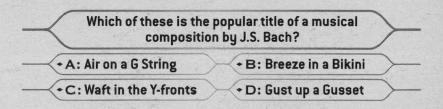

Which of these is the popular title of a musical composition by J.S. Bach?

- A: Air on a G String
- B: Breeze in a Bikini
- C: Waft in the Y-fronts
- D: Gust up a Gusset

It seemed pretty straightforward but, to my horror, Michelle said, 'I'm really sorry, but I've just never, ever heard of it.' I did point out that, bearing in mind we were talking about J.S. Bach, perhaps there were some options that she could eliminate – the great man probably didn't sit down with piano, paper and quill and compose 'Waft in the Y-fronts' for the waiting world.

She got my drift – eventually – and decided that 'Air on a G String' was the most likely answer, and the audience sighed in mild relief.

'They're only easy if you know the answer,' I said. 'Don't panic. You've still got all three Lifelines.' Michelle had no problem deciding that Aer Lingus was the national airline of Ireland for £200, but at £300 she got completely stuck again:

In which city is Everton Football Club based?

- A: Birmingham
- B: Liverpool
- C: Manchester
- D: Newcastle

'Oh God,' she said, 'football is just not my best topic. I'll have to Ask the Audience.' A surprisingly low percentage of 87 per cent could tell her that "Liverpool" was the right answer, and we moved gently on to question number four, for £500:

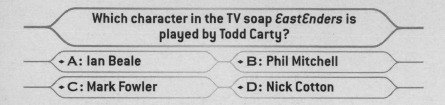

Which character in the TV soap *EastEnders* is played by Todd Carty?

- • A: Ian Beale
- • B: Phil Mitchell
- • C: Mark Fowler
- • D: Nick Cotton

'Oh, this is dreadful,' she said. 'I never, ever watch *EastEnders*. I'll have to use my 50:50.' She was left with 'Ian Beale' or 'Mark Fowler'. 'God,' she said, 'those were the two I was stuck on. I thought it was probably one of them. I really don't want to waste my Phone-A-Friend. I'll play. I'm sure it's "Mark Fowler".' We breathed easy again, as Michelle got to £500.

This was the question to guarantee her £1000:

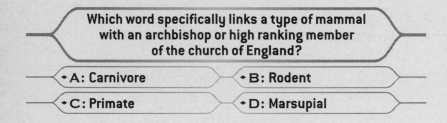

Which word specifically links a type of mammal with an archbishop or high ranking member of the church of England?

- • A: Carnivore
- • B: Rodent
- • C: Primate
- • D: Marsupial

'Oh no,' she said. 'It is so much easier at home. I'm sure the questions aren't so hard when I'm watching there.' 'This sounds difficult,' I said to her, 'but take a good look at the answers. See which you can eliminate.'

'Well, I don't think it's "rodent",' she said, 'and I don't think it's "carnivore".' This is good, I remember thinking, she's getting there. But then, to my horror, and there must have been a sharp intake of breath right across the British Isles, she said, 'And I don't think it's "primate", so it must be "marsupial".'

Up in the audience, Andy buried his head in his hands. Desperate, I reminded Michelle that she still had her Phone-A-Friend. 'No,' she said. 'I'll save that for later.' 'I'll play,' she said. '"Marsupial".' The poor girl didn't realise there now wasn't going to be a later. The look of horror on her husband's face said it all. People were screaming at their television sets all over the UK but for Michelle it was too late – 'D' had gone to orange. The right answer was "primate".

I don't think that his grace the Archbishop of Canterbury would be too pleased to be referred to by his staff as the 'Marsupial of all England', and nor was Michelle too chuffed to be the third contestant to leave *Who Wants To Be A Millionaire?* with nothing.

We coined a new phrase that night. It was what we now call 'a marsupial moment'.

Tony Emans

Tony Emans was a washing-machine repairman from Reading. He ran his own business, but told me openly that on a good week he was lucky if he made £100. He also mentioned quietly that he was going to have to move out of his house in the next few weeks. It was obvious that Tony was having a rough time, and that a few quid would certainly make life a lot more tolerable. His twin sister Maureen was cheering him on in the audience; his twelve-year-old daughter Storm was one of his Phone-A-Friends. Tony said, 'Her specialist subject is S Club 7. Any question about S Club 7 and I'm straight on the phone to her. If I do get a big win tonight,' he added, 'I'll get the *Who Wants To Be A Millionaire?* logo tattooed on my arm. But, to be honest, I just need a good night out to cheer myself up. I don't mind losing. It's only money.'

He raced to £1000 without pausing for breath, and then I asked him a question that brought back memories of a particularly grisly vision beamed on to our screens earlier in the year:

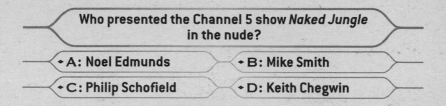

Who presented the Channel 5 show *Naked Jungle* in the nude?

A: Noel Edmunds   B: Mike Smith

C: Philip Schofield   D: Keith Chegwin

They sounded pretty frightening possibilities. 'Keith Chegwin' – 'Mr Button Mushroom' himself – was the right answer. Tony was guaranteed to go home with at least £1000. 'This means a lot to me,' he said, looking very happy.

He took his time answering every question. He was very careful not to jump the gun or misunderstand anything.

At £4000 he had to use his first Lifeline:

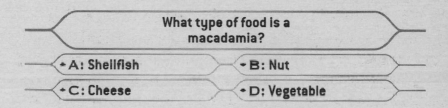

What type of food is a macadamia?

A: Shellfish   B: Nut

C: Cheese   D: Vegetable

Tony didn't think he'd ever eaten a macadamia in his life, whatever it was. He asked the audience. Seventy-six per cent said 'nut', which was, of course, correct.

For £8000 he got this:

In Edward Lear's famous verse, the Jumblies went to sea in which container?

A: Sink   B: Sieve

C: Saucepan   D: Saucer

'It's a sieve,' Tony said straight away. 'I remember learning that poem at school.' He was now on £8000.

Out of interest, I asked him, 'How long is it since you read that poem?' 'At least twenty years,' he said. 'It hasn't crossed my mind since I left school. Isn't that weird?'

For £32,000 he got a question about the single 'Macarena'. By the process of elimination he worked out that the artists who recorded it must have been Los del Rio. 'It's certainly not Rene and Renata,' he said. 'He was that fat geezer and she was the little one.' He was absolutely spot on – he was now on £32,000.

'How do you feel?' I asked Tony. 'Well, it's still only money,' he replied. But his hands were shaking – the sheer amount was starting to get to him. He was now guaranteed £32,000, and he still had two Lifelines to help him.

When the £64,000 question came up on the screen, I thought it would probably stop him dead:

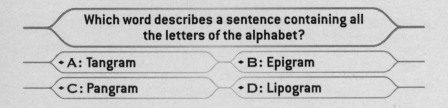

Which word describes a sentence containing all the letters of the alphabet?

- A: Tangram
- B: Epigram
- C: Pangram
- D: Lipogram

But I had underestimated Tony. He said to me without any hesitation, 'It's got to be "pangram" because "pan" means "everything". Final answer – I really think I know this.' He certainly did – and he'd just won £64,000.

For £125,000 I asked Tony this question:

Who was the father of the legendary
King Arthur?

A huge beam spread across his face. 'I'm sure this is "Uther Pendragon",' he said. 'I'm absolutely certain of it.' Up came the options:

- A: Sir Lancelot
- B: Beowulf
- C: Uther Pendragon
- D: Sir Gawain

'I've got to go for it, Chris,' he said, 'I'm absolutely certain that I'm right.' 'Tony,' I replied slowly, 'You've just won £125,000!'

We estimated it would take Tony more than two hundred years of repairing washing machines to earn the money he'd just won in twenty minutes. But there was more to come.

This was the question for £250,000:

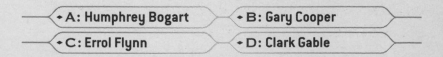

The Misfits, released In 1961, was the last film of
which Hollywood legend?

Tony's face broke into another grin. 'You're doing it again,' I said to him. 'Let's have a look at them first,' he said.

- A: Humphrey Bogart
- B: Gary Cooper
- C: Errol Flynn
- D: Clark Gable

'Has the one you wanted to see appeared on that screen, Tony?' I asked him. 'Yep,' he said, 'it's "Clark Gable".

The Misfits was definitely his last film. It was also Marilyn Monroe's. If I get £250,000 now, that's the house sorted. I'll get the *Millionaire* tattoo done, and I'll go to Sri Lanka to watch England play cricket.'

So I accepted 'Clark Gable' as Tony's final answer. It was 100 per cent the right answer: he was now on a mind-numbing £250,000. Maureen stood up on her seat and started screaming. It was fantastic – Tony Emans, a struggling, self-employed washing-machine repairman, was now just two right answers away from £1,000,000, with two Lifelines intact.

This was the question for £500,000:

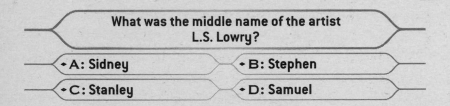

What was the middle name of the artist L.S. Lowry?

• A: Sidney	• B: Stephen
• C: Stanley	• D: Samuel

'I haven't really got a clue about this one,' Tony admitted. 'It could be Stanley, but I'll need to Phone-A-Friend,' he said. 'I'll phone Steve, but please don't tell him what this is worth.'

So I rang Steve, glossed over just how far his friend had got, and put Tony on the line. Steve was very quiet on the other end when the question had been read to him. With the seconds ticking away, he finally said, 'I've got an idea that it might possibly be . . .' but it was too late, the time had run out. The audience groaned, I groaned. Tony looked gutted. 'Come on, Tony,' I said, 'You told me it was only money.' 'Yeah,' he said, 'but this is different. This is serious stuff. I'll use my 50:50.' 'Stephen' and 'Stanley' remained. 'I have to say my instinct is still "Stanley",' Tony said. He went silent, agonising whether to play. 'No,' he finally decided, with a big sigh, 'I'm going to take the money. I'm just not sure enough.' To everybody's great pleasure, and relief, Tony Emans was leaving *Who Wants To Be A Millionaire?* with £250,000.

I was able to tell him on his way out, 'If you had gone for "Stanley" you would've just lost £218,000.' 'Oh my God,' he gasped, looking shocked, 'I was *that* close to going for it.' He walked off the set, clasping his cheque, looking numb. It had been an extraordinary night for Tony — perhaps the best night of his life — and he had earned every single quid.

Life After *Who Wants To Be A Millionaire?*

Tony has since bought the house that he was going to have to leave, and has completely renovated it. He went to Sri Lanka to see the cricket and is going to Australia later this year to watch some more.

Mike Pomfrey

Mike Pomfrey, from Derbyshire, taught bridge for what was clearly a not very handsome living. But he had an interesting claim to fame: he once played against Omar Sharif and actually beat him.

He got in the chair, leaving his daughter Lizzie looking cringingly embarrassed in the audience. She spent the entire show with the pained look on her face that daughters always have when dads are making a spectacle of themselves in public. (Mine have it more or less all of the time.) Apparently, when Mike told Lizzie he was coming on the show, she was horrified because Dad's fashion sense was at least thirty years out of date and she was terrified that he'd wear his horrendous purple suit. From her description, it did sound pretty grisly. But, instead, Mike chose to go for a nice open-neck shirt, sat upright, was very articulate and the only teensey-weensey thing for Lizzie to feel embarrassed about was Minnie the Moose, the large lucky charm that he wore in his top pocket. At one point during the show he even gave Minnie a drink of the water that we normally reserve for the contestants – a complicated business involving pushing Minnie's little head down into the cup and lifting back her fluffy little ears – sorry, antlers.

As you can imagine, it looked all set to become a strange evening. It got stranger when Mike blithely told me that he was planning to ring his ex-wife Georgie as his Phone-A-Friend. Now, each to his own, but I cannot imagine many couples, having emerged from the sadness and bitterness of divorce, prepared to risk asking their ex-partner for help to win a lot of money on a TV game show. But, interestingly, Mike said that not only was Georgie happy with the idea, but he had even tried to get them on the couples show that we had run a few weeks previously.

In fact an ex-couple would not have qualified as a couple, so it was never put to the test. Shame really – it could have been fascinating.

So, instead, Mike was playing on his own – well, apart from his lucky moose. For all the slightly potty air that Mike had about him, he was clearly no mug.

He raced through a fairly hard set of early questions and didn't need a Lifeline until £16,000, when he decided to Ask the Audience:

> **Who is the father of presenter Zoe Ball?**
>
> A: Michael Ball   B: Johnny Ball
>
> C: Alan Ball   D: Bobby Ball

Eighty per cent thought 'Johnny Ball'. Rather worry-
ingly, 7 per cent thought Bobby Ball was Zoe's father.
Mike sensibly dismissed the 7 per cent as nutters.
'Johnny Ball' was the right answer, and he got his
£16,000.

Mike knew the answer to the £32,000 question immediately and there was a roar when I handed him the cheque
that was guaranteed to be the smallest amount he would
leave with that night. Minnie the Lucky Moose was clearly
doing the trick.

When the £64,000 question came up, Mike's face immediately broke into one of those huge smiles that everybody
loves to see on the programme. It means 'I know this without being given the alternatives.'

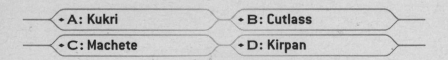

**What is the name of the knife with a curved blade
used by the Gurkhas?**

Before the answers had appeared on the screen, he said,
'It's a kukri.' 'How sure are you?' I asked. 'Virtually certain,' he said. Up came the four answers:

- A: Kukri
- B: Cutlass
- C: Machete
- D: Kirpan

Easy — £64,000 in the bank. The £125,000 question
appeared:

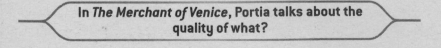

**In *The Merchant of Venice*, Portia talks about the
quality of what?**

Again Mike knew it straight away and, from my days of

English Literature, so did I. 'It's "mercy",' he said. Up they came:

- A: Kindness
- B: Charity
- C: Mercy
- D: Clemency

Preserving two Lifelines along the way, he had got all the way to £125,000. The audience, the crew and I began to get dry mouths – we knew we could be about to see a £1,000,000 winner. It's an electric feeling.

Sometimes at these moments, although it's essential that I concentrate extra hard, my mind goes off into a little flight of fancy. I suddenly became genuinely worried about where Mike would put the £1,000,000 cheque because Minnie the Lucky Moose was already filling his top pocket. It was a silly thought and I dismissed it. Mike and Minnie would manage.

This was the £125,000 question:

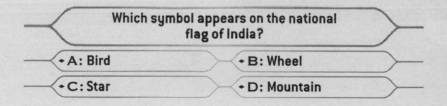

Which symbol appears on the national flag of India?

- A: Bird
- B: Wheel
- C: Star
- D: Mountain

Mike said to me, 'I think it's a wheel,' and the audience gasped. 'However,' he said, 'whether I'm certain enough that it's a wheel to risk losing £93,000, I'm just not sure.' He used his 50:50 and "wheel" and "bird" remained. Mike started visibly sweating. After all, this was for £250,000. 'I want to phone my ex-wife Georgie,' he announced. It still seemed to me a bizarre thing to do, but for Mike it obviously seemed the natural course of action. 'Do you want me to tell her that this is for a quarter of a million?' I asked him. 'Absolutely,' he said. 'She's the sort of person who would absolutely hate not knowing.' I rang Georgie. I told her the situation and Mike was right: she certainly did want to know exactly how much money was involved. It also became clear that she was on a cut, although I never did find out the percentage.

Mike told her the question and the two remaining answers. 'It's a wheel,' she said. 'I'm pretty sure.' 'I thought it was "wheel",' said Mike, then turned to me and said, 'It was *my* first impression and my ex-wife thinks it's a wheel. I'm going to play . . . "wheel".' It was the right answer. Mike had won a quarter of a million. Lizzie, in the audience, was in tears. Mike said, 'Well done, Moosey,' and gave Minnie another glass of water.

This was now very serious money. Question number fourteen, for £500,000, was this:

> **The capybara is the largest member of which animal order?**
>
> - A: Rodents
> - B: Marsupials
> - C: Carnivores
> - D: Primates

'I know this,' said Mike, straight away. 'I'm 100 per cent certain. It's a rodent.'

'Final answer?' 'Yes please, Chris.' Five hundred thousand! The audience erupted. I pumped Mike frantically by the hand and at the top of his voice, he hollered, 'They're only easy if you know the answer!'

It's always a great moment on *Millionaire* when the audience, myself and, most importantly, the contestant can see a £1,000,000 question. You could almost carve the silence in the studio with a knife as up it came:

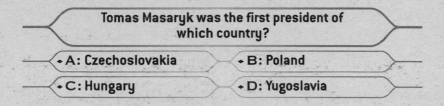

Tomas Masaryk was the first president of which country?

A: Czechoslovakia   B: Poland

C: Hungary   D: Yugoslavia

Mike looked at the question long and hard. He said to me, 'When the question appeared on the screen, three possible answers came straight into my mind. "Czechoslovakia", "Poland" and "Hungary".' Not particularly helpful. 'It's definitely not "Yugoslavia",' Mike said. 'I think it's "Poland". But I'm not certain enough to risk losing half a million.' And after more spine-chilling hesitation, he reluctantly decided, 'That's enough. It's too much money to risk. I'm taking £500,000.'

There was a huge cheer from the audience. There was an even bigger cheer when I told Mike that if he'd said 'Poland' he would have just lost £468,000. The right answer was 'Czechoslovakia'.

Minnie the Moose had worked her magic right to the end. It had been a fantastic night.

We had a Czech nanny living with us at the time and when I crawled home around midnight after the show had been recorded, I found she had stayed up especially to tell me, 'Tomas Masaryk! Tomas Masaryk! I knew the answer at once. He was one of my great schoolgirl heroes.' Apparently she had been literally screaming at the TV screen at the top of her voice. Then again, to put things in perspective, she hadn't known a single one of the other fourteen questions that Mike had got right. As he'd pointed out, at the top of his voice, 'They're only easy if you know the answer!' (Or if you happen to have been born in Prague.)

Life After *Who Wants To Be A Millionaire?*

Mike says he loved being on the show, and life since has been very nice. He has bought a nice, red, flash sports car, a new place to live five minutes walk from the golf course, had a few holidays and has invested the rest. He also says his love life has improved!

Ann Baldwin

One lady who nearly joined the small and unfortunate band of people who have left *Who Wants To Be A Millionaire?* with absolutely nothing was Ann Baldwin.

Ann seemed a lot of fun – bright and positive – when she sat down. Her husband Headley ('named after a famous Yorkshire cricketer') sat grinning proudly in the audience. She had some definite ideas on how she wanted to spend £1,000,000 if she answered all fifteen questions correctly. She wanted to rehouse the royal family in a small two-up, two-down terraced house and put television's Royle family, Ricky Tomlinson and co., into Buckingham Palace – just to see how the two families would handle the role reversal. She hoped for some money for her daughter Genevieve's wedding, and enough spare cash to buy herself a really splendid hat for the big day.

She said she wanted to grow old disgracefully, to become a mad old woman in wellies surrounded by donkeys, chickens, pigs and so on. Fascinatingly, she was the first contestant to claim that she had had a premonition about one of the questions and its answer. She said she would give me a little sign – a maniacal waggling of her thumbs in the air, when it came up.

So we started and she got £100 without a problem. On the second question, though, things suddenly came to an abrupt halt. This was the question, not too tricky, I think you'll agree:

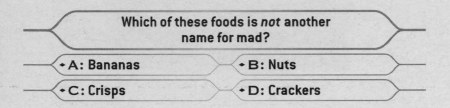

Which of these foods is *not* another name for mad?

A: Bananas   **B: Nuts**

C: Crisps   **D: Crackers**

Ann completely collapsed, started cackling like a loon, tugging at her hair, looking down at her knees as if she was about to be publicly executed and said, 'I think I'm having a nervous breakdown.' She appeared to be going through the most dreadful inner torment. Eventually she said, 'I'm really not sure. This is so embarrassing – it's either "nuts" or "crackers" but I really can't make my mind up which one.' I went terribly cold inside – I could see the wedding plans, the splendid hat and, above all, her self-respect disappearing into an abyss. If she was honestly going to tell me that 'nuts' was not another word for 'mad', she was going home with El Zippo.

Luckily, she wasn't totally confident as to whether it was 'nuts' or 'crackers' and to my enormous relief she asked the audience. I assumed that 100 per cent would give her the right answer. In fact only 89 per cent of the audience said it was 'crisps'. Sometimes it's the small minorities on Ask the Audience who give an answer that's so utterly wrong that is more intriguing than the majority who get it right. Alarmingly, 8 per cent voted for 'bananas', 2 per cent thought 'crackers' and 1 per cent believed that 'nuts' was *not* another word for 'mad'. Clearly some people in the studio that night weren't safe to walk the streets. It's amazing that some of them could even do up their own shoe laces.

With a sudden demonic scream, Ann cried, 'Oh my God, I've read the question wrong!' She certainly had. 'It's "crisps"!' she bellowed. '"Crisps!" "Crisps!" "Crisps!"' And a potential catastrophe was averted in the nick of time. It was very nearly 'a marsupial moment'.

Physically shaken, Ann ploughed on to £1000; to £4000, using the rest of her Lifelines; £8000; then a fantastic £16,000. The audience cheered her every inch of the way.

For £32,000 she got this question:

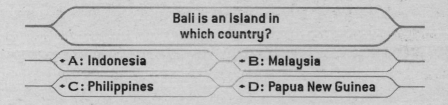

She knew it wasn't 'the Philippines'. She knew it wasn't 'Papua New Guinea'. She said to me, 'I think it's "Malaysia", but I'm just not sure enough to risk this. I'm going to take the money,' and, with a huge sigh of relief, she did the sensible thing and left us, beaming, with £16,000.

If she had said 'Malaysia' she would have been wrong. The right answer is "Indonesia". Ann had provided tremendous entertainment, although her confidence never really recovered from the near disaster of question number two.

Oh, and the premonition that she had about the fateful question, and the correct answer that she had already heard herself saying to thunderous applause? It never did come up.

Life After *Who Wants To Be A Millionaire?*

Ann still can't believe that she nearly got the £200 question wrong. She misread it, and it shook her up so much that her brain shut down and she could barely remember her own name.

She had only made one phone call to the show and although she had never previously won anything in her life, she says she felt destined for that chair! She was able to make her daughter's wedding extra special, give her some money to start married life, and take friends and family out for meals and on holiday. She is glad that she didn't win any more than £16,000, or there would have been all sorts of added pressure, and people might have felt differently about her!

Richard Deeley

One of the oddest contestants we have ever had on the show was a young guy called Richard Deeley, an accountant from Nottingham. To say he had a very strange sense of humour would be an understatement.

He described himself as 'single at the moment' and continued in a matter-of-fact tone, 'but I think there's something about getting into the hotseat on this show that could make me irresistible to women'. I have no idea whether or not he was joking, or whether the show transformed his love life, but the last I heard he was still single. Read on and you may not be surprised.

Richard waved in a rather strange way at the top of the show and when I asked him why, he told me, 'I chose a *Star Trek* Spock wave – anything else would look silly.' When I asked him what sum of money he'd set his sights on, he replied, 'I'd like £32,000 plus.' There seemed no reason why he might not achieve his target – he was obviously a bright bloke. He had dark, staring eyes and it was very difficult to predict what he was going to do or say next. He did a lot of play-acting, making a point of doing extraordinarily long pauses between questions and rubbing his chin in mock bewilderment at those to which he clearly knew the answer. He seemed vaguely amused by everything around him – and above all, himself.

He got to £1000 easily enough with this question:

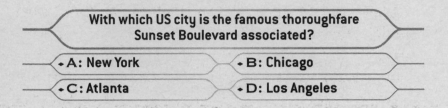

Richard made a big show of deliberating for a while, before he eventually gave me 'Los Angeles' as the correct answer.

I must say I was quite surprised that he had to use his first Lifeline on the question for £4000:

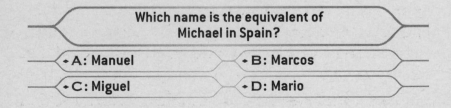

Even now I'm not sure if he was feigning ignorance – as I say Richard Deeley was a strange gentleman – but eventually he chose to Ask the Audience. Eighty-two per cent of them knew straight away that 'Miguel' was the right answer. Alarmingly, 1 per cent voted for 'Manuel'. Richard went with the majority and got to £4000.

We soldiered on. He'd said he'd like £32,000 plus, and this was question number ten:

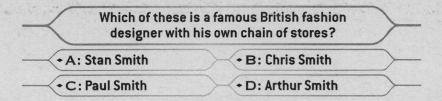

Which of these is a famous British fashion designer with his own chain of stores?

A: Stan Smith   B: Chris Smith

C: Paul Smith   D: Arthur Smith

After more hesitation he suddenly said, 'It's "Paul Smith" – final answer.' It was correct and it got him to his target.

But what happened next will be etched on my memory for ever. I wrote out a cheque in the name of Richard Deeley for £32,000 and handed it to him. To my amazement and to the disgust of the audience and the other contestants, he took it off me, screwed it up into a small ball and threw it across the studio floor. 'I don't want that,' he said. 'Give me another one.' I don't think anything quite like it has ever happened on *Millionaire* anywhere in the world. I guess he probably thought he was being very amusing, but in fact he was being hugely insulting. I'm a big boy, I can handle it, but he was insulting the show, the other contestants and, above all, the people watching at home, for whom £32,000 would be a great deal of money.

My job on *Who Wants To Be A Millionaire?* is never to show emotion and I don't think I did now, even at such bizarre behaviour, but there were audible gasps from the audience. In fact there must have been cries of anger from people watching their television sets all over the country. Inwardly, I'll happily admit, I was absolutely furious. But resisting the temptation to reach across and shake him by the windpipe, I went on to the next question, aware, in the back of my racing mind, that there was a screwed-up cheque somewhere on the studio floor and determined that I was not going to be the one to go and pick it up.

This question came up for £64,000:

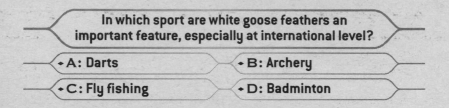

'Can I Phone-A-Friend?' Richard asked. 'Help yourself,' I said, secretly surprised that he'd got any. He rang his mate Andy and read him the question. Andy said, 'I'm not certain, but I think it's "archery".' 'Yes, thank you,' said Richard, 'that was my inclination as well.' He turned back to me with a contented smile on his face. 'He says "archery", I thought it was "archery", I'm going for "archery" – final answer.'

It was completely the wrong answer. It is the shuttle-cock in badminton that contains goose feathers. 'Never mind,' I said, trying to hide a certain amount of glee. 'You still go home with a cheque for £32,000.' 'Where is it?' he asked me, suddenly rather less full of himself. 'I've no idea,' I said. 'Presumably wherever you threw it.' So, to the delight of everybody in the studio audience, the crew and myself, Richard Deeley had to go scrabbling about on the floor to pick up his cheque. He made his way out to only the tiniest ripple of polite applause, as the audience and the other contestants went through the minimal motions.

It was a truly extraordinary display. Once he'd screwed the cheque up and thrown it across the studio there was no way that I was going to fetch it for him. I can hardly imagine Cilla or Brucie scrambling about on all fours on the floor for any of their contestants, and I was damned if I was going to.

Richard Deeley was lambasted in the press the next morning for being an appallingly arrogant man. He said later he genuinely thought he was being funny, he didn't mean any harm and it was just a joke that went wrong. Maybe that's true.

There was one fine moment after the show when he did ask Damon, our producer that evening, if he could have a replacement cheque as the one he'd got was all scrumpled up and the bank might not accept it. Damon, who is normally a very good-natured guy, really helpful with the contestants, and never remotely vindictive, took great delight in saying to him, 'I'm sorry, Richard, but I'm afraid we don't do replacement cheques. If you decide to screw it up into a tight ball, throw it in the river or even set light to it, that's very much up to you. After all, the cheque was absolutely fine when it left us.'

David Edwards

David Edwards was a physics teacher from Staffordshire. He had his wife Viv in the audience; his two kids, Richard and Louise, were at home. Whether either of them was watching the show is debatable. The morning that David had left, he'd said goodbye to the elder of the two, twenty-one-year-old Richard, who'd poked half an eye out from under the duvet, muttered, 'Good luck, Dad' and gone straight back to sleep.

But David was rather relying on Richard. He was paranoid about getting a physics question – the last thing he needed was all the kids in his class smirking behind their hands because 'sir' didn't know enough about the subject he taught – and Richard was studying physics at university. So, in theory, he should be of some use in a crisis, but his other parting words had been: 'If it's a physics question, please don't call me.' Not very reassuring for Dad.

I asked David how much money would be life-changing to the Edwards family and he replied, 'Anything in six figures would mean that I can retire from teaching.'

He quickly got up to this question, for £1000:

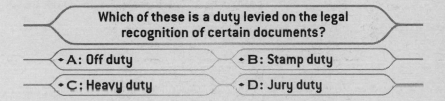

Which of these is a duty levied on the legal recognition of certain documents?

- A: Off duty
- B: Stamp duty
- C: Heavy duty
- D: Jury duty

The answer is 'stamp duty'. David knew that, and he was on a guaranteed £1000. 'Feeling better?' I asked him. 'Betterish,' he responded, 'but not great.'

For £4000 the computer dished out this question:

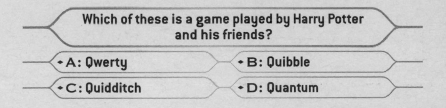

Which of these is a game played by Harry Potter and his friends?

- A: Qwerty
- B: Quibble
- C: Quidditch
- D: Quantum

'That will be "quidditch",' David said without hesitation. 'So you've read the books?' I asked him. 'No,' he told me, 'I've never read any of them, but I have a family full of people who have and they talk about little else.' It was the right answer.

For £32,000, still with all his Lifelines intact, this question came up:

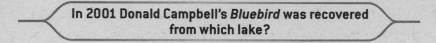

In 2001 Donald Campbell's *Bluebird* was recovered from which lake?

David smiled at once.

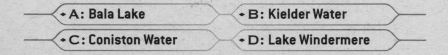

| • A: Bala Lake | • B: Kielder Water |
| • C: Coniston Water | • D: Lake Windermere |

'It's "Coniston", I'm absolutely sure,' he stated, quickly qualifying it with, 'I hope.' Viv was clapping frantically; clearly, she too thought it was the right answer, and it was. David was now guaranteed £32,000. I suggested to him that this was quite a decent amount of money for a physics teacher to earn in one night. 'Worth two or three lessons,' he said with a twinkle in his eye, 'possibly even more.'

For £64,000 the computer threw this at David:

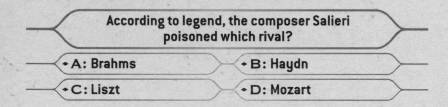

According to legend, the composer Salieri poisoned which rival?

| • A: Brahms | • B: Haydn |
| • C: Liszt | • D: Mozart |

'It's "Mozart",' he said, 'I'm sure.' Viv was nodding emphatically; again she seemed to agree. David seemed very certain. 'Were you there,' I said, 'when the poisoning took place?' 'Do I look that old?' he asked amiably, adding, 'Don't answer that.' We smiled, and David had every reason to – he'd just won £64,000. 'I feel absolutely terrified,' he said. 'This is strange but I feel much more frightened now.'

'Well, the next question is for six figures,' I warned him. 'One hundred and twenty-five thousand pounds. At the beginning of the show this was the amount which you told me would mean you could give up teaching.' 'I'll probably carry on as a physics teacher,' he said now, 'if I do win this. But not for very much longer.' 'Does that mean you'll leave tomorrow?' I asked him. 'That would be a bit of a shock for the headmaster.' 'No,' he said evasively, 'let's just say I won't continue teaching indefinitely.' What a wonderful word 'indefinitely' is. It means everything and nothing.

So, we had a look at the £125,000 question:

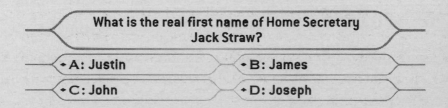

What is the real first name of Home Secretary Jack Straw?

◆ A: Justin   ◆ B: James

◆ C: John   ◆ D: Joseph

For the first time David looked genuinely puzzled. 'I think I'll Ask the Audience,' he said. It was a huge responsibility and predictably they all groaned. However, 62 per cent said they thought it was 'John'. 'It's a high percentage,' I said to David. 'Yes, it is,' he said, 'but it's the obvious one you would guess at. I think this needs a little bit of contemplation.' He paused while he did some serious thinking. 'The two most likely options are "John" and "James",' he said. '"James", of course, is "Jacques" in French, which sounds horribly like "Jack". I was thinking too: if your name was John Straw, why would you bother to change it to Jack Straw? Nevertheless, sitting there staring at David, I also thought it was probably 'John'.

'I'd better ring my comatose son,' he said. 'Well, at least he was comatose first thing this morning. Hopefully he'll be a little bit more alert by now.' 'Do you want me to tell him the amount of money involved?' I asked David. 'Yes please — it'll really concentrate his mind,' he said with a twinkle in his eye.

We phoned Richard and David read him the question. Richard sounded horrified and apologetic. 'I'm sorry, Dad,' he said, 'I really have no idea.' 'Never mind,' said David. 'Go back to sleep, son,' and the phone went dead.

David now started thinking even harder. He looked seriously ill at ease. Up in the audience, Viv also looked worried for the first time.

'The trouble is,' said David, '"John" is just too tempting. I'll use my 50:50. I'm not going to leave here with any Lifelines left.' Sickeningly, though, this left 'James' and 'John'. 'One of these could be your retirement money,' I reminded him, 'and one of them will cost you £32,000.' He looked up at me with real concern. 'Is Viv having kittens behind me?' he asked. I looked up. 'Yes,' I said, 'she certainly is.' He paused a bit longer and then said, 'Sorry, Viv.' Viv now had her eyes completely closed. 'I'm going for the one that looks less likely,' said David.

Then, for some reason, he stopped in his tracks. 'On the other hand,' he said, 'there are no trick questions on *Millionaire*, are there?' 'No, there aren't,' I reassured him. 'Perhaps it really is "John". Come on, let's go for it. Sorry, Viv. "John" — final answer.'

After all that, to everyone's great relief, 'John' was the right answer. Jack Straw's real name apparently is John Whittaker Straw, so being nicknamed 'Jack' was the least of his worries. David was now on £125,000. He'd terrified all of us — but probably nobody more than himself and his wife. 'That's it,' I said over the loud cheers of the audience, 'that's the retiring money. Now for God's sake go!'

David had made £125,000, and I suggested he might as well peep at the £250,000 question:

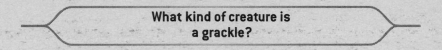

What kind of creature is
a grackle?

After the tension of the last few minutes David's face burst into a huge grin. 'I know this one,' he said. The choices were:

A: Lizard   B: Bird

C: Fish   D: Beetle

'It's a bird,' he said. 'No question, it's a bird.' I knew he was right as well – I'd seen one only days earlier on the Discovery Channel. It went to orange. It was the right answer. He'd just won £250,000.

Up came question number fourteen, for £500,000:

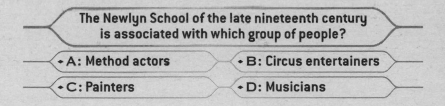

The Newlyn School of the late nineteenth century
is associated with which group of people?

A: Method actors   B: Circus entertainers

C: Painters   D: Musicians

I more or less expected David to take the money, but he looked at me with almost an apology in his eyes and said, 'I think it's painters. I'm sorry, Viv.' His wife's body language at this moment was extraordinary: she'd adopted a scrunched-up position rather like a hedgehog on a busy main road. 'Final answer,' David said. 'I'm sure I'm right – it's "painters".'

He was right! The whole place erupted. Our physics teacher was now on half a million. I showed him the cheque: 'Pay David Edwards £500,000.' He looked at it happily, but he wouldn't touch it. 'I'll keep it for now,' I said, 'but it's yours. You've just won half a million quid.' He was staring at me in disbelief.

Now, for only the seventh time since the programme first aired nearly three years earlier, we were going to see a £1,000,000 question. It's always a special moment. David said to me, 'Do you know I'm now, in a rather masochistic sort of way, almost enjoying this. I've worked out that £500,000 is more money in total than I've probably ever been paid in my whole life. This is unreal!'

This was the question:

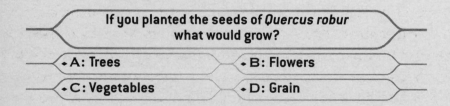

If you planted the seeds of *Quercus robur* what would grow?

- A: Trees
- B: Flowers
- C: Vegetables
- D: Grain

I think we all automatically expected David to say, 'Thank you, Mr Tarrant, I've had a very nice day, give me the £500,000 cheque and I'll be off.' But he looked at me, stunned, and muttered, '*Quercus* is a type of tree.' Viv appeared to be trying to hide under her seat in the audience. 'I think I'm going to go for it,' he said. There was a great cheer from the audience. I had to ask them to calm down and remind them, and him, that if he got it wrong he would lose £468,000.

This huge sum always brings a contestant up with a bump and I saw David's face twitch uneasily for a nanosecond. 'It's terrifying,' he said, 'but I am *almost* certain.' He added, 'Horrible word, *almost*!' Then he started rambling. 'I'm not quite sure what kind of a tree it is,' he said. 'It might be a type of oak.' 'David,' I jumped in, 'it doesn't matter what kind of a tree it is, you just have to be certain that it is a tree.' 'I'm going to play,' he said. 'I'm *almost* certain' – that word again. 'Final answer.'

I went through my usual, infuriating all-around-the-houses routine: 'If you'd said "flowers" you'd have been wrong, you'd have lost £468,000. If you'd said "vegetables", you'd have lost £468,000. If you'd said "grain . . ." I emphasised the word "grain" and I saw him look up. For a brief moment we had direct eye contact and I know that, at that second, he thought he'd blown it. 'You would have lost £468,000,' I continued, with the accent on the word 'lost'. My words, 'You've just won £1,000,000,' even at the top of my very loud voice, were already drowned. The audience stood up on their seats and applauded uproariously.

David Edwards had become the first man to win £1,000,000 on *Who Wants To Be A Millionaire?* Viv came down, grabbed him and gave him a huge kiss and then wandered off into the wings, completely dazed. 'Don't leave him now,' I said, 'after all the years you stood by him as a physics teacher, don't leave him now.' She came back sharpish. 'I don't know what to say,' David said. He was obviously numb. 'How many of those did you know, Viv?' I asked. 'I knew them all except Jack Straw,' she said. 'Which is ridiculous, because I was actually at university with Jack Straw.'

They were a really lovely, bright couple and from that moment on they were £1,000,000 better off than they had been when David walked into the studio earlier that afternoon. 'I just feel numb,' David kept repeating.

Looking back now, David remembers the huge relief of getting the £125,000 question right, as he had literally guessed it. He also does admit that when I emphasised 'grain' on the £1,000,000 question, for half a second he had a sick feeling that he got it wrong. Now it's all over, he says he loved his time on the show.

Lots of interesting opportunities and experiences have arisen because of the money. There's been no sudden transformation in the way they live, but things are evolving nicely. They've paid off the mortgage, bought a larger house, and they've replaced both their cars with new models – David's has leather seats! They are starting to spend some money on types of holidays they would not have had before, such as a long visit to Australia, where David's two uncles live and a trip to the Caribbean a few months after the show. He is also toying with the idea of buying a second house in France.

As David said on the show, his immediate reaction on winning lots of money was to give up teaching. But he realised that actually he rather enjoys it! So he and Viv held on to their jobs, though David is retiring at the end of this school year. When they both do so, he says: 'The great thing is that we won't ever have to worry about where the money will come from. All our financial worries have been taken away.'

Janie McCathie

In September 2001 Janie McCathie, from Argyll and Bute in Scotland, became the youngest contestant so far on *Who Wants To Be A Millionaire?* She was sixteen years old and studying for her A levels. Her big sister Claire was up in the audience and quite openly admitted to being deeply envious of Janie. Apparently she had phoned the show loads of times too, but had never been chosen. Janie had made only one call and got straight on.

Mum and Dad were watching at home, along with the dogs Robbie and Elsa, the cats Smokey and Sooty and Perky the goldfish. Janie's dream, if she won enough money, was to buy a car. At least that's what her school mates had instructed her to do, so that they could drive her around in it until she was old enough to pass her test. She didn't mind what kind of car it was, as long as it was better than her sister's. There was clearly some friendly-ish sibling rivalry between the two of them.

Janie was a very pretty girl with a beautiful smile. She was also very nervous. We've had some bright young kids on the show over the years, several of whom have made it into the chair. Once there, they have found it tough. We've had brilliant Oxbridge students and we've had some really high-flying school boys and girls. But usually, however intelligent they are, they just haven't been on the planet long enough to accumulate a lot of the useless baggage that older generations carry around. They don't have twenty-five-plus years' worth of trivia to draw on, and so they often find the game an uphill struggle. Dated questions; ancient sayings that have gone out of fashion; or things that happened long before they were born are generally problematic for them.

However, on the positive side, they are usually very good at Fastest Finger First, which some of our older contestants find hard. I've always loved the OAPs who get on to Cilla Black's *Blind Date* – some of them are outrageous – and we've had some equally wicked old devils who've arrived at the studios for *Millionaire*. They are too old to be fazed by anything; they are usually wonderfully irreverent; and they often have a great bank of knowledge on all sorts of subjects. But, time and again, however bright they are at rehearsal, come showtime they don't make it into the chair simply because they don't have the speed and co-ordination required to win Fastest Finger First. I've seen it night after night, and it always frustrates me.

Perhaps one day we'll do an OAPs-only show to guarantee at least two or three of them make it to the chair. It would be a real hoot.

Anyway Janie won her Fastest Finger First – a question on pop – in 4.5 seconds and raced into the hotseat. She got to £300 but was forced to Ask the Audience:

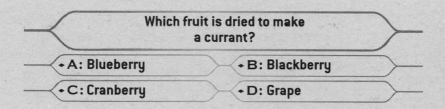

Which fruit is dried to make a currant?

- A: Blueberry
- B: Blackberry
- C: Cranberry
- D: Grape

Eighty-nine per cent said 'grape', and understandably Janie went with the majority. She murmured, 'I had a feeling it was "grape", but I'm a bit scared here.' She needn't have worried – she was on £500 still, with two Lifelines intact.

We proceeded to the first watershed of £1000:

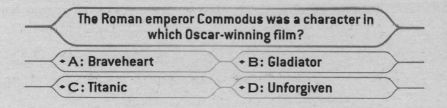

The Roman emperor Commodus was a character in which Oscar-winning film?

- A: Braveheart
- B: Gladiator
- C: Titanic
- D: Unforgiven

Janie looked puzzled but said, 'I think it's "Gladiator"'. I pointed out to her that she could still walk away with £500 but she replied, quite defiantly, 'I'm not going to do that.' 'All right,' I said, 'when did you last earn five hundred quid?' 'Never,' she admitted, and the audience let out an audible 'Aahhh'.

She decided to use her 50:50. The computer left

'Gladiator' and 'Braveheart'. She plumped for 'Gladiator', although she didn't seem very confident about doing so. Luckily. Janie had made the right choice, and was now guaranteed £1000 – a serious amount of money for a sixteen-year-old schoolgirl. She had no problem with the question for £2000, but she got this for £4000:

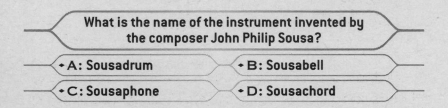

What is the name of the instrument invented by the composer John Philip Sousa?

A: Sousadrum
B: Sousabell
C: Sousaphone
D: Sousachord

'I haven't got a clue,' she said. 'I have absolutely no idea. I'm going to Phone-A-Friend. I'd like to phone Brian.' 'It's definitely the sousaphone,' Brian told her at once. Janie looked delighted – he had sounded very positive – and, sure enough, by going along with him, she had earned herself £4000. For a sixteen-year-old, this was becoming a profitable evening's homework.

For £8000, she got this question:

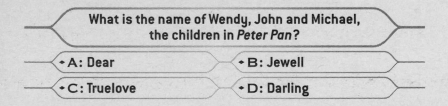

What is the name of Wendy, John and Michael, the children in *Peter Pan*?

A: Dear
B: Jewell
C: Truelove
D: Darling

'I think I read *Peter Pan* a long time ago,' said Janie. 'I know my sister will know this question. She used to read it a lot when we were both younger. I think it's "D", for "Darling". Final answer.' It went to orange and, of course, she was right. Janie, now living dangerously, with no

Lifelines left, was on £8000. Claire looked suitably impressed, but slightly envious.

For £16,000, Janie got this question:

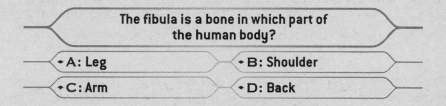

The fibula is a bone in which part of the human body?

- A: Leg
- B: Shoulder
- C: Arm
- D: Back

She looked at me in amazement as the question came up. 'This is scary,' she said. 'Why?' I asked her. 'Because you don't know the answer?' 'No, because I asked Claire this earlier today. It's really weird.' The audience and I were bewildered as to quite what she meant, but apparently Janie and Claire had been firing practice questions at each other on the journey down to the studio. To be honest, any sort of revision for *Who Wants To Be A Millionaire?* is pretty futile, as the computer has tens of thousands of questions that it throws out at random, but I suppose it never does any harm, and this was a case in point – and a weird coincidence. But, disastrously, Janie couldn't remember what the answer was. 'I think it might be "leg",' she said, suddenly. 'It's not "arm". I'm sure it's "leg". Final answer, please. "Leg", "leg", "leg".' It was the right answer – Janie now had £1000 for every year of her life.

For double the money, up came question number ten:

What is a Jack-in-the-pulpit?

- A: Plant
- B: Insect
- C: Toy
- D: Card game

Janie had no idea. So I wrote her a cheque for sixteen grand, and she skipped ecstatically out of the studio with her sister in hot pursuit, taking it back to show Mum and Dad and Perky the goldfish. Before she left I was able to tell her that a Jack-in-the-pulpit is a flower, but I don't think Janie could have cared less. And who could blame her? She was, at that moment, probably the richest school-girl in Scotland.

Robert Brydges

Robert Brydges came from Romsey in Hampshire. He described himself as a budding children's author, although it wasn't really clear whether he'd actually written a book yet. Robert was father to two kids, nine- and ten-year-old Kent and Catherine, and husband to a very glamorous wife, Marilyn, who was sitting in the audience.

They'd both once been in a similar line of business and had first met on the phone – she had been attracted to him 'because he had a lovely voice'. They'd been married for years – Marilyn said she was with Robert for the laughs. Apparently he was also a very good cook but, in his wife's words, 'extremely messy'. He had once made a magnificent apple pie, put it on the floor of their garage, where Marilyn, not necessarily expecting an apple pie to be lying around, had stepped in it. Undeterred, she told us, Robert still proudly served the remnants that night to some friends for dinner.

Marilyn drove a black taxi because it was great for the kids, who could throw everything, even bicycles, in the back. So, if he came into some money, Robert said he'd like to treat his wife to a new cab. He also said the whole family wanted to go to Las Vegas because he said, 'It's great for families.' I rather got the impression that Robert was the driving force behind that idea. The bottom line was that he wanted to go to Vegas. He added romantically that if he won £1,000,000, the first thing he would do would be to buy Marilyn a bunch of flowers.

He was very together and seemed to be thoroughly enjoying the show, even though I kept taking the mickey out of his 'lovely voice'. He got to this question, for £2000, before he paused for the first time:

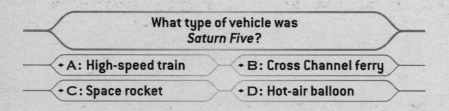

What type of vehicle was *Saturn Five*?

A: High-speed train   B: Cross Channel ferry
C: Space rocket   D: Hot-air balloon

He looked long and hard at the question, before finally deciding that *Saturn Five* had been a space rocket. It was the right answer and he was now on £2000. 'I've told the kids to expect absolutely nothing,' he said. 'They mustn't get too excited. I don't want them to get silly expectations of Daddy winning a million quid because, let's face it, it's not going to happen!' He raced on, but I was surprised that he didn't know the answer to this question for £16,000:

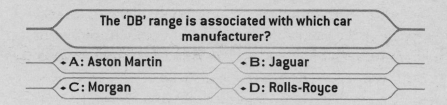

> **The 'DB' range is associated with which car manufacturer?**
>
> ◆ A: Aston Martin ◆ B: Jaguar
>
> ◆ C: Morgan ◆ D: Rolls-Royce

'So you're not a petrolhead then?' I asked him. 'No, not at all,' he said. 'I'm just not really interested in cars. I'll have to Ask the Audience.' There were some grunts of horror. I don't know why, because 81 per cent of them gave him the right answer. 'DB' is fairly widely known as the initials of David Brown – the creator of the classic Aston Martin.

For £32,000 Robert got this question:

> **In the eighteenth century, Capability Brown was best known for designing what?**
>
> ◆ A: Wigs ◆ B: Pottery
>
> ◆ C: Theatre sets ◆ D: Gardens

Robert beamed with delight. He knew it at once. 'It's gardens,' he said immediately. 'Capability Brown designed beautiful gardens for some of the most magnificent houses in the British Isles.' Robert was now on £32,000.

For £64,000 he got this question:

> **Which twentieth-century poet wrote 'The Wasteland'?**
>
> ◆ A: Rupert Brooke ◆ B: Ted Hughes
>
> ◆ C: John Betjeman ◆ D: T.S. Eliot

Again Robert was immediately positive. 'It's T.S. Eliot,' he said, with no hesitation. 'T.S. Eliot' lit up in orange, and then green. He was quite right. His conviction that that there was no way he could win a million was suddenly beginning to ring less true. He'd only struggled at all on one question and he still had two Lifelines intact.

We continued to £125,000:

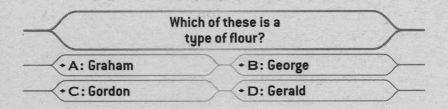

Which of these is a
type of flour?

A: Graham   B: George

C: Gordon   D: Gerald

'I think it's "Graham",' he said very confidently, but then he started to ramble: 'No, I'm not completely certain, I may be getting confused with "Gordon", Gordon crackers. No, that's nonsense,' he decided. 'I'll play. It's "Graham".' It went orange. He paused, still worried – probably about Gordon and his crackers. But, it was good news – it was the right answer.

This was now becoming a serious business. His next question was worth £250,000:

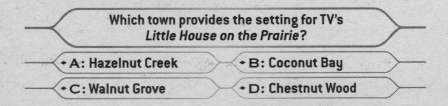

Which town provides the setting for TV's
Little House on the Prairie?

A: Hazelnut Creek   B: Coconut Bay

C: Walnut Grove   D: Chestnut Wood

'I think it's "Walnut Grove",' Robert said, 'but I'm not certain, I don't know where that's come from. I'll phone Edwina.' 'Do you want me to tell her it's for £250,000?' I asked him. 'Yes, OK,' he said coolly. I told Edwina, as instructed, what her answer was worth and she was far less cool. In fact she was horrified. 'Oh gosh!' she exclaimed. Whether the enormity of the amount of money involved put her off or not, I don't know, but after thirty seconds Edwina still had not given us an answer. 'I'm sorry,' she said and we ran out of time. 'I still think it's "Walnut Grove",' said Robert. 'I'm going to play.' Marilyn closed her eyes and two kids down in Romsey almost certainly closed theirs.

'Walnut Grove' was correct.

Robert Brydges was now £250,000 better off. 'Where on earth did that come from?' I asked him. 'I really don't know,' he said. 'It must be at least twenty-five years since I've seen *Little House on the Prairie*. It was just somewhere in the back of my mind.' As I've said, an appearance on *Millionaire* often seems to force out useless pieces of trivia from the deepest recesses of the brain, where they've been tucked away for years and years. Marilyn was now screaming and whooping with joy in the audience.

Robert had one Lifeline left, his 50:50, and the next question was for £250,000. I noticed his body language had changed. He seemed to have physically pulled himself up and started to focus even harder on the screen in front of him. This was his question:

> **Which of these African countries is situated south of the equator?**
>
> ◆ A: Ethiopia ◆ B: Nigeria
> ◆ C: Zambia ◆ D: Chad

'It's "Zambia",' he said immediately. 'I've been there.' So had I, and I too knew it was well south of the equator. So Robert was now on £500,000 with a Lifeline still there for him to fall back on. 'The next question is for a million,' I told him, and I reminded him of the consequences of getting this wrong. He looked me in the eye, deadly serious, as frankly you would be at the thought of losing £468,000. Marilyn visibly shrank when she heard the words 'lose four hundred and sixty-eight thousand pounds'.

This was the £1,000,000 question:

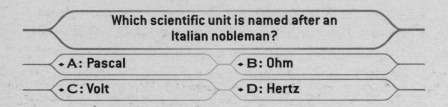

Which scientific unit is named after an Italian nobleman?

A: Pascal   B: Ohm

C: Volt   D: Hertz

'I'll go 50:50,' said Robert, with no note of real conviction in his voice. The computer took two away: 'volt' and 'ohm' remained. One of those was worth £1,000,000 and one of them would cost him nearly half a million. 'I think it's "volt",' he suddenly announced. 'Please don't ask me why.' Marilyn, up in the audience, started shaking her head in horror. 'I want to play,' he said. '"Volt" – final answer.' The audience let out a loud, involuntary gasp that sounded like a giant gas leak and it seemed a particularly good moment to take a commercial break, although Robert, Marilyn and the audience clearly didn't agree.

When we returned everyone had just about got their breath back. I held my breath, looked down at my screen to check the computer's verdict, and was absolutely thrilled to see that I could tell Robert Brydges that he'd just won £1,000,000!

Robert had been magnificent! Marilyn went berserk. A huge smile spread right across her husband's face – taking that cheque must be one of the nicest feelings in the world. Marilyn ran down and gave him an enormous smacker on the lips. Eventually, talking in a daze, she said, 'I don't believe it, I didn't think he'd get anything at all.' Robert just replied, 'I'm in shock.'

They were cheered all the way out of the studio and Robert Brydges became only the third person in the UK ever to win £1,000,000 on *Millionaire*.

Life After *Who Wants To Be A Millionaire?*

Robert's memories of the night on the show, he says now, were initially of disappointment at how useless he was at Fastest Finger First. He'd been practising at home on his laptop and thought he was prepared for anything, but when asked in rehearsal to put four letters of the alphabet in the correct order, he panicked and managed to get it hopelessly wrong.

He hasn't gone mad with the money yet, although he's had a lot of work done on his garden. The great thing, he says, is that it takes all the pressure off. He really is now in the process of writing a book, now that he has the time to make it as good as possible, without worrying about having to work to feed his family.

Joanne Welch and Fred Ellis

I've thoroughly enjoyed our various specials – over the
years we've done one-off shows for charity, with
celebrities; couples; newlyweds; twins; and a whole week
of parents and kids. I assumed that 'parents and kids'
would mainly consist of mums or dads in their mid-thirties
with older teenage offspring – legally no one under the age
of sixteen can appear on *Who Wants To Be A Millionaire?*
So, imagine my surprise and delight when one of our dads
turned out to be Fred Ellis, a remarkable man, who was
just a few months short of his eightieth birthday.

He came on the show with his daughter Joanne, who
had a husband and a baby daughter waiting at home. From
the sound of things, home was a bit cramped: they were all
still living with Fred and were desperate for a place of
their own. Fred was a tall man with a lovely twinkle in his
eye, and his main reason for coming on the show was to
win some money for Joanne. At his age his own needs

were clearly simple enough. He seemed a very contented, kind man, who just wanted a nice day out and was obviously having one.

Joanne kept grinning at Fred, who was definitely her absolute hero. She obviously adored her dad and was very proud of him. Fred was apparently sometimes rather forgetful. He told us that when Joanne was a baby, he had taken her down to the local shops and left her lying there in her pram, gurgling and waiting for Daddy. He had got all the way home, had made a cup of tea and still hadn't registered that he'd left her behind.

The great love of Fred's life, apart from his family, was Stockport County Football Club. He claimed he must be the longest-serving supporter of any club in Britain and I'm sure he was. He said, 'I've followed them for seventy-six years. It's like a marriage – you take a football team for better or for worse. The only problem is, in the case of Stockport County, I've taken them for worse.'

As the two of them were getting ready to start with the first question, Fred confided to me and the audience that they had a master plan. 'I know lots about sport,' he said, 'and dance bands, like Glen Miller. Joanne will have to know everything else.' It was to prove a better combination than it sounded.

They didn't need any Lifelines at all until they got to £8000, when this question came up:

Teams in the NHL play which sport?

- A: Ice hockey
- B: Basketball
- C: Water polo
- D: Netball

'I think it is "ice hockey",' said Fred, but Joanne wasn't so sure. She worried that if it was 'ice hockey' the letters should spell out 'NIHL'. And she wasn't sure about asking the audience either, as, amazingly, earlier that evening over 90 per cent of them had given a contestant a completely wrong answer. However, Fred suggested tentatively they try them anyway, and 61 per cent went for 'ice hockey'. They both agreed to go with this as their final answer. It was correct and there was thunderous applause from the audience – mainly out of sheer relief that they had finally got something right.

Their question for £32,000 was this:

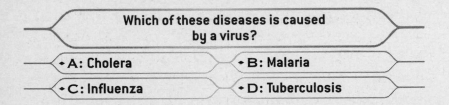

'I think it's "flu",' said Joanne. Fred looked perplexed, but Joanne was very positive. Clearly the large amounts of money were beginning to get to Fred. When you're coming up to eighty you don't go risking losing £15,000 every day of the week, but then again you probably don't win £32,000 too often either.

'I'm sure it's "flu",' said Joanne. 'Yes it is, it must be. It's "flu".' She looked anxiously at her dad. 'All right then,' said Fred, 'let's go "flu".' He was rather enjoying the gamble. It went to orange – it was the right answer. Fred looked absolutely thrilled – they now had a guaranteed £32,000.

Joanne explained that they were going to split the money straight down the middle, 50 per cent for Mum and

Dad, and 50 per cent for her and her husband and baby daughter. 'But if we get to a higher amount than this,' she said, 'Mum and Dad say we can have it for a new house for their granddaughter.' It seemed more than generous, and they were well on the way.

This was the £64,000 question:

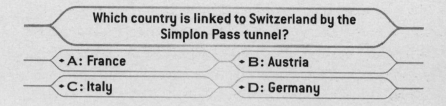

Which country is linked to Switzerland by the Simplon Pass tunnel?

A: France   B: Austria

C: Italy   D: Germany

'I remember going through the Simplon Pass on a school trip to Interlaken when I was fourteen,' said Joanne, 'but where were we?' She paused and then said, 'I'm sure we must have been going out of Italy.' 'Do we still get our £32,000?' Fred kept worrying. 'Yes,' I explained to him, 'that is absolutely guaranteed.' 'We can't lose it?' he said. 'No, Fred, you've got £32,000.'

'I'm sure it's Italy,' said Joanne. 'Phone Neil,' said Fred. 'We could go 50:50,' said Joanne. 'Oh come on, let's go for it,' said Fred. 'OK,' said Joanne, 'it's a joint decision. We are saying "Italy" is our final answer.' It was the right answer and Fred gave her a huge kiss. It was great to see such open affection between father and daughter.

'The next question is for £125,000,' I told them. 'Do we still get our £32,000?' said Fred. 'Yes, Fred, I've explained all that,' I said to him gently. 'Whatever happens, you leave here with £32,000.' Fred looked happier, but still concerned.

'Right, this is the question:'

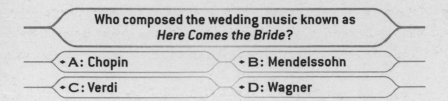

'I'm sure it's "Mendelssohn",' said Joanne, 'from *Midsummer Night's Dream*.' 'I really don't know,' said Fred, 'but we do still get our £32,000, don't we?' 'Yes,' I told him. 'Yes, Dad,' said Joanne patiently. 'OK then,' said Fred, 'shall we go for it, Joanne?' 'OK, let's go for it. Final answer – "Mendelssohn".' It went to orange, but sadly it was the wrong answer. The right answer was 'Wagner'.

'Oh Daddy, I'm so sorry,' said Joanne. 'Don't worry, dear,' said Fred. 'We've still got our £32,000, haven't we?' 'Yes,' I reassured him, and handed them the cheque.

They both went away grinning, holding hands and £32,000 better off, having had a real adventure.

Life After *Who Wants To Be A Millionaire?*

Talking about it after his eightieth birthday, Fred said their appearance on *Who Wants To Be A Millionaire?* was one of the best nights of his life and he still gets recognised all the time. They did split the money 50:50. Joanne put most of her money aside for daughter Emma. They all went on a family holiday to Austria for two weeks, and Fred is going to Italy soon with his wife. Doubtless while he is there he'll take time out to have a little drive through the Simplon Pass.

Peter Spyrides

Peter Spyrides came from Brentwood in Essex. His wife Catherine was with him in the audience; their two-year-old daughter Emma, who was clearly the pride of Peter's life, was back at home. Peter told me with obvious pride that Emma's joy at weekends was to go shopping with Daddy to the supermarket – not Mummy, or Mummy and Daddy – just Daddy. He said he used to work in 'cash management', whatever that is, but not any longer, he said. He'd got fed up with handling big cheques for other people.

His aim was to get up to the £32,000 mark – the family house desperately needed an extension and it was going to cost them around £30,000. If Peter did really well, he said, he also wanted a new car, a home cinema and a DVD player, while Catherine had put in a bid for an eternity ring. Peter wasn't sure about this because, he said, 'I don't think we've been together long enough.'

The early questions seemed fairly straightforward, although Peter was quite nervous. He kept looking at the computer screen as if it was full of gremlins. I've seen this a lot over the past four years. However much I reassure people that there are no trick questions on *Millionaire*, they often look most terrified in the early stages, and only calm down later – even though the money and the degree of risk is going up.

Peter got to £1000 by knowing that Barry, Maurice and Robin made up the Bee Gees. For the first time he relaxed and his face opened up in a great big grin. 'I feel much better now,' he said. 'I've got £1000, so I haven't made a complete fool of myself.' Peter was a big *Star Trek* fan, so the next question, for £2000, on just that subject gave him no problems either. Catherine also now seemed to be enjoying herself as she sat behind her husband smiling in the audience. Presumably she was thinking that the eternity ring was now a serious possibility – whether they'd been together long enough or not.

For £8000 I asked Peter:

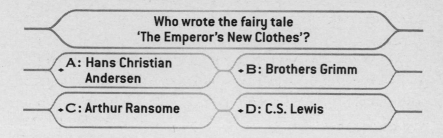

**Who wrote the fairy tale
'The Emperor's New Clothes'?**

A: Hans Christian Andersen   **B: Brothers Grimm**

C: Arthur Ransome   **D: C.S. Lewis**

'I'm fairly sure it is "A",' he said, 'but I think I'll check with the audience.' Sixty-eight per cent agreed with him and indeed 'Hans Christian Andersen' was the right answer. Catherine's grin was getting wider all the time.

But, at £16,000, Peter had to use a second Lifeline.

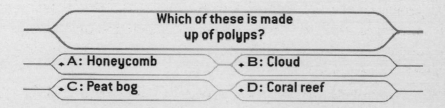

**Which of these is made
up of polyps?**

A: Honeycomb   **B: Cloud**

C: Peat bog   **D: Coral reef**

I admit unashamedly that I would have got this question wrong. 'I think it is "coral reef",' said Peter, 'but I'm not certain enough to risk it. I'm going to phone my friend Bruce.' Bruce also thought it was "coral reef", having emphasised to Peter he was not 100 per cent sure. Once the phone line went dead, though, Peter had no hesitation at all. 'I'll go with him,' he said. '"Coral reef" — final answer.' It was correct. I'd have been on my way home, but Peter had just won £16,000.

Question number ten was for the extension — £32,000:

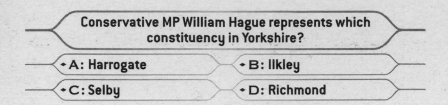

Conservative MP William Hague represents which constituency in Yorkshire?

- ◆ A: Harrogate
- ◆ B: Ilkley
- ◆ C: Selby
- ◆ D: Richmond

Peter had no doubts about this one. 'It's "Richmond", Chris,' he said. 'No question, final answer.' He was now guaranteed £32,000: the builders could start work on the extension and there might even be a couple of grand spare for a nice ring for Catherine. She was looking like the cat who got the cream.

Peter just sat very quietly smiling to himself, but his eyes opened wide at the next question:

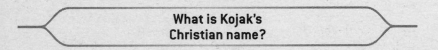

What is Kojak's Christian name?

Peter reminded me, 'My surname's Spyrides, which, as you may have guessed, is a Greek name: I have a Greek family. This is one of my father's favourite TV shows. Kojak's first name was Theodore.'

The stakes were getting higher. We had a look at the £125,000 question:

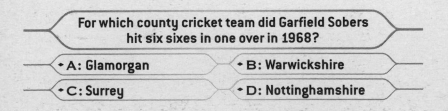

For which county cricket team did Garfield Sobers hit six sixes in one over in 1968?

- ◆ A: Glamorgan
- ◆ B: Warwickshire
- ◆ C: Surrey
- ◆ D: Nottinghamshire

Peter stared at me again with his great big eyes. 'I believe it is "Nottinghamshire",' he said, very slowly and deliberately, 'and I am going to play.' It was the right answer. Every cricket fan must have seen Gary's amazing over played again and again. It was one of the greatest feats of batting the world has ever seen.

At this point Peter was delighted, but Catherine was in tears. In fact she was so distraught that I didn't dare look up at her again. Her husband was on £125,000. I showed him the cheque. 'I'll just touch it,' he said, 'but I don't want to take it yet.'

For £250,000 he got this question:

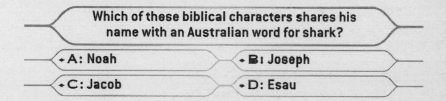

Which of these biblical characters shares his name with an Australian word for shark?

- A: Noah
- B: Joseph
- C: Jacob
- D: Esau

After some thought, Peter said to me, 'I'm thinking "Noah", but I'm just not sure how confident I am.' Catherine looked increasingly horrified. 'I'm going to play, Chris,' he decided. 'I'm sure the answer is "Noah".' It went to orange. Catherine now had her eyes clenched tightly shut – she seemed to be crying and praying all at the same time. 'It's the right answer!' I told Peter, really chuffed, and we did high fives. 'You've just won £250,000.' It is in fact rhyming slang. Noah – Noah's ark – shark.

Peter still wouldn't hold the cheque. 'I'm very superstitious,' he said. 'I didn't mind taking the £32,000 cheque because that one was guaranteed, but I don't want to touch any of these until I leave.'

This was the £500,000 question:

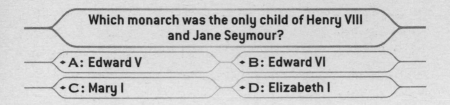

Which monarch was the only child of Henry VIII and Jane Seymour?

A: Edward V
B: Edward VI
C: Mary I
D: Elizabeth I

Peter eyeballed me again and said, slowly and precisely, 'It's "Edward VI", Chris.' There was a gasp from the audience at the enormity of what he might be risking; more tears were pouring down Catherine's cheeks. It went to orange. It went to green – right answer. Peter had just won £500,000. For a guy with a wife and a young daughter, who'd come on the show hoping to win just enough to build his extension, this was becoming unbelievable. 'It seems like a dream,' he said. 'I'm not really here.'

'Well, let me make your situation absolutely clear,' I said to him, with butterflies in my stomach, 'I'm now going to show you question number fifteen. You have got £500,000, if you give me the right answer to this you win £1,000,000. But if you give me a wrong answer you lose £468,000.' Peter let this sink in. 'Yes, Chris, that is absolutely crystal clear, thank you.'

We looked at the £1,000,000 question for only the sixth time in three years:

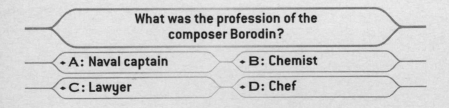

What was the profession of the composer Borodin?

A: Naval captain
B: Chemist
C: Lawyer
D: Chef

Peter looked at me again with that huge grin on his face, but I couldn't read him. He either knew it or he was going home. He soon put me out of my misery: 'I can categorically tell you that I don't have a clue. I'm going to take the money.' The audience gave him a standing ovation, and he strode off the set to join Catherine, who looked like a woman who'd seen a vision of hell, and then one of heaven!

Incidentally, the right answer was 'chemist'.

Life After *Who Wants To Be A Millionaire?*

Peter says his most vivid memory of the show is the look on Catherine's face at the very end when she came down to join him on the studio floor. I think if he had been sitting where I was sitting and had seen her face all the way through, he would have cut and run a lot earlier.

The Spyrides didn't bother with an extension – they bought a whole new house instead. They gave away some of the money to family and friends, and have invested the rest. Peter says, 'I still have to pinch myself about what actually happened that night. I now have a safe and secure future and I hope to take early retirement when I'm fifty. The great thing for both of us is that we have no need to worry about Emma's future.'

Colin Hallett

Colin Hallett was a window cleaner from Shoeburyness in Essex. One of the programme's strengths has always been the huge range of people that get on – and 'huge' was certainly one word for Colin. His appearance was further undermined by his very few teeth, which made him quite hard to understand. I suspect he has been the victim of a lot of mickey-taking and insults over the years. He certainly lacked self-confidence and, to be truthful, he seemed an unlikely candidate to make much money on the show. Never mind *Who Wants To Be A Millionaire?*, it seemed more likely to be *Who Wants To Make Enough Money to Buy a New Bucket*. Colin had a car well over twenty years old and he clearly had very little money. Window cleaning was his only source of income and 'These days,' he said, 'because of back trouble I can only do downstairs windows or bungalows.' He confided that he only earned, on average, about £5 a house and didn't manage to get round many houses in a week. We estimated that, at his rate of work, it would take him 128 years to make £1,000,000.

Colin was wearing what he described as his lucky green shirt, because he'd observed that green seemed to be what a lot of the big winners on the show wore. I must admit I hadn't ever spotted this, although since then I've noticed that, bizarrely, it does appear to be true. Then again, perhaps subsequent contestants have followed 'the lucky pattern'. Colin said to me that £32,000 would completely change his life. Frankly, he looked as if a hundred quid would change his life. With his great big frame squeezed into the chair, he looked strangely downtrodden and ill at ease as he kept peering at me uneasily through his glasses. But he got to £1000 with no real problems, answering questions on a range of topics, from AstroTurf to Ronald Reagan, to creatures that hunt truffles. I could tell that the audience were beginning to warm to him: they applauded him loudly when he got his first guaranteed amount. He responded with his big, toothy grin, but still he had a hunted look about him.

Nevertheless, the money for which he was playing kept quietly going up and up. On £8000 he got this question:

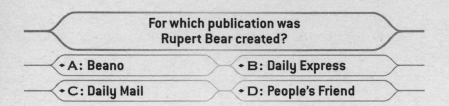

**For which publication was
Rupert Bear created?**

A: Beano

B: Daily Express

C: Daily Mail

D: People's Friend

Colin said, 'I think it's the "Express", but I'd better go 50:50.' This was the first Lifeline he'd used. Two wrong answers were removed by the computer and he was left with 'Beano' and 'Daily Express'. '"Daily Express",' he said with certainty. 'It's my final answer.' He'd won £16,000, having used only one Lifeline. For anybody, this was becoming a great night's work; for a window cleaner it was the stuff of dreams.

Colin had said quite openly at the top of the show that £32,000 would transform his life, so when the next question appeared we all held our breath:

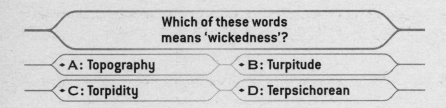

**Which of these words
means 'wickedness'?**

A: Topography

B: Turpitude

C: Torpidity

D: Terpsichorean

Colin looked terrified: he obviously wasn't at all sure of the answer. Words like this are hardly the sort of vocabulary you need when you work all day with a bucket and sponge. So he asked the audience what they thought. Fifty per cent of them said 'turpitude'; 40 per cent said 'torpidity'. Not a huge help. Having got up to £16,000, there now seemed to be a horrible possibility that Colin could lose £15,000, which would take him years to earn any other way.

'I'll Phone-A-Friend,' he decided. 'I'll phone Peter.' So we phoned Peter, who was amazed that I was calling. Like every Phone-A-Friend, he knew that he had to be on standby in case he was needed, but he clearly hadn't rated Colin's chances of making it into the hotseat. His first words were, 'You're joking, Chris – I never thought Hallett would make it.' 'Well, he has,' I told him, 'and your help could get him £32,000.'

Colin had thirty seconds to read out the four possible answers, but here was another problem. He obviously had real trouble reading. For such a bright bloke, I'm sure it's been a source of embarrassment to him all his life, and reading words like 'topography' and 'terpsichorean' is not exactly easy for anybody. For Colin it was a nightmare: he had to spell out every letter of every word and it took twenty-nine seconds for him to complete the question. With a second to go, Peter screamed, 'I think it's turpitude!' . . . and then the phone cut off.

It was the most frantic thirty seconds I can remember on the show. The audience and I were completely drained. 'I think it's "turpitude" as well,' said Colin quite calmly. 'I'm going for it.'

He was right! The audience went crazy and, for the first time, he looked really relaxed and gave everybody his enormous toothy grin. By now he had the whole country on his side and he had won the amount of money that he'd said would change his life. 'Will you carry on cleaning windows?' I asked him. 'Yes, I think I will,' he said, 'but only for exercise.'

'What else will you do?' I asked. 'I'll definitely move out of Shoeburyness,' he said. He clearly wasn't very happy there. 'Where will you go?' I said. 'Just somewhere that's not Shoeburyness,' he replied, with total honesty.

For the tourist board in Shoeburyness, this was a nightmare, but for Colin it was now the happiest night of his life.

The £64,000 question came up:

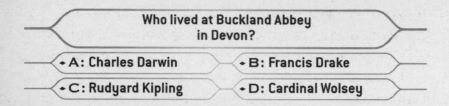

'I've got nothing to lose,' he said. 'I think it's "Sir Francis Drake".' He was absolutely right. Our window cleaner with his bad back and very few teeth, who could only clean downstairs windows for £5 a house, was now on £64,000. This was the very essence of what *Who Wants To Be A Millionaire?* is about.

The next question was for £125,000:

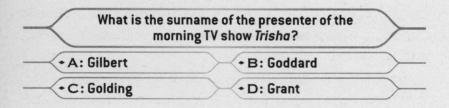

'I think it's "Goddard",' said Col. The audience gasped. I reminded him, very carefully, that he had £64,000 at this moment and that if he got this wrong he would lose £32,000. It was obviously a huge risk, but Colin Hallett saw it differently. 'That's all right,' he said. 'I only really wanted £32,000 anyway. I'm gonna play and I'm gonna play "Goddard". That's my final answer,' he mumbled at me through his gappy teeth.

I left him hanging, as I have done to so many others before, and we went for a commercial break. The audience were on the edge of their seats. When we came out of the break, I announced to Colin, 'You've just won £125,000!'

He could barely take it in – such a sum of money was clearly just too huge for him to get his head round. He looked distinctly punchy. He was still adamant that he was going to carry on cleaning windows, just for exercise, of course. With £125,000, I said to him, he could buy his own gymnasium. He grinned one final time. 'This is like a dream,' he said. 'I'll probably wake up in a minute.' But it wasn't – it was for real.

We peeked at the question that would take Colin to £250,000:

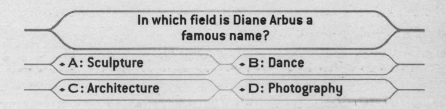

In which field is Diane Arbus a famous name?

A: Sculpture   B: Dance

C: Architecture   D: Photography

Colin, understandably, had no idea and he baulked at taking a punt on this one. (As all you photographers out there will know, 'D' was the correct answer.) So I got out my pen and happily wrote him his cheque, and off he went back to Shoeburyness, probably only to pack a case and get the hell out of there – £125,000 better off.

Paul Cleary

Paul Cleary was an amiable minicab driver from Peckham, south London. Just as he'd won Fastest Finger First, the klaxon went for the end of the show, so, although he knew he'd got into the hotseat he had to wait twenty-four hours to see his very first question.

He came back the following night really up for it. His girlfriend Belinda was sitting in the audience, her face lit up in anticipation of his big night. Paul had led a very diverse life. He'd travelled a lot; he had been a toilet-roll salesman and he'd worked in casinos as a blackjack dealer. He related the story of a single infamous night in one casino when a customer had won eight million quid, only to lose the whole lot a few hours later. All Paul Cleary wanted to do was make one million quid in a single night, and keep it.

He said if he won lots of money he would first clear Belinda's and his mortgages, and then he would take her for a night at the opera, but not just any old night at the opera – this one would take place at the Sydney Opera House. It was a beautiful dream and Paul was deadly serious about it. But his biggest ambition was, in his own words, 'to stop minicabbing as soon as I possibly can. If I win £32,000 tonight I'll be jumping for joy.'

He got to £1000 with no problem at all on this question:

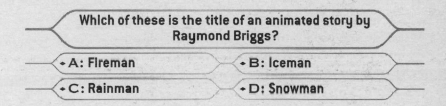

Which of these is the title of an animated story by Raymond Briggs?

◆ A: Fireman ◆ B: Iceman
◆ C: Rainman ◆ D: Snowman

Paul knew the answer straight away: it was 'Snowman'. 'A thousand pounds is a few days' minicabbing,' I said to him. 'Several weeks minicabbing actually,' he confided. Paul was clearly thoroughly enjoying his evening on the show. He kept grinning at me from behind his glasses.

The first time he paused at all was on the question for £2000:

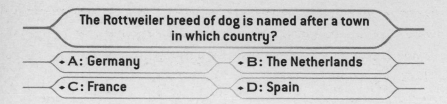

The Rottweiler breed of dog is named after a town in which country?

- ◆ A: Germany
- ◆ B: The Netherlands
- ◆ C: France
- ◆ D: Spain

Paul looked at his monitor long and hard and, after a long pause, said, 'I am tempted to Ask the Audience but I'm pretty sure I know what they'll say. I think it's "Germany" and I'm sure they all think it's "Germany" as well, which would make it a bit of a waste of a Lifeline!' This was a brave tactic, which was to become more significant later in the show. He was absolutely right – the Rottweiler dog does come from the German town of Rottweil.

He then steamed ahead to the £32,000 question, which was:

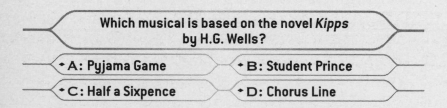

Which musical is based on the novel *Kipps* by H.G. Wells?

- ◆ A: Pyjama Game
- ◆ B: Student Prince
- ◆ C: Half a Sixpence
- ◆ D: Chorus Line

Paul was clearly a widely read man and he knew this at once. 'It's "Half a Sixpence,"' he told me, delighted. Belinda broke into a huge grin in the audience. Her boyfriend knew now he was going home with at least £32,000 and could probably knock minicabbing on the head as soon as he liked.

His face lit up as soon as the £64,000 question came up on his screen:

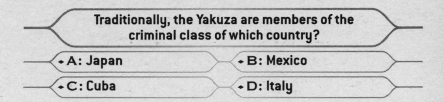

Traditionally, the Yakuza are members of the criminal class of which country?

◆ A: Japan   ◆ B: Mexico

◆ C: Cuba   ◆ D: Italy

'I've actually seen a film called *The Yakuza* and it's set in Japan,' Paul said, looking pleased. He was absolutely right. Like many taxi drivers, he had a lot of spare time on his hands and he obviously hadn't wasted it. He was now on £64,000, with all three Lifelines still available to him. 'How do you feel?' I asked him. 'Deliciously terrified,' he replied, which probably encapsulates perfectly the mixed emotions of so many contestants over the years on the show. He was on a roll – but it was going so well as to be frightening.

For £125,000, he got another movie question, which is quite rare on *Millionaire*: usually the computer tends to pick out a particular topic once during any given run of fifteen questions. But it does happen from time to time and with the knowledge of the movies that he'd already demonstrated, and no Lifelines used, it seemed likely that Paul was about to storm up to really big money. I liked him. He was a good lad and clearly very bright.

This was the question for £125,000:

In which 1985 film did Michael J. Fox play Scott Howard?

◆ A: Back to the Future   ◆ B: American Graffiti

◆ C: Teenwolf   ◆ D: Fame

Paul looked at the question for a long time and said to me, 'He's definitely not in 'American Graffiti', because that's one of my all-time favourite films. And he's certainly not in 'Fame'. He *is* in 'Back to the Future', but I really don't know about 'Teenwolf'. 'You're only three away from a million after this,' I told him. 'You've still got three Lifelines.' 'I know,' he said, thinking hard. 'No, I want to play. I'm sure it's "Back to the Future". Final answer.'

It was the wrong move, and wrong moves at this level are disastrous. I knew, and as I discovered afterwards, a large number of the audience knew, that the right answer was 'Teenwolf'. The movie had actually been on TV just a few nights before. I was absolutely gutted to have to break this to Paul and the whole of the audience gave a horrified gasp. I think we all thought we were about to make a Peckham minicab driver a millionaire. 'I can't believe I did that,' said Paul. 'Nor can I,' I said. I think I was almost as disappointed as he was.

He still went away with £32,000, but the tragedy was that he had had all three Lifelines to draw on. This was the highest amount of money anyone's ever got to and then lost without touching a Lifeline. We've had people using Lifelines on £200 and going on to win £125,000. Paul tried to hang on to his Lifelines for just one question too many, and the result was tragic.

However, as he said to me afterwards, 'Any night you go home £32,000 better off has got to be a good night.' Then again he knows, and we know, how close it was to being a 'great' night.

Life After *Who Wants To Be A Millionaire?*

Paul says that after the show he found he had two kinds of friends: those who congratulated him on his win, and those who called him a plonker for losing so much! But, as he says, he had the last laugh – he was the one who went home £32,000 better off, which has enabled him to buy a new house.

Roger Walker

Roger Walker was a printer from the little country village of Holmbury St Mary in Surrey. He had brought along his daughter Alex, who had that coy look that daughters get when they are concerned that their father is about to embarrass them. He told me, 'I went to the hairdressers especially for tonight. Alex refused to come with me unless I had my hair cut.' His son Rupert was at university and his wife Margery was at home with a cold. Roger didn't seem very sympathetic about this. In fact he said, 'I'm glad she's not here, because she would almost certainly come down from the audience and attack me if I give a wrong answer.' A scary-sounding lady. He said, 'I've been phoning the show on and off for years. I ring you up every time I feel broke and I'm particularly delighted that I've finally got on today as I've just had a really sniffy letter from my bank manager. To be honest,' he continued, 'I'm just here for a bit of cash. If I was lucky enough to get a decent amount, I would love to go to New York, walk the streets of Woody Allen's *Manhattan* and hire a car so I could drive Tony Soprano's route home.'

So Roger's plan was to make himself a few quid, get himself out of trouble with the bank manager and cut and run at the earliest opportunity. However, things didn't quite turn out like that.

He quickly got to £1000 answering this:

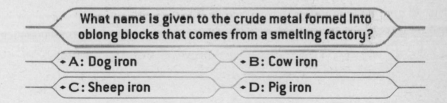

What name is given to the crude metal formed into oblong blocks that comes from a smelting factory?

A: Dog iron   B: Cow iron

C: Sheep iron   D: Pig iron

Roger knew straight away it was 'pig iron' and was tickled pink to find himself now a guaranteed £1000 better off. I got the impression that he hadn't won quite enough to placate the bank manager, but he still had three Lifelines, so there was every chance that there was more to come.

He had no problem with the next couple of questions either and said in disbelief that it felt very strange to be earning so much money so easily.

The first question that slowed him up was for £8000:

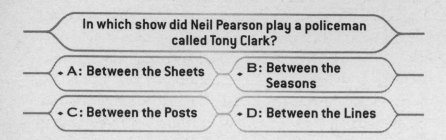

In which show did Neil Pearson play a policeman called Tony Clark?

A: Between the Sheets   **B: Between the Seasons**

C: Between the Posts   **D: Between the Lines**

He wasn't sure about this and decided to Ask the Audience. Eighty-five per cent chose 'Between the Lines'. A small percentage went for 'Between the Sheets'. Roger ignored such strangeness and went with 85 per cent of the audience to find himself on £8000.

But for £16,000 the computer threw up this stinker of a question:

Which of these is the name of a Roman palace in West Sussex?

Roger looked pretty confident when he saw the question, but the colour slowly drained from his cheeks as the four possible answers emerged:

A: Manbourne Palace   **B: Oxbourne Palace**

C: Fishbourne Palace   **D: Catbourne Palace**

'To be honest,' he said, 'I was expecting completely different choices and they're not there, so I haven't got the foggiest idea. I have heard of Fishbourne but I don't know if it is a palace and in fact I don't even know if it is in West Sussex. I'll Phone-A-Friend,' he said. 'I think I'll phone

Sarah.' Sarah wasn't very happy with this question either. 'I really don't know,' she said. 'As a guess I'd probably go for "Fishbourne". But,' she emphasised, 'it is only a guess.' Unsurprisingly, Roger was very hesitant about whether to play. 'I'll use up my 50:50,' he decided. 'Oxbourne' and 'Catbourne' were removed. 'Manbourne' and 'Fishbourne' remained. He ummed and erred. 'I'm still not at all sure,' he said eventually, 'but I did think it was "Fishbourne" and "Fishbourne" is still there, so I think I will go for it.' It was the right answer.

Roger now had £16,000 but no Lifelines. I could see he was itching to get out of that chair. However, the next question seemed to settle him somewhat:

What was the nickname of the actress of Lillie Langtry?

- A: Guernsey Lily
- B: Alderney Lily
- C: Sark Lily
- D: Jersey Lily

'It's "Jersey Lily" – final answer,' he said, sounding very sure. Roger was suddenly on a guaranteed £32,000. His bank manager must have been pleased, and Alex was certainly looking a lot less embarrassed by her father. Roger kept shaking his head in amazement. 'This is not happening to me,' he said. 'This is somebody else.'

He dispatched the £64,000 question with no problems and suddenly found himself looking at this, worth £125,000:

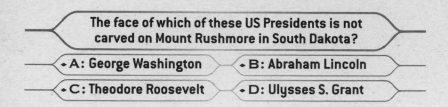

The face of which of these US Presidents is not carved on Mount Rushmore in South Dakota?

◆ A: George Washington   ◆ B: Abraham Lincoln

◆ C: Theodore Roosevelt   ◆ D: Ulysses S. Grant

Roger looked unhappy. He paused for what seemed an age. There was total silence in the studio. Then he started to articulate his thoughts: 'Washington and Lincoln are both definitely on Rushmore. My gut feeling is Ulysses S. Grant, but I don't know about Roosevelt.' He kept laughing in disbelief. 'I can't believe I'm even thinking about risking this sort of money,' he said. 'Then again, I'll be very happy if I leave here with £32,000. I'm going to go for "Ulysses S. Grant".' It went to orange. I wasn't at all sure myself, but eventually I dared to look down at my monitor, and there were the magic words 'right answer'.

Roger's head-shaking routine went into overdrive. 'I don't believe this,' he said. 'I'm pinching myself.' 'Get ready to run,' I said, 'but have a look at this next question first – it's worth £250,000.'

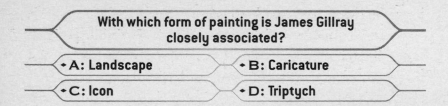

With which form of painting is James Gillray closely associated?

◆ A: Landscape   ◆ B: Caricature

◆ C: Icon   ◆ D: Triptych

'I think it's "caricature",' he said, 'but am I confident enough to risk losing this sort of money?' Alex certainly had hoped not. She had stuffed both hands into her mouth. I think she wanted to go home very badly. 'I'm 90 per cent sure it's "caricature",' said Roger, 'I have to say I'm so tempted, I'm going to play. "Caricature" – final answer.'

And with this Roger Walker, who'd only come 'for a bit of cash', was now £250,000 better off than just a few minutes before.

'You are amazingly brave,' I told him. 'Slightly mad but very brave. I think you'll find your bank manager will have a whole new attitude to you when you see him tomorrow morning with this cheque in your hand.'

Roger continued to shake his head in disbelief. 'You might as well have a look at this,' I told him, 'It's worth £500,000.'

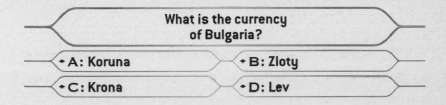

What is the currency of Bulgaria?

A: Koruna   B: Zloty
C: Krona   D: Lev

'It's "the lev",' said Roger immediately. There was a simultaneous intake of breath from two hundred people in the audience. '"Zloty" is Poland, "krona" is Denmark or somewhere up there in Scandinavia, and "koruna" I've never heard of. I'm going to go for "lev".'

To wolf whistles and applause, I told Roger he had just won £500,000. He was about to join the very small band of contestants who have looked at a £1,000,000 question.

Which of these is a butterfly not a moth?

A: Mother Shipton   B: Red underwing
C: Burnished brass   D: Speckled wood

'I've really no idea,' he said. 'If I was brave I would go for "Red underwing", but I think I've been too brave already. I'm going to take the money. It's been absolutely fantastic.' He was still shaking his head as he left the studio. But before he left, I was able to tell him, 'If only you had been a little bit braver and had gone for "Red underwing" – and you have to admit your hunches have been pretty good right through this evening – you would have . . . lost £468,000! The right answer was "Speckled wood".'

Life After *Who Wants To Be A Millionaire?*

Roger says the money has made an enormous difference to his life. It has alleviated the horrendous financial pressures that were weighing on him, and has meant that he can actually enjoy his work. He and his wife have finally been able to do up their family home – an old, derelict stables – and turn it into the house they've always wanted.

Den Hewitt

Den Hewitt, a civil servant from Chester-le-Street in
County Durham, must be one of the biggest fans of
Millionaire we've ever had on the show. He had been
trying to get on for nearly four years. He'd been trying
even before we had even started broadcasting – he had
seen some publicity about it and had immediately rung up
to see if he could be a contestant. Somebody explained to
him that it wasn't quite as simple as that and he would
have to wait until we opened the phone lines. Den had
been ringing on and off ever since.

He worked as a computer programmer but his real ambition was to be an actor – he'd done a few bit parts and his
life's dream was to go into acting full time. He still lived at
home with his mum Vera, who was up in the audience. He
told me that of course the money would be handy, to put it
mildly. But more than anything he wanted to get to the
£1,000,000 question for a sense of achievement. I've

encountered this with quite a few of the contestants over the years – rich or not, they want to get all fifteen questions right and beat the computer almost more than winning a million.

Den was clearly a bright guy. He was very focused and he didn't pause for breath until he got to £2000:

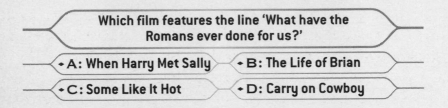

Which film features the line 'What have the Romans ever done for us?'

- A: When Harry Met Sally
- B: The Life of Brian
- C: Some Like It Hot
- D: Carry on Cowboy

Den broke into a big grin for the first time. 'I know this one, no problem. It's one of my favourite films. It's the Monty Python team in "The Life of Brian".' Absolutely correct, for £2000.

He sailed through questions on David Ginola and Dostoevsky, so, on £8000, I remarked to him that things were looking very promising – perhaps he could now afford his career change and think about starting life all over again as an actor. 'I'd love to,' said Den, 'but I don't want to end up like Robert De Niro or Mel Gibson. What I would really love, my absolute dream, is to become someone like Sam Kidd – the greatest actor of all time.' For those of you who don't know about Sam Kidd – probably rather a lot of you – he was a famous character actor in the forties, fifties and sixties who seems to pop up briefly in pretty well every film of that era. He played anything and everything, from a bicycle-repair man to a hot-dog salesman. Den, who had already had two small parts on television as a policeman and a corpse, was adamant that if he did make enough money, he would do his best to replicate Kidd's career.

At £8000 he got this question:

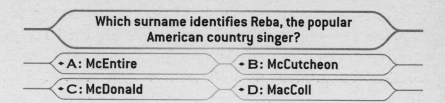

Which surname identifies Reba, the popular American country singer?

◆ A: McEntire ◆ B: McCutcheon

◆ C: McDonald ◆ D: MacColl

Den paused and thought about using a Lifeline. 'No, I'll save them for later,' he decided. 'I think it's "McEntire". It rings a bell. I'm gonna play. Reba McEntire.'

He was riding his luck, but he was absolutely spot on. He'd got to £16,000 and he still had three Lifelines intact. Then the klaxon rang out for the end of the show and Den and Vera went away for an early night, knowing that he was just one question away from £32,000.

As we started recording the following evening, Den said something very odd: 'I've had a premonition about the £1,000,000 question and my premonitions are surprisingly good.' Ignoring my look of surprise, he continued, 'I genuinely believe that I know what the question will be, if I get that far . . . and I've gone to the trouble of writing it down on a piece of paper, with the correct answer. It's in my trouser pocket.'

This was spooky stuff. None of us have any idea what a £1,000,000 question will be on any particular night because it's locked away in the computer. But if it had mirrored whatever was in Den's pocket the press would have had a field day. It would have looked like the most enormous fix, yet there was no way that Den could have got the information from any source, short of witchcraft. It was riveting. I was dying for him to get to £500,000 so we could compare my computer screen with the contents of his trouser pocket. In the meantime, the £32,000 question:

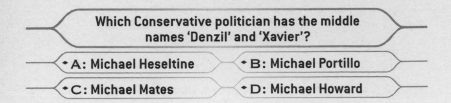

Which Conservative politician has the middle names 'Denzil' and 'Xavier'?

- A: Michael Heseltine
- B: Michael Portillo
- C: Michael Mates
- D: Michael Howard

At last Den had to resort to using a Lifeline. He asked the audience and 84 per cent remembered that 'Denzil Xavier' were the middle names chosen by the parents of Michael Portillo. Poor Michael, but lucky Den! Right answer, he'd got to £32,000. The audience clapped as enthusiastically as Den, and Vera smiled.

The next question was brought up on the screen:

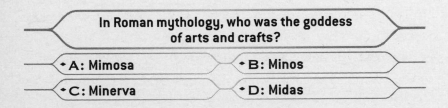

In Roman mythology, who was the goddess of arts and crafts?

- A: Mimosa
- B: Minos
- C: Minerva
- D: Midas

'I think I know this,' said Den, 'but I want to use my 50:50.' The computer took two away; 'Mimosa' and 'Minerva' remained. 'My answer's still there,' he said. '"Minerva" is the only one I've ever heard of and I'm going to go for her.' It was the right answer. He had won £64,000. Perhaps we were going to see the contents of his trouser pocket after all.

His next question for £125,000 was:

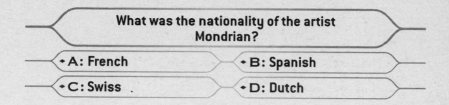

What was the nationality of the artist Mondrian?

- A: French
- B: Spanish
- C: Swiss
- D: Dutch

'I've no idea about this one,' said Den. 'I'll phone John,' 'OK,' I said. 'Do you want me to tell him how much money is involved?' 'Absolutely not,' replied Den, 'it might spook him.' So I phoned John and used my usual formula of saying Den was doing 'quite well' without actually telling him how well.

When Den had finished reading the question John said, very positively, 'He's Dutch – absolutely definitely.' 'I'll play "Dutch" then,' said Den, and it was correct.

We went to the £250,000 question. As soon as it came up on the screen Den smiled. So did I, inwardly, because if he got this right, we were only one away from seeing the secret bit of paper in his pocket.

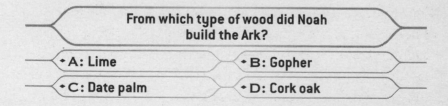

From which type of wood did Noah build the Ark?

- A: Lime
- B: Gopher
- C: Date palm
- D: Cork oak

'I know this one,' said Den. 'It's "gopher".' 'Are you a very religious man?' I asked him. 'I am now,' he quipped at the top of his voice, to howls of laughter from the audience. It was the right answer.

By now, half the British Isles were dying to see Den's

little £1,000,000 memo. We were almost there, and this was the £500,000 question:

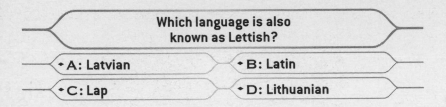

Den looked at it long and hard and then said to me, disappointed, 'I'm really sorry, Chris, but you're not going to see my piece of paper.' I was gutted. 'It's just too much money,' he said. 'I'm going to cut and run. But if you did push me, I would say "Latvian".'

It was a shame I didn't push him, since if he had said "Latvian", he would have been cheered away £500,000 better off, and my curiosity about Den's premonition would have been satisfied. To my eternal regret, he never did tell me what was written down in his pocket – even in the bar afterwards with celebrations in full swing.

Life After *Who Wants To Be A Millionaire?*

Den says his lasting memory of the night was trying to push the buttons on Fastest Finger First and missing one first time around, so he was sure it wasn't going to be his night. He has bought a brand-new car and is looking for a new house. He has invested some of the money so that it is, in his own words, 'out of harm's way'. He wants to do a lot more TV and film work now that he can get the time off that he needs to pursue his dream of becoming an actor like Sam Kidd.

Carol Vorderman

arol Vorderman was the first celebrity ever to come
on *Who Wants To Be A Millionaire?* to play for charity. Paul Smith and I had big reservations about charity
programmes. Not, of course, because we have any problem with making donations to charities, but because we
dreaded somebody answering a string of questions correctly and then losing the lot on behalf of their chosen
charity. It had already happened in a couple of other countries and we didn't think it was fair on the show, the
celebrity or the charity.

However, we agreed to try it as a one-off experiment,
very much on the understanding that the celebrities could
cut and run at any level they liked and that no allowances
were made in how we played the game. The credibility of
the show would be completely undermined if I'd been
given the chance to say, 'Well, you said "B". The right
answer is actually "D", but it's for charity so, hey, that's

near enough.' So my brief was to give no extra help whatsoever.

Having Carol for the first-ever charity show was a huge bonus. She is obviously very intelligent but also has a lot of common sense – she would know exactly the right point to bite her lip and take the money. She came on looking magnificent in leather – why do I still remember that? – and I asked her how she felt. 'Absolutely desperate,' she replied.

The show was to be a major focal point of ITV's Year of Promise, in which many different celebrities promised to do all sorts of things to raise money for charity. Carol was committed to a charity called Express Link-Up, of which she is a patron. Their goal was to buy at least five hundred computers for children in hospitals, many of them with long-term, even terminal illnesses. She explained to us that with diseases like leukaemia kids were stuck in hospital for months, even years, and some of them, tragically, for the rest of their lives. Computers made a huge difference to the quality of their lives, enabling them to communicate with their friends via email and continue their education on the internet, both of which gave them a huge psychological boost. Carol told us that each computer cost about £1000, so every correct answer she might give would be quantifiable in terms of equipment for the kids.

In the audience were her mum Jean and her sister Trixie. She confided to us that her weak areas of general knowledge were movies, but then added, 'I'm not great at pop music either. And I'm not very strong on sport.' I did point out to her that this cut out most of the questions she was likely to get and unless something came up about algebra or logarithms, it was going to be a bit of a thin old night. It didn't help either that her first question, for £100, was about films. She looked at me in horror. I pointed out that it was probably quite good to get a film question this early, because the earlier they are the easier they should be. This was certainly a good example.

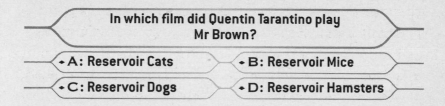

In which film did Quentin Tarantino play Mr Brown?

◆ A: Reservoir Cats   ◆ B: Reservoir Mice

◆ C: Reservoir Dogs   ◆ D: Reservoir Hamsters

As the possible answers came up on the screen her look of horror changed to one of relief. 'It's "Reservoir Dogs",' she said. 'Of course it is – it certainly wasn't going to be "Reservoir Hamsters", was it?' I asked, and Carol was on her way with a hundred quid.

For £1000 she got this question:

Which creature is the larval stage of a butterfly?

◆ A: Tadpole   ◆ B: Caterpillar

◆ C: Hopper   ◆ D: Leatherjacket

She said, 'I know this, it's a caterpillar.' Express Linkup were now one computer better off.

Carol raced on to £8000 and this was the first time she got stuck:

Muhammad departed from Mecca to which city?

◆ A: Medina   ◆ B: Jerusalem

◆ C: Damascus   ◆ D: Bethlehem

Carol looked worried for the first time. 'It's not "Bethlehem",' she said, 'and it's not "Jerusalem". I don't think it's "Damascus" either. I think it must be "Medina",' she said, 'but the worry is, I'm just not certain. Perhaps I'll Phone-A-Friend.' 'Who are you going to phone?' I asked. 'Richard Whitely,' she announced, to strange, excited giggles from women in the audience. What is the magic of Whitely, or, as one tabloid headline called him: 'Richard "Twice-Nightly" Whitely'? How come some women see him as some kind of love god? It's a great puzzle to me! 'Will he still be awake?' I asked her, bearing in mind this was an early-evening recording. 'Oh yes,' she said, 'he'll be waiting for my call – pipe, slippers and a mug of cocoa by his side.' I rang Richard, a really nice bloke whom I've known for years, and I told him, 'I've got Carol Vorderman here, she's playing for charity.' 'That's marvellous,' answered Whitely. 'How's the old bird doing?' 'She's doing OK,' I told him, 'but this is now serious money, it's worth £8000 and a wrong answer could mean the end of a beautiful relationship that's lasted more than eighteen years.'

Carol came to the phone to read Richard the question and the four possible answers. He erred and ummed but, staggeringly, never actually managed to give her any indication of the answer before the thirty seconds ran out. It was almost unbelievable. We all stared aghast. It was a terrible waste of a Lifeline and Richard Whitely had been a total waste of space. Urgency is clearly not one of his greatest strengths.

'Well, I'll have to go 50:50 now,' Carol said. The computer left 'Medina' and 'Damascus'. 'It would be so embarrassing if I guessed the wrong answer,' she said. 'Well then, don't,' I told her.

I offered: 'Four thousand pounds is still four computers and a great result.' 'No,' said Carol. 'If I'm wrong I'll raise it some other way. I'm so sorry, kids, I really can't walk away from this, I cannot bottle out at £4000. I think it's "Medina". I've never, ever been there, I'll probably never want to go there after this, but I'm still going to go for "Medina" – final answer.'

We went to orange on the computer – it was the right answer. Carol Vorderman had got to £8000 and I gave her a great big snog – for purely professional reasons, you understand.

For £16,000 she got this question:

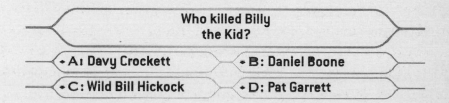

Who killed Billy
the Kid?

A: Davy Crockett   B: Daniel Boone
C: Wild Bill Hickock   D: Pat Garrett

'I've absolutely no idea,' said Carol. 'I think I'll Ask the Audience.' Seventy-five per cent of them said 'Pat Garrett'. Carol still looked unconvinced. 'The trouble is, it means nothing to me.' 'It's a very high percentage,' I said, having read all my cowboy comics as a kid and knowing full well that 'Pat Garrett' was the right answer. 'Yes,' Carol replied, 'but Pat Garrett could be a footballer for all I know. My problem is that I'm very impulsive. Seventy-five per cent is very high. Using my mathematical training, the elements of probability are considerable. It's therefore probably right. If I lose £7000, kids, I promise somehow I will work extra hard to get it back for you . . . OK, my final answer is "Pat Garrett".'

It was the right answer. She had now won £16,000.

Carol began to wave her arms at me like some sort of demented duck. I made no comment, just sat there looking bemused.

The next question would guarantee her £32,000, but could also lose her charity Express Linkup £15,000:

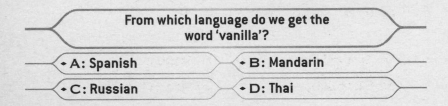

From which language do we get the word 'vanilla'?

A: Spanish   B: Mandarin

C: Russian   D: Thai

'Well, I think it's "Spanish",' she said. 'It just sort of sounds Spanish – *vanneeeeyyya*.' I wasn't sure of the answer myself on this one, but I reckoned she was probably right. 'If I don't play and it is "Spanish",' she said, 'frankly, Chris Tarrant, I can't be responsible for my actions.' This was quite alarming. I began to sympathise with Richard Whitely having to put up with this every day. Carol could be a scary woman! 'I think I have to play,' she said. 'Final answer – "Spanish".' 'You've just won £32,000!' I told her.

Trixie and Mum stood up on their seats and cheered wildly; Carol looked absolutely blissful – battered but blissful. And £32,000 meant thirty-two new computers. 'I'm so happy,' she said and then suddenly punched the air with her fist and went, 'Yes! Yes! Come on, ask me who painted the *Mona Lisa*. "Leonardo da Vinci" is the answer, Chris. Thank you.'

This was all very well but it was sadly nothing to do with the next question. However, for £64,000, with no Lifelines remaining, she did get this question, which was nearly as good:

In which county is the city of Lichfield?

'I know it,' she said. 'It's near Stoke.' 'So what's the answer,' I asked her?' 'Not sure,' she said. 'Put them up on the screen.' So dutifully up they came:

- ◆ A: Cambridgeshire
- ◆ B: Staffordshire
- ◆ C: Shropshire
- ◆ D: Gloucestershire

'It's Staffordshire,' she said straight away. She was quite right. For the first ever of our charity specials, this was magnificent. 'Sixty-four thousand pounds,' said Carol in wonder. 'This will make such a big difference. Sixty-four computers for those kids. We need a million, but sixty-four is a brilliant start.' It certainly was, but up came the next question for £125,000.

'You don't have to play this,' I said to Carol, 'but you might as well have a look before you take your nice big cheque away.'

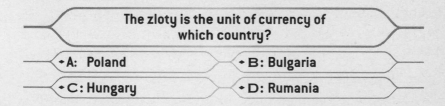

The zloty is the unit of currency of which country?

- ◆ A: Poland
- ◆ B: Bulgaria
- ◆ C: Hungary
- ◆ D: Rumania

Carol looked carefully at the question. 'It's "Poland",' she murmured. 'It's "Poland", it's "Poland", it's "Poland". It's going to be "Poland". I'm sure it's "Poland". My final answer is "Poland".' She closed her eyes. Trixie and Mum also closed their eyes and crossed themselves. It was the right answer. Carol Vorderman had just won a fantastic £125,000! There were tears in her eyes, and she really did look as if she had been through the Spanish Inquisition, but that's the sort of effect I seem to have on women!

I was really impressed by what she'd done and how she'd handled the stress of playing for money that wasn't hers. The next question was for £250,000, but she said to me straight away, 'I'm not playing unless I know the answer.'

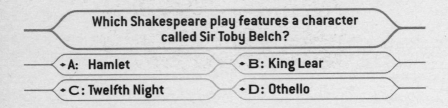

Which Shakespeare play features a character called Sir Toby Belch?

◆A: Hamlet ◆B: King Lear
◆C: Twelfth Night ◆D: Othello

Carol couldn't help but be tempted by the prospect of even more money for the kids. 'It's not "Hamlet",' she said. 'It's not "Lear". I think it's probably "Twelfth Night".' Then a look of real fear came into her eyes. 'It's too much,' she said. 'I'm not prepared to risk losing whatever £125,000 is minus £32,000.' 'You should know,' I said, 'you're sup-posed to be the mathematician!' 'Oh yes,' she said, '£93,000. I really, really can't risk it. I'm going to take the money.'

If ever there was a personality who could make the first of our celebrity specials such fun, perhaps not for herself but for us, and certainly for Express Link-Up, it was Carol Vorderman. She had been magnificent. She went away with £125,000 and the kids who benefited in hospitals all over the United Kingdom are now at least 125 brand-new computers better off.

Oh, and incidentally, 'Twelfth Night' was the right answer.

Jonathan Ross and Jane Goldman

'This is the single worst moment of my life!' These were the words of Jonathan Ross, who came on *Who Wants To Be A Millionaire?* with his beautiful wife Jane Goldman and got stuck solid at £8000.

Considering the pressure he's lived under for years, presenting countless hours of live TV and radio, effortlessly fronting unpredictable nights like the Comedy Awards, Jonathan seemed to be feeling a great deal of stress from the moment he walked into the studio. He described Fastest Finger First as 'a torture chamber', and when he finally got into the chair, looked horrified. Jane, a writer and journalist, seemed altogether more composed. But then after living with Jonathan, their kids Betty, Harvey and Honey, two iguanas, a cat, a ferret, various chinchillas, a python and two salamanders (Mulder and Scully), coming on *Who Wants To Be A Millionaire?* must have been an oasis of calm from the chaos of her normal world.

Their aim was to earn as much as they could for two charities — Tommy's, a charity that researches into and counsels on premature birth, miscarriage and stillbirth, and the Lowe Syndrome Trust, who try to do whatever they can for families of those suffering from this rare genetic condition that causes physical and mental handicap.

Jonathan and Jane watch the show regularly. 'We often play along at home,' he said, 'and I always pretend I know the answers. Even when I don't, I lie and pretend that I do. We've even got the computer game.' Considering he had had so much practice, and is an intelligent bloke, I couldn't think why Jonathan looked so worried. But once he'd started playing, it slowly became clear.

The two of them had no problems with the first few questions, and for £1000 up came this:

> **Which is the only one of these sports to use a ball?**
>
> A: Ice hockey   B: Squash
>
> C: Badminton   D: Curling

'That'll be number "B" then,' said Jonathan, from which I took it that he meant 'squash'. It was the right answer and they were guaranteed at least £1000.

But at £2000 this question came out of the woodwork and stopped both of them in their tracks:

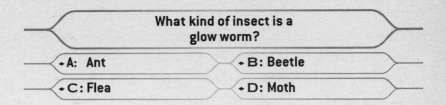

What kind of insect is a glow worm?

- ◆ A: Ant
- ◆ B: Beetle
- ◆ C: Flea
- ◆ D: Moth

'I'm not certain,' said Jonathan, 'but I'd guess it's a kind of moth. If only we could phone David Attenborough – he'd know!' 'We could Ask the Audience,' said Jane brightly. 'A complete waste of time,' Jonathan retorted. 'I've seen these people with the lights up! Let's go 50:50.' He was clearly the master tactician of the two, and though it had seemed pretty certain that they would go for 'moth', it was lucky they went for 50:50 instead, as the computer left 'beetle' or 'flea'!

'I said it was a beetle or flea,' said Jonathan, fooling nobody. 'It won't be a flea,' said Jane. 'A flea would be too small to glow!' Frankly they were making less sense by the second and I told them so. 'When did you last see a glow worm?' Jane asked me. 'Last night,' I shot back, lying through my teeth.

'We'll Phone-A-Friend,' Jonathan decided for them. 'But who on earth could we phone? There's no point ringing Mum, she only knows about *EastEnders*. What about Frank Skinner – he knows the oddest things. We could try Vic Reeves, but he'll probably say the answer's "cheese".' Frankly, sitting opposite the pair of them, I was beginning to lose the will to live!

'Why didn't I stay in bed tonight?' said Jonathan. 'We're idiots. Why didn't somebody warn us? How can we be in such a state at two grand?' However, eventually they agreed to go for it. 'Final answer – "beetle", "beetle", "beetle", "beetle".' Mercifully, after all that, 'beetle' was the right answer!

Everything went swimmingly for at least another couple of minutes and then, on £8000, they got asked this:

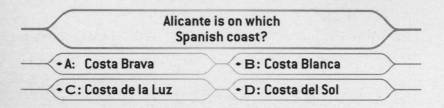

Alicante is on which
Spanish coast?

A: Costa Brava

B: Costa Blanca

C: Costa de la Luz

D: Costa del Sol

'We've never been on a Spanish sunshine holiday,' said Jonathan. 'But I wish we had now. Paella. Donkeys. If only we'd tried them. We're going to have to use a Lifeline. OK, I'm going to Ask the Audience, and if you get this wrong we'll never, ever speak to any of you again.'

The vote was fairly split among the four possibilities, but the majority – 52 per cent – went for Costa Blanca. 'This is desperate,' said Jonathan. 'We can't risk losing £7000. We might have to Phone-A-Friend. Let's ring your dad,' he said to Jane. 'He might know about Spain. He's called Stuart – he's a bit of a party animal. Knows where all the raves are. Stays up all night. Let's ask him.'

We rang Stuart. He spoke to me politely in an educated voice. Jane told him the question and four possible answers, but after thirty seconds Stuart had come up with nothing and we were none the wiser. Jonathan was almost apoplectic. 'Your bloody father!' he exclaimed. 'He knew nothing, and he put on a posh voice. He's never, ever spoken like that before in his life. This is desperate. We have done so pathetically badly. And as for your father – and I thought your *mum* was bad. I'll never talk to any of your family again!'

'Oh, come on, let's go for it', said Jane briskly. 'Fifty-two per cent of the audience say "Costa Blanca", we should at least try and get these poor charities £8000. Final answer – "Costa Blanca".'

Fifty-two per cent of the audience were right! Jonathan and Jane had somehow clawed their way to the princely sum of £8000.

But the computer was not finished with them yet. For £16,000, up came this little beauty:

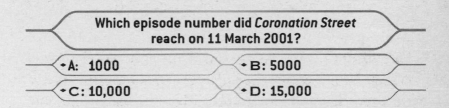

Which episode number did *Coronation Street* reach on 11 March 2001?

A: 1000   B: 5000
C: 10,000   D: 15,000

If I'd asked them the formula for splitting the atom, they couldn't have been more horrified. 'I haven't the foggiest idea,' said Jonathan. 'I haven't seen *Corrie Street* for months. But hold on, perhaps we can work this out. Fifty weeks in a year . . .' 'Fifty-two,' corrected Jane pedantically. 'I'm just rounding it up to fifty,' said Jonathan impatiently, 'so the audience can try and follow this. So, fifty weeks in a year; it's on about twice a week; it's been going for forty years. I think it's "10,000".'

'I feel sick,' said Jane. 'I feel ashamed of ourselves,' countered Jonathan. 'You don't have to play this question,' I reminded them. 'It must be "B" or "C",' said Jonathan. 'It can't be "D". "D" would just be silly. "D" is nonsense. Five thousand seems too few. It's gonna be "C" – 10,000 episodes. Please let it be the right answer. God have mercy on our souls.'

Their final answer went to orange and they both closed

their eyes in prayer. When they opened them again, it gave me no pleasure at all to pass on to them the disastrous news that it was completely wrong. There was a disappointed groan from the audience. Jonathan's face took on the startled, terrified look of a rabbit caught in headlights. 'I'm afraid the right answer is "5000". You've just lost £15,000.' They both looked genuinely devastated.

They had been immensely entertaining, though, and by taking a risk and going for it, with great courage and real humour, they'd done something that we'd always feared might happen one day – lose a charity a lot of money. But then the charities understand the risks; they start with nothing and anything they receive as a result of the celebrities is a bonus. Jonathan and Jane were still able to hand over a cheque for £1000 to Tommy's and the Lowe Syndrome Trust.

In fact it was a great night for charity: on that one evening alone, we raised £129,000. One thousand pounds came from Jonathan and Jane . . . and £128,000 came from the other contestants!

David Baddiel and Frank Skinner

Two of the most entertaining celebrities that we've had on a charity special have to be David Baddiel and Frank Skinner. The whole show, which spread across two nights, was a hoot from beginning to end but, just like everybody else, once the money started getting serious, the strain was written all over their faces.

David and Frank were playing for the Catholic Children's Society and the Imperial Cancer Research Fund. I was surprised at how well they both knew the show. For some reason I always assume that showbiz people are too busy to watch television – I know I usually am. But Baddiel and Skinner seemed to be great fans. So much so that Frank could even sing the theme music, which he insisted on doing throughout the early questions. (He was actually rather good!)

They began by complaining about how high the chairs were. David claimed he had a real fear of heights, and said that the hotseat wasn't helping his nerves one bit; Frank accused me of making him feel like a Thunderbird. I had no idea whether they were going to be any good or not. 'I'm the more intelligent one because I wear glasses,' said David – which, looking at Frank's inane grinning expression, I decided might not be too hard!

This particular show was made at Christmas, and at £500 they got this question:

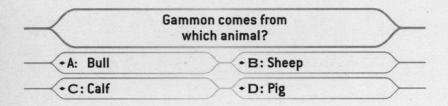

Gammon comes from which animal?

- A: Bull
- B: Sheep
- C: Calf
- D: Pig

'You're not allowed to answer this one,' Frank joked to his Jewish mate. 'It's Christmas after all – it's our time! It's "pig",' he proclaimed to a wincing Baddiel, and 'pig' was the right answer.

For £1000 they got this question:

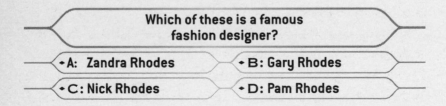

Which of these is a famous fashion designer?

- A: Zandra Rhodes
- B: Gary Rhodes
- C: Nick Rhodes
- D: Pam Rhodes

'As you can tell,' said David, 'we are at the very cutting edge of fashion.' To be honest, they looked more like a couple of dossers who'd ambled in off the streets of Borehamwood, but they did manage to answer correctly. 'It's Zandra Rhodes,' they told me. They had £1000, we all cheered and the klaxon rang.

They came back on Boxing Day, and chatted amiably about how scary they'd found the night before. They also described their famous flat-sharing years together, when they'd lived in a pigsty of a place, talked non-stop about football and had eventually decided to turn the experience into a TV show. They were now living in the same road. 'We bought a road,' said Frank rather grandly. Well, not quite – David lived at number one and Frank lived at number five. You had to feel deep sympathy for the poor devil living at number three.

After more ramblings, we got back to business and Frank 'n' Dave went skipping through a couple of early questions until they got to this for £8000:

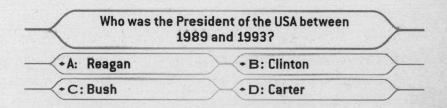

Who was the President of the USA between 1989 and 1993?

A: Reagan
B: Clinton
C: Bush
D: Carter

'I'm fairly sure it's "Bush",' said David. Frank didn't look so convinced. 'Who was the one with the small beard who was shot at the theatre?' asked Frank. 'That was Abraham Lincoln,' I said, with just a hint of exasperation in my voice, 'and he's not one of the choices.' 'I'm sure that George Bush followed Ronald Reagan,' said David. 'That was just a rumour,' replied Frank. 'Even if the answer's wrong,' David threw back, 'at least it gave you a chance to get that joke in. We'll go 50:50.' This was the first Lifeline they had actually needed. It left Clinton or Bush. 'It's definitely "Bush",' said David. 'Final answer.' It was the right answer.

They were now starting to get rather excited. Suddenly,

after a slow but entertaining start, they were playing for a cheque for £32,000 with this question:

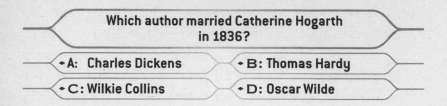

Which author married Catherine Hogarth in 1836?

A: Charles Dickens   B: Thomas Hardy

C: Wilkie Collins   D: Oscar Wilde

'I'm not very good at marriage,' said Frank sadly. 'Mine only lasted ten months. We still had cake left!' 'Let's Phone-A-Friend,' said David, ignoring Frank's marital woes. 'We should ring Tracy,' said Frank. 'Who's going to talk to her?' I asked. 'Me,' said David. 'No, me,' said Frank. 'Why should you talk to her?' I have to say that who is going to talk to the Phone-A-Friend has never been a problem before. With these two everything became a problem.

Eventually Frank won and it was agreed that he would talk to Tracy, whoever she was. After all the build-up Tracy didn't know the answer, and so we were back to square one. After some consultation Frank announced, 'It's "Dickens" or "Hardy", and Dave's sure it's not "Hardy", so it must be "Dickens". Go on, that's our final answer.' 'We'll take a break,' I replied to the horror of both of them.

We try to do the breaks in real time, so it's a genuine two and a half minutes. The contestants stay seated throughout, while I go for a walk round the back to talk to the floor manager. When I sat down again to face the lads, Frank looked absolutely terrified. 'This is terrible,' he said when we were back on air. 'It's such a huge amount of money to lose, not for me you understand – £32,000 to me, well, pah, £32,000 for me – I'd spend that on a jacket, but for those poor charities . . .' He was hilarious, but clearly very much on edge. 'Stop talking,' I told him. 'You've just won £32,000.'

Frank and David were doing brilliantly and had made me and the audience laugh pretty well non-stop, but they weren't finished yet. I did remind David that he had a university double first in English. 'Oh don't bring that up now,' he said, 'not after the last question.'

The next one, for £64,000, was on an altogether different topic:

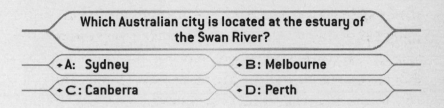

Which Australian city is located at the estuary of the Swan River?

A: Sydney
B: Melbourne
C: Canberra
D: Perth

Frank said, 'I'm really not sure, let's Ask the Audience. There's some policemen in the audience tonight. A lot of criminals were sent to Australia. They are bound to know.' Thirty-nine per cent of the audience, a majority but only a small one, thought it was 'Perth'. 'Hang on,' said Frank, 'when you are in Australia there are big signs everywhere for Swan lager, so wherever this place is, it will be the home of the big Swan brewery right next to the Swan match factory.' He was rambling, but it got a lot worse. 'Canberra is the capital city. A lot of people get very thirsty in capital cities – they'd need a drink, so they'd think of this, can . . . can of lager . . . canbeera, can of beer. It's a sign,' he said. 'There's something coming through to me from the other side.'

David looked at him blankly and said, 'This is all very well, but I think it's "Perth".' Frank looked suitably crestfallen. 'Hang on,' he said, 'isn't "Perth" what Chris Eubank keeps his money in?' Ignoring this, David said, 'I think it's "Perth".' Frank relented: 'Yes, in fact I'm sure I remember test cricket being played next to the Swan River, and I don't remember any test match ever being played at Canberra.' 'We'll go "Perth",' they agreed. 'Final answer.' They both closed their eyes. 'It's correct!' I told them.

Huge cheers resounded around the studio. So much for Frank's 'can-o-beer' theory. 'I wish I'd given the money to a local hospital,' said Frank, 'because that's where I'll be when Chris Eubank catches me.' He asked me to hurry up with the questions, now convinced that an angry Eubank, outraged at his mickey-taking, would already be on his way to the studio to beat him to a pulp. 'Come on,' he said, 'Get a move on – next one. Quick! He's on his way – he's in a taxi.'

So we rushed on to £125,000 with this question:

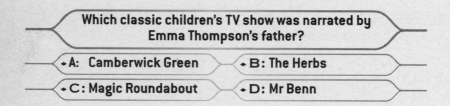

Which classic children's TV show was narrated by Emma Thompson's father?

- ◆ A: Camberwick Green
- ◆ B: The Herbs
- ◆ C: Magic Roundabout
- ◆ D: Mr Benn

'It's "Magic Roundabout",' said David at once. Frank looked bewildered at the speed of David's answer, but then said, 'OK, let's not hang about. Chris Eubank will be here any second – final answer.' It was the right answer! They now had £125,000.

For £250,000 – the biggest amount that anyone had ever won for a charity – Frank and David were asked:

> **Which poet wrote the words to the hymn 'Jerusalem'?**
>
> A: John Donne
> B: Robert Browning
> C: John Keats
> D: William Blake

They started whispering to each other again and then turned and grinned at me. 'Chris, we both know this – it's "William Blake",' they said. 'Final answer – come on now, hurry up.' It was the right answer. They were up to a staggering £250,000.

For once, the two of them were almost lost for words. 'This is just incredible,' Frank declared. 'When you get a question right it's better than sex,' and then, as memories clearly came racing back into his evil little mind, he added, 'In fact it's miles better than sex.'

The next question was for £500,000:

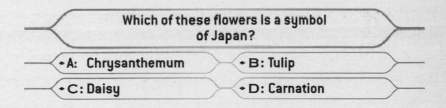

> **Which of these flowers is a symbol of Japan?**
>
> A: Chrysanthemum
> B: Tulip
> C: Daisy
> D: Carnation

Frank looked horrified. 'I've just been to Japan,' he said. 'I've only been back for about ten days. I do remember seeing chrysanthemums everywhere, but then they could have just been flowers around the place, not a national symbol.' 'I have a feeling it's "tulips",' said David, whose instincts had been so good all evening. They had another hushed consultation after which Frank announced, 'It's just too much money. We really can't risk this. We just don't know.' So, to huge cheers from the audience for the bravery, skill, knowledge and hilarious entertainment that these two had given us over two riotous nights, they left the studio with a cheque for £250,000. It was a tremendous result that would make a vast difference to both charities. They were also probably our funniest shows ever.

Oh, and incidentally, Frank, chrysanthemum *was* the right answer!

Neil and Christine Hamilton

Having seen the Hamiltons in all sorts of situations, on television newsreels when their lives seemed to be going from bad to worse, and only the week before in the documentary that Louis Theroux made about them, I didn't quite know what to expect from Neil and Christine.

I didn't know if they'd seen the show before, or whether they even knew what it was about or how it worked. But they told me that yes, they had seen it many times, they knew all about it. They had carefully prepared their Phone-A-Friends even though, as Christine told me, quite matter-of-factly, 'Most people probably don't think we've got any friends left.'

I certainly didn't expect them to be so extraordinarily nervous. Neil was looking preoccupied and worried; Christine was in the most dreadful state. She kept saying to me, 'We are going to make complete fools of ourselves.'

Having just emerged from the clutches of Mr Theroux, I should have thought they'd have considered *Who Wants To Be A Millionaire?* a breeze, but clearly Christine didn't see it that way.

Her biggest concern, she told us, was that they knew nothing whatsoever about popular culture and, with hindsight, frankly she was right! Neil was polite and amiable towards myself and the production team but strangely distant; despite her nerves Christine was the much more extrovert of the two.

Just before we were about to start filming I had to call the floor manager to stop the tape and the music, because Christine had burst into tears. It's the only time this has ever happened. 'It's going to be a disaster,' she sobbed. 'Why are we here?' I kept reassuring her that even if they just got to £1000 that would be a great result for their chosen charities – the Children's Wish Foundation and the Mid-Cheshire Sheltered Workshop for Disabled Children. Gradually she calmed down, the make-up lady dried her eyes and powdered over the redness, and we got them both back into the chair.

Once the show had started they were very amusing about their relationship. Christine, who told us she was busy writing a bumper book of battleaxes, said, 'In spite of the public image that I am the dominant one, Neil will be the boss on this programme. He is much better at these sorts of things – he'll have the final word.' Neil clearly didn't believe a word of this and nor did I.

The £100 question gave them no problem:

> Which of these means someone's plans and efforts were frustrated?

A: Foiled   B: Clingfilmed

C: Stickytaped   D: Kitchen Rolled

Even at this point Christine made clear the extent to which Neil would be the boss. 'It's one for you, darling,' she said, 'but I'd go for "A".' The audience laughed and Christine seemed to have relaxed. But at £300, her fears were realised, with this question:

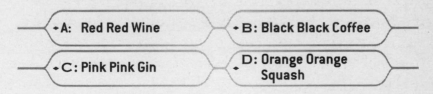

Which of these was a UK number-one single for UB40 in 1983?

She gasped out loud and started shaking her head, 'Oh my God, I really don't know – we haven't a clue.' I pointed out to her that it was a big hit around about the time they got married. 'Oh for goodness sake,' she said. 'We didn't have time for that, we were far too busy, and in any case we had trumpet music in the background.' The mind boggles. The four alternatives were:

A: Red Red Wine   B: Black Black Coffee

C: Pink Pink Gin   D: Orange Orange Squash

'You've got three Lifelines,' I reminded them. 'You can Ask the Audience.' They did, and, unsurprisingly, 86 per cent voted for 'Red Red Wine', though, bewilderingly, 11 per cent thought UB40 had a big hit with 'Orange Orange Squash', and 3 per cent thought it had been with 'Pink Pink Gin'.

'Are you going to go with the majority of this

audience?' I asked them. 'Oh yes, always trust the popular vote,' said Neil. 'Unless, of course, they vote to throw you out,' he added. It went to orange, then green. They had clawed their way up to three hundred quid.

But Christine was still terrified. 'It's even more nerve-racking than I expected,' she said. 'And we've been through such a lot as well.'

Mercifully they got to £1000 with this question, which Christine knew straight away:

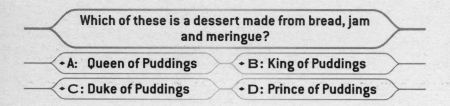

Which of these is a dessert made from bread, jam and meringue?

- A: Queen of Puddings
- B: King of Puddings
- C: Duke of Puddings
- D: Prince of Puddings

It was, of course, 'Queen of Puddings' and the Hamiltons breathed a huge sigh of relief. They were going home with at least £1000 for charity.

The question for £2000 was much more to their liking:

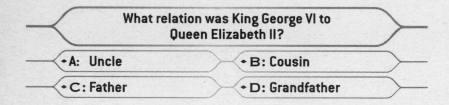

What relation was King George VI to Queen Elizabeth II?

- A: Uncle
- B: Cousin
- C: Father
- D: Grandfather

Christine graciously allowed Neil to answer, and he said quite rightly, 'It's got to be "father".' The audience applauded and they now had £2000. This was getting better.

They achieved the £4000 mark easily too, with a question about beetles. But when she saw the £8000 question Christine groaned again, and looked almost sick:

It'll be OK, I thought. Hundreds of contestants have been faced with this level of question at about this stage in the game, and they still had two Lifelines. These were the four choices:

- A: Jessica Lange
- B: Geena Davis
- C: Meryl Streep
- D: Whoopi Goldberg

'I've never ever heard of anyone called Geena Davis,' said Christine. 'Nor me,' said Neil. 'You can go 50:50 and you can still Phone-A-Friend,' I reminded them. Christine completely took over the strategy. 'Right, let's phone Shaun and you talk to him,' she instructed Neil, 'and cut out any long bits of the question as well. Never mind all that waffle at the beginning, keep it short.' After this thorough briefing she sat there with her hand over her eyes. Shaun came on but he wasn't a huge help. 'Well, I'd probably go for Jessica Lange,' he said before the phone cut off, 'but I'm really not very good at this kind of subject.' 'Oh God,' said Christine, 'I knew we would come unstuck on a question like this.'

I did remind her that they had £4000 and that they could still walk away. 'Not yet,' said Neil. 'Let's use our 50:50.' 'But it's such a waste of 50:50,' said Christine. 'Well, we might as well use it,' said Neil. 'It's no use to us when we get home, is it?' Again the audience laughed. But Christine's nerves were going from bad to worse, and she suddenly announced at the top of her voice, 'I've had enough stress in my life without this sort of thing.' Anyway, following Neil's advice, we went 50:50. It left Jessica Lange and Geena Davis.

I kept reminding them they could take the money and go. 'No,' Christine said. 'We really ought to try harder.' Neil thought the answer must be Jessica Lange. 'Come on, let's play "Jessica Lange" – final answer.' But they both said it with no real confidence and as they closed their eyes to hear the verdict, I had to tell them that, regrettably, it was the wrong answer. They'd just lost £3000. The answer was 'Geena Davis'.

What happened next was extraordinary. They were still going away £1000 better off, but Christine burst into floods of tears again! 'I knew this would happen,' she sobbed. 'We've failed. We've failed. I knew we'd fail.' It was actually quite distressing: she was really inconsolable. We had to try to gently get her out of the studio and she couldn't stop murmuring, 'We've failed, we've lost so much money for all those charities, all those poor little kids.' 'You haven't failed, you've won them £1000,' I comforted her. But she would have none of it, she was completely distraught.

We had to edit quite a lot out of the final show, especially as it was going out on Christmas Day – it was hardly a barrel of Yuletide laughs. Christine seemed to see them losing money on *Who Wants To Be A Millionaire?* as yet another symptom of how everything always went wrong for them. But in the end they had done the best they could. They had gone away with a lot more than quite a few people, and their kids' charities were £1000 better off. The crew and I discussed it afterwards. We are a fairly hardened bunch, but the bottom line was that we had found the whole thing really rather sad.

Andy Gray and Richard Keys

Andy Gray and Richard Keys, sports commentators for Sky Television appeared on *Who Wants To Be A Millionaire?* playing for Sparks children's charity and for Macmillan Nurses. Andy is one of my favourite football commentators: he combines real knowledge of the game with great passion and commitment, having been there at the sharp end, and that was just how he played *Millionaire*. Famously, Andy had once been Britain's most expensive footballer – his record-breaking transfer fee was £1.5 million, so you can see how much times have changed. These days you probably wouldn't even get a Division Three defender for that sort of money! For a Scotsman he was surprisingly complimentary about the English team heading out to the 2002 World Cup in Japan and South Korea, commenting, 'I do think they're a very good side, they could actually be a fantastic side, but possibly not just yet: I have a feeling that this World Cup might just be a year or two too early for them. But they are a really promising team with a great manager.' As I said, complimentary words from a Scot!

Richard Keys, whom I'd known since we both worked at TV-am, is a very smooth, unflustered live-TV presenter. He is also one of the hairiest men I've ever met. I haven't worked with him since the early eighties, in the heady days of Ann and Nick and Roland Rat, but for some reason this is etched in my brain. I seem to remember once being with him when he stripped to the waist – it was like standing next to a yak! He could easily have been a werewolf in a previous life.

Andy picked me up on this when I mentioned it. 'Correction, Christopher,' he said. 'Richard's not *one* of the hairiest men in the world, he is *the* hairiest man.' 'We've got a plan,' said Richard, ignoring both of us. 'I'm going to take the first five questions, Andy's going to do the second five, and after that we just won't care. We've also got Alan Shearer as our Phone-A-Friend. We're hoping that he'll be so bad that people will forget how feeble we were. Alan Shearer has been picked specifically to be hopeless if required.'

It was a unique strategy, but perhaps it would work. They did get up to question five without a problem. For £1000 I asked them:

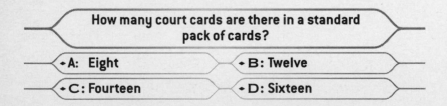

How many court cards are there in a standard pack of cards?	
• A: Eight	• B: Twelve
• C: Fourteen	• D: Sixteen

'Do aces count as court cards?' said Richard. 'Of course they don't,' said Andy. 'In that case it's "twelve".' It was the right answer.

Andy was now starting to get excited, as sportsmen do. But for £4000 they got this:

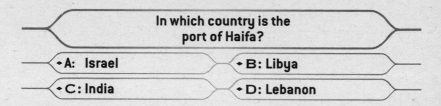

In which country is the port of Haifa?

- A: Israel
- B: Libya
- C: India
- D: Lebanon

Andy looked worried. 'I've never seen Andy Gray so nervous in all the years that I've known him,' said Richard. 'This is terrifying,' Andy retorted. 'It's Israel,' said Richard. 'Our final answer.' It was correct. At that point the klaxon signalled the end of the show and the boys left for the night with £4000 and all three Lifelines remaining. Andy looked relieved; Richard just looked hairy!

When they came back the next evening I asked them how they felt, looking back on their first day's performance. 'We did all right,' said Richard. 'We saw off the opposition and now we look forward to a great second half.' Andy said, 'I do feel a bit better, I had visions of doing worse than the Hamiltons.' This amused the audience greatly.

This was their question for £8000:

Which boxer was known as 'the Clones Cyclone'?

- A: Lloyd Honeyghan
- B: Chris Eubank
- C: Nigel Benn
- D: Barry McGuigan

'I thought "McGuigan" before the answers even came up,' said Andy. 'Let's play – final answer, "Barry McGuigan".' It was the right answer!

To get their charities to £16,000, I asked the lads:

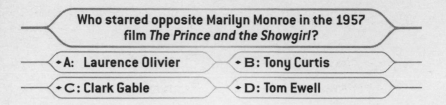

Who starred opposite Marilyn Monroe in the 1957 film *The Prince and the Showgirl*?

- A: Laurence Olivier
- B: Tony Curtis
- C: Clark Gable
- D: Tom Ewell

Andy looked devastated. 'I can't believe this,' he said, 'I'm a real Marilyn Monroe fan, I've got loads of books about her at home. I'm ashamed that I don't know the answer to this question.' They asked the audience and a small majority, 42 per cent, thought it was Laurence Olivier – not enough of a majority to convince Andy or Richard to risk losing the money they'd clawed their way up to so far.

Suddenly Richard announced very grandly, 'One of our Phone-A-Friends came here and won £1,000,000.' 'Hang on,' I said, 'I thought your Phone-A-Friend was Alan Shearer.' 'We've got him on standby,' said Richard, 'but we think we may prefer to go to another friend on this. We'll call Judith Keppel.' 'Don't be daft – you don't have Judith Keppel's phone number,' I said. 'How would Judith Keppel know a couple of oiks like you?' They grinned and shot back, 'We've got her number, and frankly if it's a choice between her and Alan Shearer we're going to use it.' This made a lot of sense.

We phoned Judith. Richard decided he would speak to her, because she wouldn't understand a word that Andy said. As soon as Judith came on the line, Richard read her the question. Before he'd even given her the choice of answers, she said, 'It's "Laurence Olivier".' That's why Judith won £1,000,000, and she had just enabled Andy and Richard to play for a possible £32,000.

This was question number ten:

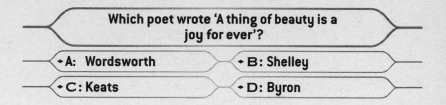

Which poet wrote 'A thing of beauty is a joy for ever'?

A: Wordsworth

B: Shelley

C: Keats

D: Byron

Andy let out a horrified cry, 'Oh God.' 'We're not really experts on poetry,' said Richard. 'I think I could have guessed that,' I replied. They used their 50:50 – 'Keats' and 'Byron' remained. 'Oh dear, that's my two choices gone,' said Richard. I'm not sure if he was joking or not – probably not. 'This is feeling like a penalty shoot-out now,' he said. 'Yes, and we're playing like Chris Waddle,' said Andy. 'I think it's "Keats" all of a sudden,' said Richard. 'Why on earth do you think it's "Keats",' I said to him. 'Just moments ago you thought it was either "Wordsworth" or "Shelley".' 'I know,' he said, 'but it sounds a bit like "Keys".'

The gambler in Andy clearly really wanted to have a stab at it, but Richard wasn't so sure. 'My instinct is to stop,' he said. 'If I had to, I'd go for "Keats", but we have got £16,000.' 'I really think we should have a go,' said Andy. 'We're going to get some terrible stick whatever happens. If we don't play this one all our mates back at Sky will tell us we bottled it. If we do play this one and get it wrong we'll get stick for losing £15,000.' 'I can't believe you're going to risk £15,000 just because "it sounds a bit like 'Keys'",' I said to them. 'Nor can I,' said Richard, 'but I think we are.' 'We definitely are,' said Andy. 'Final answer.' It went to orange and I felt it was about time to take a commercial break. 'I knew you'd do that,' said Andy in horror. I thought he was going to chin me.

We came back out of the break, both Andy and Richard white with fear. I think they both thought they'd blown it. After a certain amount of teasing I told them, 'You've just won £32,000!' Andy erupted into the air as if he'd just scored a hat-trick. 'Fantastic!' he screamed. I handed over the cheque, but Andy wouldn't touch it. 'It's like the FA Cup, son,' he said. 'You never touch it before you've won it.'

All their Lifelines were gone. For £64,000 they got this question:

> **Ewart was the middle name of which Prime Minister?**
>
> ◆ A: Disraeli   ◆ B: Gladstone
>
> ◆ C: Canning   ◆ D: Palmerston

Richard said to me, 'I think it's "Gladstone", but honestly I've got no idea why.' 'Do you want to play?' I asked him. 'We might as well,' said Andy, 'we've got nothing to lose on this question,' and they went for 'Gladstone'. Incredibly, they were correct! 'Yes! Yes! Yes!' shouted Andy. I think, in his delirium, he felt as though Scotland had just won the World Cup, beating France 5–0, having knocked out Brazil 10–0 in the semi-final. He was absolutely hyped up, ecstatic. I love it when players react like this.

For £125,000 they got this question:

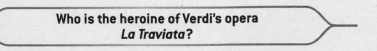

> **Who is the heroine of Verdi's opera**
> ***La Traviata*?**

'I'd say "Rosetta",' said Andy, 'but I'm not going to 'cos I haven't got a clue. We're going to take the £64,000.' So they did, and after all this entertainment, Sparks and Macmillan Nurses were £64,000 better off. Many charities stage events all through the year for a lot less money than Andy and Richard had raised in a single evening.

They were probably one of the most exciting combinations we've ever had on the show; they were certainly the most excited! There's something about sports people — they are always passionate, and love living on the edge. Incidentally, if Andy had said 'Rosetta' he would have been completely wrong. The right answer was 'Violetta'. But I don't expect that too many footballers are well up on their opera.

'The Major'

Of my most memorable contestants on *Who Wants To Be A Millionaire?*, there is one who is an especially controversial figure. He is the well-known Major who won £1,000,000 on the show one night in September 2001. After our Production team had viewed the tape carefully many times in the small hours of the morning, they formed the opinion that he had been cheating during his time in the hotseat. The £1,000,000 cheque was immediately stopped by Celador, and several arrests have since been made. Of course, that programme has never gone to air.

He denies that he has done anything wrong or had any form of illegal assistance from the audience. There have been all sorts of press theories ever since about the alleged scam, but as the case is pending at the time of writing I am unable to go into any more detail. The full story of the Major's fateful appearance on the show will emerge in court some time in the next few months – and perhaps it will one day warrant a whole book of its own!

WHO WANTS TO BE A MILLIONAIRE?®

The US Experience

Brian Fodera

One of the most famous of all the contestants on the US *Who Wants To Be A Millionaire?* is not one of the several who have gone away $1,000,000 better off, but a gentleman from Massachusetts called Brian Fodera. He was a good-looking, clean-cut kind of a guy, wearing a sharper suit than even Regis Philbin, the host over there. However, it turned out he wasn't as smart as he looked.

Regis started him on his way with the first question, for $100:

> **According to the nursery rhyme, what did Little Jack Horner pull from a pie?**
>
> • A: Ribbon • B: Plum
>
> • C: Blackbird • D: Little Jill Horner

Brian considered the question for a few moments and then said, 'I'm really not too happy about my knowledge of nursery rhymes, but I'm pretty sure it's "C: Blackbird".' Regis looked as though he'd been punched by Mike Tyson, and the audience held its breath. 'Is that your final answer?' he asked, incredulously, adding, 'Don't forget, you've got three Lifelines you can use.' Brian looked at the question hard. 'Yes,' he decided, 'that's my final answer.' 'D' went orange, and Regis had to break the news to Brian that Little Jack Horner pulled a plum from his pie. It was a fantastic TV moment.

The following day every talk show in America, every radio host, was discussing poor Brian Fodera – the man who had failed to answer even one question correctly on *Who Wants To Be A Millionaire?*. It certainly stopped them crowing at us for a while about their superior number of $1,000,000 winners! No English contestant had ever proved to be quite so daft as Brian!

John Carpenter

Jerry Springer, who spends a lot of his time flitting backwards and forwards across the Atlantic, once told me that the questions on the US version of *Millionaire* are much easier than the ones that contestants are faced with here. It's difficult for us to tell, because they would obviously find questions about popular culture in America that we would find difficult, very easy, and vice versa.

But see what you think. These are the questions that faced John Carpenter, a taxman from Connecticut, who made history on the US show in 1999.

Question number one for $100:

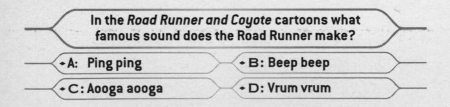

In the *Road Runner and Coyote* cartoons what famous sound does the Road Runner make?

- A: Ping ping
- B: Beep beep
- C: Aooga aooga
- D: Vrum vrum

'Beep beep' is the right answer.
For $200:

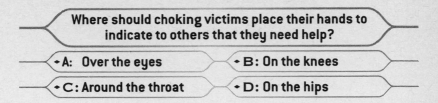

Where should choking victims place their hands to indicate to others that they need help?

- ◆ A: Over the eyes
- ◆ B: On the knees
- ◆ C: Around the throat
- ◆ D: On the hips

The answer is 'around the throat'.
For $300 John was asked:

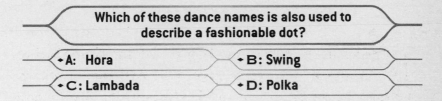

Which of these dance names is also used to describe a fashionable dot?

- ◆ A: Hora
- ◆ B: Swing
- ◆ C: Lambada
- ◆ D: Polka

The answer is 'polka'.

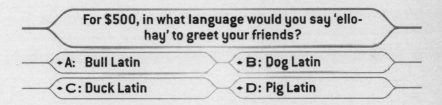

For $500, in what language would you say 'ello-hay' to greet your friends?

- ◆ A: Bull Latin
- ◆ B: Dog Latin
- ◆ C: Duck Latin
- ◆ D: Pig Latin

The answer is 'pig Latin'.

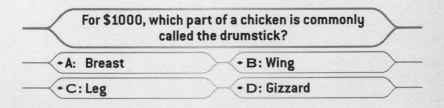

For $1000, which part of a chicken is commonly called the drumstick?

- ◆ A: Breast
- ◆ B: Wing
- ◆ C: Leg
- ◆ D: Gizzard

The answer is 'leg'.

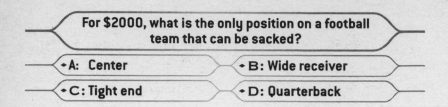

For $2000, what is the only position on a football team that can be sacked?

A: Center

B: Wide receiver

C: Tight end

D: Quarterback

The answer is 'quarterback'.

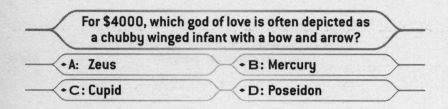

For $4000, which god of love is often depicted as a chubby winged infant with a bow and arrow?

A: Zeus

B: Mercury

C: Cupid

D: Poseidon

The answer is 'Cupid'.

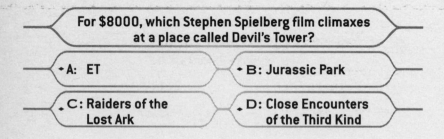

For $8000, which Stephen Spielberg film climaxes at a place called Devil's Tower?

A: ET

B: Jurassic Park

C: Raiders of the Lost Ark

D: Close Encounters of the Third Kind

The answer is 'Close Encounters of the Third Kind'.

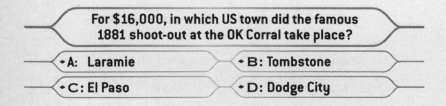

For $16,000, in which US town did the famous 1881 shoot-out at the OK Corral take place?

A: Laramie

B: Tombstone

C: El Paso

D: Dodge City

The answer is 'Tombstone'.

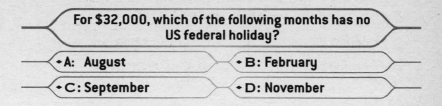

For $32,000, which of the following months has no US federal holiday?

- A: August
- B: February
- C: September
- D: November

The answer is 'August'.

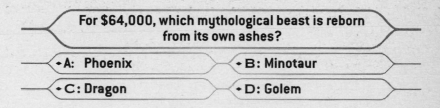

For $64,000, which mythological beast is reborn from its own ashes?

- A: Phoenix
- B: Minotaur
- C: Dragon
- D: Golem

The answer is 'Phoenix'.

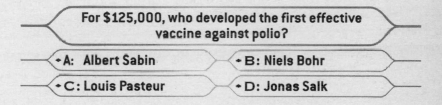

For $125,000, who developed the first effective vaccine against polio?

- A: Albert Sabin
- B: Niels Bohr
- C: Louis Pasteur
- D: Jonas Salk

The answer is 'Jonas Salk'.

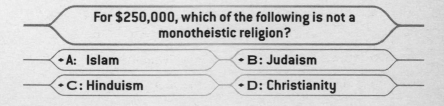

For $250,000, which of the following is not a monotheistic religion?

- A: Islam
- B: Judaism
- C: Hinduism
- D: Christianity

The answer is 'Hinduism'.

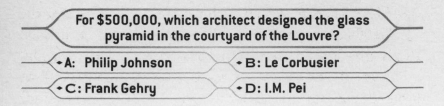

For $500,000, which architect designed the glass pyramid in the courtyard of the Louvre?

- A: Philip Johnson
- B: Le Corbusier
- C: Frank Gehry
- D: I.M. Pei

The answer is 'I.M. Pei'.

If you're wondering how many Lifelines the taxman had used up to this point, John Carpenter had climbed to $500,000 without using a single one!

To win $1,000,000 he was asked:

Which of these US Presidents appeared on the television series *Laugh-In*?

- A: Lyndon Johnson
- B: Richard Nixon
- C: Jimmy Carter
- D: Gerald Ford

Now, as a Brit, I have to say that I was unsure about this, but it must have been a widely publicised event in the USA, of which I would have thought most people over a certain age would have been aware. And what happened next with John was quite extraordinary.

He looked blankly at Regis and said, 'I'd like to Phone-A-Friend, please. I want to phone my father. He's called Tom.' This is exactly what was said between father and son:

'Hi, Dad.'

'Hi, son.'

'Dad, I'm using you as my Phone-A-Friend, but I don't really need your help. I just want you to know that I'm about to win $1,000,000!'

There was a shocked murmur from the audience, which quickly turned to a roar. John continued, 'I've got the $1,000,000 question in front of me and I know the answer. Regis, my final answer is "Richard Nixon".' He was right!

He was the first person in the US to win $1,000,000 – the largest one-off game-show prize in the history of American television; and the only person anywhere in the world to get all fifteen questions correct with no help whatsoever.

A last thing: as you will have gathered by now, in the UK our contestants pay no tax on their winnings. In the US they are heavily taxed, so out of $1,000,000 a contestant in the States would probably only go away with the equivalent of about £350,000. Still, not a bad night's work.

Showtime

The Host

We have some strange rituals on *Who Wants To Be A Millionaire?* For example, every night at 7.29pm, as I leave my dressing room and head for the studio with the floor manager and the lads from Sound, Wardrobe and Make-up, we march down the corridor playing air guitars leaping around manically to the noisy chords of the Who's 'Pinball Wizard'.

Anyone who's witnessed this Pete Townshend-esque display is convinced we are all barking mad. I think they are probably right, and none of us can even remember why we do it, but it does give us a tremendous adrenalin rush, even when we're exhausted. Plus it would, of course, be an unlucky omen to change it now.

Moments before this little performance, at about 7.28, Billy Kimberley, my wardrobe co-ordinator and an old friend, takes a Polaroid of me in the suit, shirt and tie I'm wearing that day. It's called a 'continuity shot' and is purely for reference, in case we have to repeat a small segment of a particular show days later, or for some reason we record a few shows out of sequence.

It means that by now Billy has got an enormous file of about three hundred pictures of me, some of which would not be out of place on *Crimewatch*! Here is a small selection:

349

The Contestants

Finally, I must give a big thanks to all the contestants who have gone through the heaven and hell of sitting in the *Who Wants To Be A Millionaire?* hotseat since September 1998. They have had to bear the sight of my ugly mug at close quarters, and my teasing, but I hope that I've made up for that by handing some of them very large sums of money! However agonising it was at the time, I hope that you all thoroughly enjoyed your time on the show and that your lives, if not all your bank accounts, are a lot richer for the experience. In order from day one, here you all are:

Contestant	Money won	Contestant	Money won
Graham Elwell	£64,000	Matthew Asbury	£64,000
Rachel Mendez de Costa	£8,000	David Thompson	£8,000
Arlene Harper	£1,000	Eva Whittam	£64,000
Ross Jackson	£64,000	Derek McMorrow	£1,000
Tina Bird	£1,000	Donna Minors	£2,000
Samantha Thomas	£16,000	Dave Regan	£64,000
John Stewart	£16,000	Andy Woodcock	£1,000
John McKeown	£64,000	Donna Clark	£1,000
Craig Logue	£2,000	Cheryl Turner	£500
Judith Beacroft	£1,000	Jason Vaughan	£16,000
David McNab	£1,000	Tony Carey	£1,000

Contestant	Money won	Contestant	Money won
Paula Wellfair	£4,000	Mark Mills	£32,000
Victoria Kaye	£16,000	Phil Fiddler	£16,000
Paul Beverley	£32,000	Roger Bannock	£4,000
Sarah Woodier	£1,000	Martin Smith	£125,000
Donna Blake	£1,000	Richard Hale	£32,000
David Yule	£32,000	Davy Young	£125,000
David Hogg	£64,000	Mike Stokes	£32,000
Neil Muir	£64,000	June Woods	£16,000
Fiona McKenzie	£16,000	Andrew Stewart	£8,000
Pat Linehan	£16,000	Keith Burgess	£64,000
Fiona Wheeler	£32,000	Andrew Lavelle	£16,000
Martin Skillings	£125,000	Geoff Aquatias	£32,000
Ian Horswell	£125,000	Kenny Allen	£4,000
Gary Cunning	£16,000	Peter Thomson	£1,000
Tristan Burt	£16,000	Jonathan Green	£250,000
John Davidson	£0	Graham Hooper	£32,000
Karen Ozdemir	£16,000	Tony Stanton	£125,000
Mark Manley	£16,000	John Evans	£1,000
Roger Maynard	£32,000	Neil Reid	£64,000
Lisa Hixson	£16,000	Peter Turner	£16,000
Len Munday	£1,000	Tony Watt	£16,000
Denis Burton	£1,000	Annie Locke	£32,000
Matthew Norways	£1,000	Andy Evans	£16,000
Paul Ricketts	£2,000	Steve Jackson	£16,000
Dave Snaith	£0	Allen Langer	£4,000
Michelle McGeachy	£1,000	Sonia Davis	£16,000
Paul McLoughlin	£64,000	Jayne Bentley	£8,000
Martin Smith	£4,000	Val Fitzsimmons	£8,000
Fe Wisher	£16,000	Gary Wilson	£8,000
Bernie Waspe	£8,000	David West	£16,000
Tony Kennedy	£125,000	Mike Cooke	£1,000
Sheridan Booth	£500	Peter Arnold	£64,000
Eddie Holland	£4,000	John Penn	£16,000
Steve James	£16,000	Perry Poole	£32,000
Michelle Furnell	£1,000	Steve Fleming	£16,000
Paul Marr	£16,000	Tracy Pike	£2,000
Eileen Robinson	£16,000	Nicole Lovatt	£8,000
Daryl Arnold	£32,000	Peter Alderson	£32,000
Peter Callaghan	£1,000	Adele Bateman	£1,000
Fred Jones	£64,000	Neil Hathaway	£64,000

Contestant	Money won	Contestant	Money won
Simon Murray	£64,000	Tony Birkby	£64,000
Di Newberry	£32,000	Mike Sackett	£64,000
Mick Baines	£1,000	David Neale	£250,000
Ian Yule	£16,000	Peter Lee	£500,000
Edd Wilkinson	£1,000	Margaret Whittaker	£250,000
Garry Wilkins	£8,000	Jan Garner	£8,000
Calum Davidson	£16,000	Denise Fowler	£32,000
Rick Lawless	£8,000	David Guest	£1,000
Dave Ferguson	£64,000	Sarah Black	£16,000
Keith Rumney	£8,000	Vik Manek	£1,000
Ben Bartle	£125,000	Mick Deery	£8,000
Gerry Lennon	£125,000	Jane Wicks	£64,000
Craig Jefford	£8,000	Steve Baldwin	£1,000
David Crombleholme	£4,000	Alli Hamilton	£64,000
Liz Whitlock	£32,000	Fiona Whatley	£4,000
Pete Walsh	£32,000	Chris Hatton	£8,000
Barbara McGhee	£64,000	Tina Nicol	£16,000
Bernard Marco	£64,000	Leslie Palmer	£125,000
Gene Hunt	£8,000	Judy White	£32,000
Peter Burnes	£64,000	Sue Davies	£16,000
David Shill	£64,000	Tommy O'Donnell	£16,000
Zulma Dudgeon	£4,000	Brian Jones	£125,000
Lee Cartwright	£16,000	Jeff Arundell	£1,000
Mark Rogers	£4,000	Richard Kendall	£32,000
Lance Jones	£64,000	Dennis Evans	£1,000
Malcolm Cawley	£64,000	Paddy Spooner	£250,000
Sarah Vallaton	£64,000	Lise Greenwood	£16,000
Kate Brookes	£16,000	David Phillips	£32,000
Ted Cadman	£16,000	Richard Westlake	£32,000
Mike Walters	£16,000	Keith Morgan	£125,000
Jon Underwood	£32,000	Paul Chaplin	£1,000
James Williams	£4,000	John Hudson	£16,000
Charlie Pryde	£16,000	Alistair Macnaughton	£125,000
Robert Hipkiss	£64,000	Ian Larner	£1,000
Damian Partis	£16,000	Stuart Watson	£64,000
Sylvia Nixon	£125,000	Sandra Presland	£8,000
Mark Bowerman	£64,000	Nick Osborne	£1,000
Jane Pritchard	£1,000	Ian Cordiner	£8,000
Jim Barwick	£125,000	Gary Luckhurst	£4,000
Dennis North	£1,000	Jim Titmuss	£32,000

Contestant	Money won	Contestant	Money won
Stephen McCrudden	£16,000	John McCormick	£32,000
Harry Nock	£1,000	Ian Hodgetts	£4,000
James Markwick	£32,000	Richard Nichols	£8,000
Phil Davidson	£16,000	John Bullivent	£125,000
Carol Vorderman	£125,000	Jean Thompson	£8,000
Kirsty Young	£64,000	Bav Patel	£16,000
Roger Neuberg	£64,000	Pete Day	£1,000
Edd Oliver	£1,000	Jo Webb	£125,000
Patrick Lidierth	£125,000	Tony Welsh	£64,000
Clive Thornley	£8,000	Phil Davison	£16,000
Mark Townsend	£250,000	Matthew Stephenson	£64,000
Mark Swift	£16,000	Steve Wayland	£1,000
Don Williams	£8,000	Duncan Bickley	£32,000
Rod Jordan	£16,000	Mike Hanson	£1,000
Robert Richland	£8,000	Joe Fletcher	£32,000
Nick Hand	£64,000	Roger Tozer	£125,000
Ken Harrison	£32,000	Ann Cronin	£16,000
Andy Dalton	£32,000	Alan Bennett	£4,000
Ange Seymore	£1,000	Pete Joslin	£16,000
Peter Gaynor	£64,000	Ryan Wilkinson	£16,000
John Cunningham	£32,000	Dorothy Bramham	£64,000
Andy Down	£32,000	Deb Hunter	£32,000
Phil Nicholls	£32,000	Caroline Hughes	£32,000
Tania Edgar	£32,000	Dan Hotchin	£125,000
Dave Bailey	£16,000	Richard Phillips	£16,000
Alun Wadlow	£8,000	Kate Heusser	£500,000
Elaine Briggs	£125,000	Peter Pycock	£16,000
Graham Hickin	£250,000	Josette Haviland	£1,000
Steve Cornfield	£125,000	Gary Barthram	£1,000
Margaret Roberts	£16,000	Ken Davison	£1,000
Peter Dauncey	£125,000	David Turner	£125,000
John Sedeno	£64,000	Mac McCallion	£16,000
Ann Stanley	£32,000	Debbie Sutcliffe	£1,000
George Arnold	£16,000	Nick Strickland	£64,000
Peter Hughes	£32,000	Maureen Calder	£1,000
Gill Glover	£8,000	Sarah Bunby	£1,000
Michelle Hawes	£32,000	Jon Lewis	£16,000
Nadeem Tufail	£125,000	Chris Squires	£16,000
John Ward	£16,000	Andy Martin	£250,000
Jeremy Fewster	£32,000	Pete Ingle	£1,000

Contestant	Money won	Contestant	Money won
Andy Conner	£32,000	Wesley McGookin	£8,000
Dave Hunter	£16,000	Beverley Angell	£8,000
Jane Rider	£32,000	Rod Arkle & Vicky Kirkham	£64,000
Darren Symonds	£8,000	Sheila Wilde & John Carlson	£64,000
Rowland Hughes	£64,000	Trudi Palmer &Andy Hall	£8,000
Paulette Newby	£16,000	Laraine & Russell Thomas	£125,000
Dave Chapman	£16,000	John & Karen Hannaford	£125,000
Judith Keppel	£1,000,000	Rob & Corinne Sawyer	£125,000
Chris Elliot	£125,000	Rod & Ann Gray	£64,000
Jim Parker	£32,000	Richard Godefroy	£64,000
Ben Whitehead	£125,000	Greg Carter	£4,000
Linda Allan	£32,000	Paul Leigh	£32,000
Martine Knight	£1,000	Jonathan Hughes	£125,000
John Randall	£500,000	Tom Davies	£32,000
Elsa Oliver	£64,000	Stephen Chandler	£8,000
Hywel Harris	£125,000	Sharon Moss	£64,000
Steve Hayward	£32,000	Terry Yeomans	£16,000
Paul Nicholas	£32,000	Andy Clark	£8,000
Terry Davis	£32,000	Jill Howard	£1,000
Dave Tromp	£1,000	Steve Devlin	£500,000
Paul Cole	£64,000	Debbie Allen	£64,000
Steve Edwards	£32,000	Paul Nolan	£8,000
Gen Broadbent	£125,000	Chris Lea	£32,000
Karl Duerden	£64,000	Andrew Packman	£1,000
Mike Collins	£1,000	David Stainer	£64,000
Dave Anderson	£64,000	Bryan Williams	£16,000
Andy Gillies	£16,000	Tony Stevens	£32,000
Simon Rosenberg	£16,000	Innes Scott	£32,000
Gareth Welch	£64,000	Ravinder Rai	£32,000
John McCool	£32,000	Keith Wilcock	£250,000
Gary Bishop	£8,000	John Tuff	£4,000
Stephen Jappy	£8,000	Arrol Toplin	£125,000
Gerald Cooper	£32,000	Brian Adams	£32,000
Wik Stankiewicz	£32,000	Jon Powell	£64,000
Roger Waldron	£250,000	Peter Burke	£16,000
Tim Brown	£1,000	John Stockdale	£1,000
John Brandon	£32,000	Anton Johnson	£8,000
Adrian Pollock	£32,000	Peter Williams	£1,000
Rob Knapman	£16,000	Ged Taylor	£16,000
Val Bradley	£16,000	Sam Smith	£1,000

Contestant	Money won	Contestant	Money won
Mike Ratcliffe	£1,000	Lin & Ste Morris	£32,000
Pete Pearce	£16,000	Peter & Valiene Tungate	£0
Dave Pink	£1,000	David & Meriel Redd	£16,000
David Crossley	£32,000	Jason & Julia Stathan	£16,000
Sheila McHale	£32,000	Steve & Loraine Brownless	£64,000
Malcolm Knight	£32,000	Ken & Wendy Clark	£64,000
Charles Walton	£64,000	James & Vi Cochrane	£1,000
Sue Coles	£64,000	David Anderson &	
Stewart Crawford	£8,000	Victoria Best	£32,000
Howard Brooks	£32,000	Gail Egan &	
Carolyn Lysons	£1,000	Colin McGiffert	£64,000
John Bolus	£16,000	John & Doreen Lawrence	£250,000
Richard Scott	£16,000	Tom & Sally Naylor	£64,000
Tim Whelan	£16,000	Peter & Anne Jenkins	£125,000
Simon Wardill	£64,000	Dave Bowles	£64,000
Michelle Simmonds	£0	Phil Keane	£16,000
Joanna Karatas	£1,000	Nathan Birtle	£250,000
Andy Barnes	£16,000	Trevor Luscombe	£8,000
Majella Maher	£8,000	Angie Reddy	£1,000
John Sexton	£250,000	Peter Inwood	£32,000
Jim Whitaker	£64,000	Mike Bradshaw	£1,000
Tony Emans	£250,000	Mark Starkey	£64,000
Paul Everitt	£1,000	Steve Butler	£64,000
Alistair McDowall	£8,000	Adam Swart	£8,000
Stewart Duncan	£32,000	Steve Lacey	£125,000
Alan Scrutton	£64,000	Ady Lee	£8,000
Ceri Andrews	£32,000	Julia Freer	£8,000
Chris Jones	£32,000	Ann Baldwin	£16,000
Jo Blacker	£32,000	Jonathan Gladwin	£64,000
Matt Freeman	£64,000	Diana Ingram	£32,000
Liz Richards	£64,000	Richard Deeley	£32,000
Sue McCord	£32,000	Martin Jenkins	£250,000
Alison Grinney	£8,000	Bob Hitchin	£32,000
John Ramsden	£125,000	Julia Kitson	£64,000
Simon Steer	£16,000	Julie Gibson	£32,000
Dave McGregor	£8,000	Steve Keen	£1,000
Norman McKenzie	£8,000	Chris Hamer	£32,000
Mike Pomfrey (+Moose!)	£500,000	Dee Richards	£1,000
Mike Willcock	£1,000	Michael McGinty	£16,000
Alan Ritchie	£8,000	David Edwards	£1,000,000

Contestant	Money won	Contestant	Money won
Ian Farmer	£16,000	John & Ben Garside	£64,000
Nick Carrelli	£4,000	Sue & Graeme Williamson	£8,000
Maureen Warrilow	£64,000	Neil & Ken Hodgkiss	£32,000
Sean Wilson	£32,000	Vanessa Hains &	
David Neilson	£64,000	Jenny Tonks	£1,000
Claire McGlinn	£16,000	Ian & Mo McDonald	£32,000
Richard Brown	£2,000	Mark & Margaret Cooper	£16,000
Graham Lay	£1,000	Steve & Darryl Morgan	£8,000
Stephen Parker	£32,000	Ian & Lauren Gibson	£16,000
Chris Millard	£4,000	Terry & Kerry Parker	£32,000
Ian Saunders	£125,000	Stephen Parker	£64,000
Craig Tasane	£16,000	Peter Spyrides	£500,000
Tracey Allen	£16,000	Trevor Sumerling	£64,000
Darren Caunt	£8,000	Isobel Thompson	£64,000
Tecwen Whittock	£1,000	Philip Yale	£16,000
John Norton	£125,000	Charles Middler	£64,000
Janie McCathie	£16,000	Dave Wood	£16,000
Nick Hulse	£8,000	Muir Smillie	£125,000
Jasper Carrot &		Nicola Yeoman	£8,000
Jenny Davis	£64,000	Jeff Gross	£64,000
Martin Frizell &		Paul Thurlbeck	£1,000
Fiona Phillips	£64,000	Sara Moloney	£64,000
Jane Goldman &		Ray Smith	£16,000
Jonathan Ross	£1,000	Cristina Bas	£64,000
James Amos	£64,000	Julian Bloom	£32,000
Adam Smillie	£32,000	Colin Hallett	£125,000
Suzi Boyle	£8,000	Stuart Reid	£125,000
Miles Robson	£125,000	Jayne Duncan	£16,000
Robert Brydges	£1,000,000	Chris Verity	£16,000
Michael Donnelly	£8,000	Emma Carter	£64,000
Suzanne Barton &		Aine McLarnon	£4,000
Tom Lynch	£1,000	Nicola Farley	£32,000
Joanne Welch & Fred Ellis	£32,000	Sue Neale	£32,000
Graham & Jack Routledge	£8,000	Diane Hallagan	£250,000
Alan & Kim Dancer	£1,000	Yvonne Wade	£1,000
Caroline & Brian Wright	£2,000	Julie de Rosa	£64,000
Colette & Eileen Doyle	£16,000	Kate Mathieson	£250,000
Derek & Delia Banks	£250,000	Liz Martin	£64,000
Chris & Dave Bramley	£32,000	Russ Wright	£16,000
Martin & Dave Newbolt	£64,000	Karl Shuker	£250,000

Contestant	Money won	Contestant	Money won
Colin Mitchell	£125,000	Josephine Millett	£1,000
Briony Poole	£250,000	Vivienne Hamilton	£64,000
Richard Wolfenden	£16,000	Alasdair McLean	£16,000
Taz Poole	£250,000	Helen Brook	£8,000
Steve Greatbatch	£64,000	John Franks	£16,000
Phil Bushe	£32,000	Alan Fiddes	£4,000
Nathan Pritchard	£32,000	Ray Peters	£32,000
Ian Parkes	£64,000	Liz Perch	£1,000
Suzanne Disley	£125,000	Duncan Sirkett	£32,000
Andy Hargreaves	£16,000	Nick Hodgson	£8,000
Kirsty Orman	£64,000	Jo Everett	£16,000
Sandra & Fraser Mackay	£8,000	Ted Procter	£8,000
Joe & Carole Ball	£8,000	Giles Haynes	£1,000
Stuart & Lizzie Martin	£32,000	Alan Crompton	£125,000
Mike & Karen Taylor	£1,000	Ian Mehrer	£1,000
Judy & David Cairns	£64,000	Kieron Smyth	£125,000
Cliff & Catherine D'Arcy	£1,000	Steve Wynne	£16,000
Andrea & Peter Smith	£1,000	Rob Dodds	£125,000
Chris Rennie & Anita Anderson	£1,000	Geraint Evans	£64,000
		Peter Holden	£1,000
Philip & Linda Barnes	£64,000	Brian Barlow	£1,000
Barry Gibbs & Joanna McMahon	£8,000	Chris Knox	£64,000
		Iain Henderson	£16,000
Caroline & Neil McDonald	£64,000	Simon Narramore	£8,000
John & Sally Salter	£125,000	John Sigsworth	£1,000
Dave & Kath Burmingham	£1,000	John Holman	£16,000
Grant King & Coral Caulton	£16,000	Jane Domleo	£64,000
		Kevin Towler	£1,000
Liza & Jimmy Tarbuck	£16,000	Paul Keegan	£8,000
Julie Peasgood & Kate McEnery	£16,000	Brian Rigby	£64,000
		Keith Prophet	£4,000
Frank Skinner & David Baddiel	£250,000	Julie White	£16,000
		Anthony Byrne	£32,000
Neil & Christine Hamilton	£1,000	David Martin	£125,000
Doug Kelly	£250,000	Chris Henry-May	£8,000
Graham Brown	£32,000	Paul Cleary	£32,000
Nigel Wackett	£125,000	Patrick Calthrop	£250,000
Paul French	£64,000	Kevin Bowman	£8,000
Kathryn White	£64,000	Chris Martin	£32,000
Steve Silverman	£125,000	Eric Skilton	£1,000

Contestant	Money won	Contestant	Money won
Bill Wilson	£1,000	Phil Middleton	£8,000
Richard Bliss	£16,000	Sue Mitchell	£8,000
Andy Collin	£8,000	Den Hewitt	£250,000
Phil Leiwy	£125,000	Edward Dingle	£8,000
Andrew Harkins	£1,000	Brian & Alan Simpson	£16,000
Graham Richardson	£16,000	Alex & Cecilia Roberts	£1,000
Roger Walker	£500,000	Julie Rodgers & Stephanie	
Davina McCall &		Moss	£8,000
Matthew Robertson	£16,000	Ray & David Prior	£250,000
James Redmond &		Rick & Paul Bakker	£1,000
Kate Redmond	£1,000	Andy & Steve Burton	£16,000
Andy Gray &		Steve & Lyn Garnett	£32,000
Richard Keys	£64,000	Martin Clayton & Claire	
Dermot O'Leary &		Zincke	£32,000
Sean O'Leary	£32,000	Kazim & Anita Khan	£16,000
Kaye Adams &Ross Kelly	£125,000	Nick & Amy Salway	£16,000
Eric Fitzgerald	£32,000	Steve & Theresa Taylor	£8,000
Chris Skinner	£32,000	Paul & Julie Roxbotham	£1,000
Chris Hopkinson	£16,000	Greg & Lois Allon	£16,000
Beverly Chesterton	£16,000	Paul & Sheila Kelly	£16,000
Kevin Purcell	£8,000	Mat & Jo Newman	£8,000
Kim Totman	£250,000	Mark & Becky Truman	£16,000